Golf *Links*

Golf *Links*

Chay Burgess, Francis Ouimet, and The Bringing of Golf to America

by

Charles D. Burgess

Rounder Books
Cambridge, Massachusetts

Golf Links:
Chay Burgess, Francis Ouimet, and The Bringing of Golf to America

Published by Rounder Books

an imprint of:
Rounder Records
1 Camp Street
Cambridge, MA 02140

ISBN 1-57940-105-8
Library of Congress Control Number: 2004097779

Cover design by Steven Jurgensmeyer
Cover photos courtesy of the Burgess collection & The Country Club, Brookline, MA.

Burgess, Charles D.
Golf Links: Chay Burgess, Francis Ouimet, and The Bringing of Golf to America

1. Golf – History I. Title

First Edition

2004097779
796.352'09
ISBN 1-57940-105-8

Production & design by Windhaven Press
www.windhaven.com

Printed in Canada

9 8 7 6 5 4 3 2 1

Contents

Preface 1

Chapter 1: From the Beginning—1903
Historic Links 4
Montrose 6
Tom Morris and Bob Dow, "Grand Old Men" of Golf. 8
Scottish Independence. 10
Growing Up Linkside 12
Montrose Tournament of 1888 15
Fieldstones, Football, and Golf 18
Playing for Pay 21
Life in Professional Football. 24

Chapter 2: 1903–1905
The Birth of American Golf 29
Alex Findlay, American Golf Pioneer. 30
Willie Campbell, Donald Ross, George Wright, and Golf's Roots in Boston 32
A Golf Pro at Twenty-Eight 36
A New "Merky" Clubhouse 42
Election to The PGA 44

Chapter 3: 1905–1908
The International Links of Montrose 46
"The Great Triumvirate" Taylor, Vardon, and Braid. 49
Charlie's First Open 50
News of the World. 52
Coronation Tankard. 53
Links Championship 54
Vardon, Burgess, and Braid 55
Becoming a Teacher. 57
Surprising Setback 59

Chapter 4: 1908–1909
Findlay Returns . . . 65
America Beckons . . . 69
The Crossing and Arrival . . . 72
Chapter 5: 1909–1913
American Professionals and the USGA . . . 77
Setting Up Shop . . . 81
Finding Francis . . . 84
Francis Ouimet . . . 86
Lessons from Charlie . . . 89
Back to School . . . 92
Up in Flames . . . 94
A Championship at Harvard . . . 96
Chapter 6: 1913
Ouimet's Prelude to Prominence . . . 102
A Star-Studded Field Gathers in 1913 . . . 104
The 1913 U.S. Open: The Match that Changed Golf Forever . . . 108
Chapter 7: 1913–1914
A Tribute to Francis . . . 127
Pinehurst Privileges . . . 132
Another Championship . . . 133
Success and Celebrity . . . 136
Most Pros Still Languish . . . 138
Walter Hagen, "the Haig" . . . 139
Charlie Burgess and "the Bambino" . . . 141
Challenging Charlie . . . 142
Chapter 8: 1914–1919
The 1914 U.S. Amateur and Jesse Guilford . . . 144
Francis Banned . . . 147
The PGA of America . . . 149
The Great War . . . 151
Young Charlie . . . 152
Opposition to Golf . . . 154
Chapter 9: 1920–1921
The Twenties Begin . . . 158
Jock Blair's Misfortune . . . 160
A Return to Scotland . . . 162
Two Kinds of American Pros . . . 165
Chay's Second National Champion . . . 168
Professional Team Play . . . 170

A Rebellion in the PGA 172
New England Professionals Prosper 175
The Tragedy of Tellier 178

Chapter 10: 1921–1929

An Anniversary Back in Scotland 180
The Golf Center Shifts to America 184
The PGA Reforms 187
Jesse, Francis, and the Walker Cup 189
Golf Grows in the Twenties 190
Guilford and Burgess Win New England Crown 192
The PGA, the USGA, and the Open 195
America's Forgotten Champion 196
Saving the Ryder Cup 198
A Tribute from Francis 203
The End of the Decade 206

Chapter 11: 1930–1934

Ouimet and Guilford Challenge Von Elm and Burke 208
Ouimet's Great Comeback 213
A Hero's Return 218
The Nicoll Brothers 219
A Champion in Defeat 224
The Deepening Depression 226

Chapter 12: 1935–1960

Ruth Returns 232
Bing Crosby 237
Big League Sluggers 238
A Special Order 241
Snead Shunned 242
The Other Babe 244
Ted Bishop 245
Charles the Third 245
Retirement 247
Back to Duty, WWII 250
A Third National Champion 252
Final Rounds 254

Acknowledgments 259
Works Cited 262
Index 267

This work is dedicated to the memory of my father,
Charles D. Burgess, Sr.
(August 26, 1923–November 17, 2003)

And to my wife,
with love and appreciation for her
encouragement and support

Preface

Golf Links was inspired by the discovery of a long forgotten letter found among the papers of Charles "Chay" Burgess, a Scottish born golf professional and great teacher who immigrated to the United States in 1909. The letter was from Francis Ouimet, one of America's first sports heroes who won the United States Open in 1913 as a 20-year-old amateur.

Ouimet, a former caddie just out of his teens, was a virtually unknown entrant among the strongest field of international golf stars ever assembled for the prestigious U.S. Open. In a "Rocky"-like drama, he shocked the sporting world of his day as he battled his way across rain drenched fairways to finish in a three-way tie and then win the coveted championship in a patriotically charged play-off against the great British stars, Harry Vardon and Ted Ray. His improbable victory inspired a popular revolution in golf as thousands of average Americans took up the sport that had previously been the province of only the wealthy class.

Ouimet went on to win the American National Amateur Championship twice and was an original member and the captain of America's Walker Cup team. He was also the first American ever elected captain of The Royal and Ancient Golf Club in St. Andrews and was an original inductee into the PGA Hall of Fame. He continues to influence

American golf today through the Francis Ouimet Caddie Scholarship that was established in 1947.

In the hand written letter dated April 1929, Ouimet repeatedly gave his mentor full credit for his knowledge, success, and progress in the game of golf. This previously unknown testimonial tribute, from the man whose accomplishments impacted the course of golf in his time as dramatically as Arnold Palmer and Tiger Woods have done in theirs, clearly establishes Charlie Burgess as one of the country's most influential pioneer teachers of the game.

As a youth Charlie perfected his craft as he played upon the ancient links of Montrose, Scotland, tutored and influenced by Montrose's first professional, Bob Dow and by legendary professional "Old" Tom Morris of nearby St. Andrews. At the beginning of the twentieth century Charlie was a contemporary of the world's greatest golfing trio, the "Great Triumvirate" of Harry Vardon, James Braid, and John H. Taylor. He competed in many of the major tournaments of the era while he worked as a club and teaching professional. It was not his ability to win championships that changed the course of golf history but his extraordinary ability to teach the game to others. After coming to America, he became the coach of three national champions—Ouimet, Jesse Guilford, and Ted Bishop—and teacher to thousands of ordinary Americans. His reputation as a great instructor also attracted many celebrity pupils, such as Babe Ruth and Bing Crosby, during the golden age of American golf.

His role as a teacher of American champions is only a part of the story. Working-class roots as a trade unionist in Scotland made him deeply committed to organizing professional golfers and to improving the serf-like working conditions endured by most of the early American professionals. At the turn of the century, the lot of the early pro at the prestigious and wealthy country clubs was generally a poor one. Often forced to use the back door of the clubhouse and to take their meals in the kitchen with the servants, the early professionals had few rights, little job security, and no benefits except for those that each could negotiate on his own. The early professionals in America worked in conditions often better equated with indentured servitude instead of the celebrated life we associate with the modern golf professional today. Charlie was instrumental in the development and support of homegrown American stars during the teens and twenties, and counted men like Bobby Jones, Walter Hagen, and Gene Sarazen among his friends as they captured the attention and imagination of the American public. His independent reform and organizing efforts on behalf of the golf professionals of New England improved the fortunes of PGA club professionals nationwide just as the bold and often theatrical antics of Walter Hagen later did for the touring pros in the 1920's.

Charlie Burgess began his lifelong association with golf as a child in Victorian Scotland and experienced a remarkable career as a professional athlete that spanned over five decades. He witnessed the beginning of golf in the United States and its evolution through the First World War to the dawning of the Space Age. "Chay" was a well-traveled, multi-talented, interesting man. He also happened to be my great-grandfather and the events in this book are based upon the many remarkable remembrances that he, my grandfather, and father have shared with me since I was a young boy. These recollections help enrich this look at the life and times of one of the founding fathers of American golf.

1 From the Beginning—1903

"There are certain fundamentals necessary to develop an orthodox swing. If you begin by being taught rhythm, relaxation, grip, stance, and a schooling in mental confidence correctly, you are launched in the right direction. Have patience and diligently practice what you have been taught. Don't start out for a score. In fact, there are so many don'ts for the new golfer that I could fill a book."

—Charlie Burgess

• Historic Links •

How and where the game of golf began has been debated for decades. There is evidence that some simple games using clubs and balls were played in medieval Holland, France, other parts of Europe, even ancient Rome. But undoubtedly the game of golf that we play today began in Scotland, possibly as far back as the fourteenth century. Perhaps, as some historians have speculated, Scottish shepherds on seaside grazing lands may have played the first version of the game using their crooks to hit rocks or hardened sheep dung toward a target as amusement to pass the time. The ubiquitous rabbit holes that dotted the grass-covered dunes along the Scottish coast can easily be imagined as the target of the shepherds' shots, and the first sand traps may have been where the grazing sheep wore away the fragile grass.

If golf as we know it began in Scotland, the question becomes just where in Scotland did it start? The answer is that no one really knows. There is no absolute evidence of exactly where in Scotland golf began. However there are several towns on the East Coast of Scotland that could make a claim as the birthplace of Scottish golf because of their ancient links and the uninterrupted existence of golf on them over the centuries. The linkslands of coastal Montrose where Charlie Burgess was born could certainly qualify as one of the select few places where the Scottish game of golf may have originated and the course there is one of the oldest recorded in history.

In his book *Golf in Montrose*, Scottish golf historian William W. Coull, asserts that the course at Montrose is at least the fifth oldest in the world, and cites references to early written accounts of golf being played there in 1562 by Reformation minister William Gray and his boarding school student James Melville. James later left Montrose to study at St. Andrews University and he continued his pursuit of golf on the St. Andrews links that lie just south of Montrose across the Firth of Tay. John Graham, the Fourth Earl of Montrose, was another early Montrose golfer, who in 1624, as the Marquis of Montrose, left behind records of his involvement with the sport played on the fields near the sea in his noble domain.

The course in Montrose, like its cousins at St. Andrews, Prestwick, and Carnoustie, is located on a narrow, treeless, and windswept coastal plain. These narrow strips of oceanfront land known as linkslands were created during the retreat of the last Ice Age. The deposits of sand and soil that were left behind slowly turned to fields covered with vegetation. Short grasses developed and grew abundantly between stands of thickset spiny bushes of gorse, tall straw-like plants of broom, and the other small bushes (collectively called the "whins") that evolved along the coastal lands. Pockets of subtly multihued heather, majestic purple thistle, and hardy wildflower contrasted dramatically with the green fields, small hills, and gentle streams—the braes and burns along the sandy Scottish coast. When the early golfers used these wide-open acres for their sport, the primitive courses had no clearly defined fairways, tees, or greens. They were simply a series of starting and finishing points laid out and linked together in sequence following the lay of the land. As time went on, the courses gradually evolved and were modified only slightly by the hand of man. The links course of Montrose and the other seaside Scottish villages were the original and natural home of our game of golf.

Because the links were common land, the early Scottish game was a surprisingly democratic activity, allowing all social classes to participate. Well-to-do merchants and noblemen using custom-made clubs and expensive feather stuffed leather balls would share the links with the poorest of youths playing with a crooked stick and a round stone or other makeshift ball.

Less than two dozen courses and established golfing societies or clubs existed in Scotland before 1860. But after that time, during the middle of the Victorian Era, a period of rapid development began and new courses and clubs spread throughout the empire. By virtue of the dues required for membership and the need for capital for the building and maintenance of clubhouses, these clubs were originally the domains of the upper classes and aristocracy. The lower classes still had access to the links on common lands, however, and the average Scotsman's ability to enjoy golf in the late 1800's fostered a great interest in the game and in following the exploits of many well-known Scottish golfers of the time.

• Montrose •

On January 20, 1860, twenty-three-year-olds David Burgess and Anne Campbell were joined in marriage, according to the rites of the Church of Scotland, in the Royal Burgh of Montrose. The groom was a carter, or teamster, and the son of a successful contractor and landowner in the community. The bride was the daughter of the late Montrose innkeeper John Campbell, so her mother Mary had to give the bride away that day. Within the year the newlyweds began their family with the birth of their son John, the first of nine children David and Anne raised in their small stone and timber village home that sat along side the golf links of the town. Some thirteen years later their seventh child Charles, destined to distinguish himself in Scotland's game, would be born.

Montrose was then a thriving commercial community of about 10,000 people located in northeastern Scotland situated on a semi-peninsula formed by the North Sea to the east, the River Esk to the south, and a tidal basin to the west. Southeast of the river entrance, a headland called Scurdie Ness sheltered the waters and created a tranquil natural harbor safe from the often harsh and stormy sea. Fishing, shipping, farming, and manufacturing ventures provided a livelihood for many Montrosians.

The countryside around the central town is very much the same today as it was then. Pastures and farmlands cover gently rolling hills. Sheep and dairy farms interspersed with fields of grains—barley, wheat, and oats—reach down to the dunes beside the coastal plain. Constant summer sea breezes create ripples of gold in the farmer's fields mimicking the waves on the cold vast sea to the east.

The seven boys and two girls of David and Anne grew up in a comfortable working-class home during an era when the ancient game of golf was enjoying a period of revived growth and interest among all levels of Scottish society. This was due in part to the development of better and more affordable equipment, particularly the gutta percha golf ball that had recently replaced the costly hand stuffed and stitched leather ball known as a feathery. Working-class golf club societies were being established as trade union advances provided workers more leisure time for recreational pursuits. Another popular sport in Scotland, association football (or soccer, as it is commonly known today) was also developing in popularity as an activity that would, like golf, soon offer career opportunities to a new generation of Scottish youth. Soon both sports became as synonymous with Scotland as bagpipes and kilts.

The rapid expansion and evolution of both golf and soccer in Great Britain gave rise to official organizations created to govern them beginning in middle of the 1800's. In golf, each local club or golfing society had traditionally formed its own rules that varied in innumerable ways as the game evolved over the years, even as to the number of holes required for a match. The written rules of golf followed by The Royal and Ancient Golf Club of St. Andrews since 1812 became accepted as the standards for the entire British Empire at this time. Likewise, the Football Association was formed in England around 1863 to print and distribute a uniform set of rules to teams in and around London, and within a few years the rules were adopted by teams in Northern England and finally in Scotland. As the games spread around the world, these formalized standards for the sports were generally adopted wherever the games were played.

All of the Burgess children enjoyed playing both sports in their early years, learning the game of golf from their father who was a renowned amateur golfer and later a committeeman of the Montrose Mercantile Golf Club. Two of the younger boys, Charlie and James showed signs of above average athletic skills at an early age. Jimmy excelled at football and played for the Montrose Football Club as a teenager and was just twenty-two when Montrose won the coveted Forfarshire Cup, emblematic of the Northeast Scottish Championship. But it was Charlie who became known throughout the world for his skills in both football and golf. Affectionately called Chay by his family and friends, he was born on November 20, 1873 and was considered a golfing prodigy and an extraordinary football player as a very young boy. As he grew older, his ability to master both sports and his remarkable talent for teaching them to others eventually took him from Scotland to the United States as an emissary of these Scottish pastimes and passions. He became a member of the elite vanguard of Scottish professional golfers who left their native land to develop and profoundly influence the incredibly swift advance of American golf at the beginning of the twentieth century.

•Tom Morris and Bob Dow, "Grand Old Men" of Golf •

During the time that Charlie Burgess began his development as a golfer, the most famous figure on the links of Scotland was "Old" Tom Morris of St. Andrews. Morris has sometimes been credited with inventing the game and is often referred to as the "Father of Golf." While no one person can be credited with inventing the game, it can be said that during Charlie Burgess's lifetime there were certain men who, through their play and influence, popularized the sport and ushered it into the modern era. Old Tom Morris was the leading figure among a handful of men historians call the "Grand Old Men" of golf who fit those criteria.

Born in 1821 at St. Andrews, Tom Morris became known as Old Tom after the birth of his son Tom Junior in 1850. Both Morrises were skillful practitioners of the early game, and between them dominated the world's oldest golf championship, the British Open—officially called The Open Championship—inaugurated in 1860. Old Tom was runner up to Willie Park, Sr. of Musselburgh in the first Open but won the second in 1861 and won it again in 1862, 1864, and 1867, competing annually in the event from 1861 to 1896 until the age of seventy-five. Young Tom won his first golf tournament at age thirteen and won The Open in 1868 just before he turned eighteen. He won it four times in a row from 1868 to 1872 (there was no contest in 1871). Tragically, young Tom died in 1875 at the age of twenty-five and one can only imagine the additional accomplishments he may have been able to achieve.

Old Tom Morris's link to Montrose was through his contemporary, Robert Dow, the Montrose professional who can also be counted among the esteemed Grand Old Men of golf. Dow was a man of average stature who possessed a genial temperament that made him very popular with the golfers of Montrose. He had a rugged countenance and a broad face accentuated by a beard worn in a very distinct style, which favored a cleanly shaven chin and upper lip similar to the one favored by America's President Abraham Lincoln. Dow originally hailed from Aberdeenshire but came to Montrose as a youth in 1840 and was a caddie, amateur golfer, and apprentice to a shoemaker before turning his attention to golf full-time. His shoemaking stitching skills were easily transferred to the highly specialized trade of ball making during the late feathery era when each leather ball stuffed with compressed feathers had to be hand-stitched. He was hired as the first official head professional of the Royal Albert Golf Club in 1863 and was appointed by the Town Council to act as the Superintendent of the ancient links. He became known throughout Scotland as an excellent teacher, as well as a great competitor, because of his many duels with the famed Morris at St. Andrews and in Montrose. One such match occurred on the Montrose Links in 1866 during a competition that featured both old and young Morris, Dow, and several other notables who had or would eventually win the British Open. Among them were James Anderson of St. Andrews, Andrew Strath of Prestwick, and Willie Park, Sr. These founding fathers of the sport were among the many illustrious golfers who influenced the development of young Charlie Burgess as he grew up to witness their exploits on the links that abutted his family homestead in Montrose.

When he was just a small boy, Charlie would play his Montrose course, late into the long Scottish twilight, with a well-worn gutta percha ball and child-sized clubs handed down from his older brothers. He was a robust and healthy child who showed an aptitude for sports and athletics at a surprisingly young age. He had an amiable personality and was, as one of the younger children in a large family, quick to learn from his siblings. Light blue eyes and a sandy blond head of hair, along with a scattering of freckles across his nose and cheeks, hinted strongly of his Celtic heritage. Always cheerful, he also had a talent for making other people laugh because of his inherent good nature and sense of humor. As early as age ten, his golfing skills caught the attention of Bob Dow who took him under his wing and began a tutorial and informal apprenticeship of the boy that lasted for many years. Dow's good friend Morris also established an instructional relationship with the young Montrose golfer and shared Dow's interest in developing the boy's skills. But Charlie's development did not come without great sacrifice, patience, and hard work. A young working-class lad like Burgess did not have the means to live what we might imagine today as anything like a leisurely life. Time for sports, whether on the links or on the soccer field, came only after all of his other responsibilities had been met. Family obligations, chores, schooling, and eventually his vocational training and work all came before recreation.

• Scottish Independence •

Young Charlie Burgess was born and raised in a Scotland that had not been a sovereign nation since its union with England in 1707. At least insofar as its ability to govern itself, it was no longer independent. But, to the minds of many Scotsmen, that was just a technicality. Although a nationalistic independence movement has always existed, the average Scot seemed able to abide British rule because in many respects he still thought himself to be autonomous. Scotland's sense of self and nationhood was fueled by the patriotic and romantic literature of Robert Burns and Walter Scott. The poetic vision of Bonnie Scotland endured through their writing. Young Charlie grew up in a culture that was shaped by the mystique of Scottish heroes like MacBeth, Robert the Bruce, Mary Queen of Scots, Rob Roy MacGregor, Flora MacDonald, and Bonnie Prince Charlie. He had often heard the patriotic story of how in 1296 King Edward I of England completed the construction of a substantial fortified castle in Montrose and how a year later Scottish hero William Wallace burnt it to the ground. Even the language Charlie spoke, although technically English, was a dialect so pronounced that it gave Scotland her own independent tongue. Influenced over the centuries by the Ancient Picts, Celts, Normans, Scandinavians, and Saxons, the language of Scotland was and is unique.

Economically, the fortunes of Scotland benefited from her historic ties with England and were also linked to the United States in a number of ways. As a member of the British Union, Scotland was the beneficiary of some important trading arrangements with the American Colonies until the American independence movement. Tobacco grown in the southern United States was shipped to Scotland for re-exportation to continental Europe. Scotland also had a thriving textile industry. Wool products and the processing of linen goods were the mainstays of a flourishing industry. Cotton shipped from the United States after its independence gradually replaced linen as the leading textile product. For nearly the next one hundred years, cotton manufacturing dominated the Scottish economy until events in Europe and America began a shift in the economic, cultural, and social climate of the nation. The American Civil War cut off the raw supply of cotton from the U.S. South. The Scottish cotton industry collapsed and forced a shift from textiles to heavy industry just at the time when Charlie's parents were beginning their life together in Montrose. The unprecedented industrial development that followed created a need for skilled tradesmen all over Scotland, especially in population centers like Montrose. Hard-won advances by the trade union movement followed and allowed the working classes to enjoy relative prosperity that markedly increased recreation and leisure time activities for the average Scotsman.

It was anticipated that young Charlie Burgess would enter a trade as soon as he was of the proper age. Victorian Scotland built her homes, factories, and churches with stone, brick, and mortar. After a few years of formal schooling, Charlie would be apprenticed to a stonemason for his vocational training. Construction sites, not golf links or football fields, were where the young lad was expected to ply his trade. Nevertheless, his obvious athletic skills, ambitions, and dreams inevitably drew him back to the playing fields of Montrose at every opportunity and his passion for the Scottish games would someday lead him to new and unimagined horizons.

• Growing Up Linkside •

Charlie quite literally grew up on the very same golf links and soccer fields that would later provide him with an occupation. The Burgess family owned several pieces of property in Montrose, adjacent to the golf links, and surrounding their Wellington Street home. It was on Wellington Street that the Montrose Football Club built its Links Park Stadium, named for its close proximity to the ocean-side golf links of Montrose.

Charlie had to walk only a few blocks past the soccer fields to the aptly named North Links School where he received his primary education. The schoolmaster, Mr. Jock Davidson, was a gruff although not unkind, somewhat eccentric, and easily distracted master. Born with a clever sense of humor, Charlie spent more than a little time scheming various ways to engage Old Jock in childish antics that relieved some of the tedium of a Scottish schoolhouse in the 1880s.

One story that Burgess himself frequently recounted with amusement in his later years gives us a comical look at antics that are probably entirely contrary to our image of Victorian schoolboys. It seems that Davidson, after setting the pupils to some laborious task, such as penmanship or solving arithmetic problems, would often exit himself from the class to make use of the outhouse. The master was quite regular in his habits, so Charlie and his chums would sneak out of the class as soon as Old Jock was settled in the privy, and prepare their prank. The outhouse was built at the top of a small slope that ran down and away from the school yard. The user would enter the privy from a door at the top off a walkway from the school, while the bottom or business end of the privy was accessed by a door set into the downside of the slope for easy cleaning out of the straw bed compost material. Just when the schoolmaster took off his waistcoat and vest, unhooked his suspenders, lowered his breeches, and sat himself down onto the privy seat, the boys would make their mischief. They opened the lower "clean-out" door and took a long twig to reach up to the bottom side of Master Davidson giving the poor old master the startle of his life! Unable to rush out of the privy in time to see who his tormentors were, poor Old Jock never caught on to the identity of the culprits.

Despite the occasional distractions caused by the silly mischief of the children, Master Davidson and his colleagues provided their pupils with the sound education in reading, writing, and mathematics that was necessary to function as a literate adult in society. Because the Montrose economy was heavily dependent on farming and produce, the young schoolchildren would regularly be dismissed from their lessons in the early summer and again in October for the community's annual harvesting of the important berry and potato crops. The fertile yet loose and sandy coastal soil of the area produced abundant and incredibly large and sweet strawberries and raspberries. The temptation for the youths to eat more than they picked was so great that all pickers were required to whistle while they worked. If the foreman or straw boss could not hear the whistling then the picker was suspected of breaking the no-eating rule. In the fall another two-week hiatus from school allowed the youngsters to assist with the harvesting of the "taties " or potatoes that also grew in abundance around Montrose. This time the pickers could work in silence if they chose, as a mouthful of dirt-covered spuds was not a very great temptation to the children.

Young Charlie's scholastic education ended after elementary school, which was common in those days for children from a working-class background. At age eleven, Burgess began an apprenticeship to a stonemason. For a period of six years, until he became a journeyman, he was expected to do the lowest levels of work in the masonry trade. He dug ditches, hauled rocks and stones, carried the mortar hod on his strong young shoulders, and gradually learned the finer points of constructing stonewalls, monuments, bridges, homes, and cathedrals in Montrose.

As time-consuming and tedious as his training was, he still found the time to play and have fun. Physically good-sized and strong from his hard work, Charlie was not only a remarkable young golfer but also began to be noticed for his soccer skills by the officials of the local Montrose Football Club.

Charlie sometimes was able to combine his love for sports with the chance to make a few pence now and then as a caddie. There was an abundance of golfers from the several clubs in Montrose which stood side-by-side overlooking the shared links like a row of fraternity houses at an American college. The Royal Albert Golf Club, a club originally formed by the gentry, was the oldest of the clubs in Montrose during Charlie's boyhood. Founded as simply the Montrose Golf Club in 1810, it is known today as the Royal Montrose Golf Club and is among the ten oldest golfing societies in the world. In 1845 the club was renamed the Royal Albert Golf Club in honor of Britain's Prince Albert. Albert granted the club its royal status by proclamation after two years of lobbing by the citizens of Montrose, who felt that their club should have the same status as the other ancient golfing societies of the realm. In their petition to the Throne, they stressed that the quality and beauty of the links of Montrose was "unequaled by any in Scotland."

Many other golf clubs operated in Montrose during the time of Charlie's development as a player and suggest the high level of interest in the game and the keen competition that he must have experienced. The Keithock Club was started in 1822, the Victoria in 1864, the Mechanics Golf Club in 1846, the Caledonia in 1848, the Star Club in 1868, and the Union Golf Club in 1879. Each of the clubs had a different membership, social network, rules, and golfing hierarchy. However, each one of the clubs used the same famous links of Montrose. Even today, the successor to the Royal Albert, the Royal Montrose, sits along side the working-class Mercantile Golf Club (founded in 1897), and members of both clubs still share the ancient coastal course.

• Montrose Tournament of 1888 •

Throughout the years, the layout and number of holes in Montrose has varied, as was the case with many early golf courses. Originally any number of holes were allowed, depending on the circumstances and conditions at each locale. At one time, Montrose had a record 25 holes while St. Andrews only had 18, but when the Royal and Ancient Golf Club became the ruling body of golf, the 18 holes at the links at St. Andrews became the standard for the rest of the world.

In 1886, a reconfiguration of the Montrose course took place and famed Tom Morris, Sr. was summoned to advise on the construction of what was called the new "circular" course layout. One of his suggestions was to move the finishing hole of the Montrose Links to the other side of a busy street to make the course safer and also to make it "more like St. Andrews." For his professional services as an early golf course designer, Morris was paid the relatively princely sum of one pound per day plus expenses. It took two years to complete the work on the new course, and in the autumn of 1888, two special tournaments were held to mark the grand opening of the new layout.

Excitement was widespread. Everyone in Montrose was swept up in the hubbub that accompanied the first match held for the regional golfers, and then the anticipated arrival of world-famous golfers for the second tournament. The first contest was held on a surprisingly warm and humid day in late September when over 100 Montrose amateurs joined the local professionals in what was billed an "All Comers Event." The Royal Albert Club put up prize money for the pros and the amateurs played for medals. In those days, the prize money or the sweepstakes was not the only reward for the players and spectators. The practice of side bets between the golfers and among the gallery was common and added a financial interest for all.

The young lads of Montrose were out in force as caddies or as spectators if they weren't lucky enough to be hired by a golfer during the matches. Charlie Burgess was almost fifteen, his once-fair skin ruddy from his many hours outdoors at work and at play. His light-colored hair had changed to a sun-bleached brown in the summer that gave way to a much darker hue during the long winter months. At nearly six feet tall, his shoulders had broadened and his legs had grown strong from his masonry work. The adolescent spent the last Saturday of September 1888 carrying the clubs and watching the exploits of men he himself would soon be challenging on the links. One such person was Alex "Sandy" Keillor, who won the event and received an outstanding purse of thirteen pounds prize money—an amount equal to at least ten weeks' wages for the average Scotsman! Keillor was one of Montrose's greatest sporting heroes and excelled in both golf and football. His soccer prowess brought him to fame as an international player for Scotland six times between 1891 and 1897, and he was also one of the finest golfers that Montrose ever produced.

The September tournament had featured mostly local Montrose players, but in October, young Charlie and his mates had the chance to witness the greatest gathering of Scottish golf professionals ever to assemble in Montrose. For a youngster growing up in Scotland, the three-day event was the equivalent of an American teenager having the Major League Baseball All-Star Game held in his own backyard and being one of the batboys to boot! Young Charlie and his friends were able to see golf's greatest players first-hand. This time, the temperature was more appropriate to the calendar and the cooler weather made for much more comfortable rounds for the distinguished assembly of golfers dressed in the customary golfing attire of the period. Long woolen trousers and the increasingly popular "plus fours" or knickers with long argyle socks were worn along with tweed jackets and vests as the uniform of the day. Linen or cotton shirts with various fashionable neckties and assorted caps with small brims were worn by almost all of the participants. Nearly all of the early golf clubs in Scotland had dress codes that enforced the wearing of the proper clothing for play. Many clubs required the golfers to wear brightly colored jackets, such as the traditional red jacket of St. Andrews, to distinguish them as they played in matches against other clubs. The jackets were originally worn to insure that they could be clearly seen and to minimize injuries, as the links were sometimes used for other activities such as hunting and archery practice even as the golfers were making their rounds.

Young Burgess and the other caddies carried the clubs of the players in a neat and convenient manner by using the recently introduced leather and canvas device called a golf bag, which was an improvement over trying to cart a half-dozen loose clubs around. However, the bag had to be carried in a most awkward position under the arm, rather than by use of a shoulder strap, which was introduced later.

Among the 52 noteworthy professionals that competed, Willie Fernie, the professional at Troon and Open Champion of 1883 captured the first prize of twelve pounds with a record-setting score of 74 on the new course. Some of the other illustrious professional figures present that day were Andrew Kirkcaldy of St. Andrews, Archie Simpson of Carnoustie, and Ben Sayers representing North Berwick. Sayers was a colorful competitor who entertained the Montrose spectators in a most delightful way. He was only about five feet tall and had once trained as a circus acrobat. It was said that if he sank a good putt, he would sometimes propel himself into a series of handsprings across the green!

Willie Campbell, originally from Musselburgh, was another Montrose participant that day. Campbell was then an excellent match player who several years later gained fame throughout Scotland by making good on a bold challenge of a one-hundred pound wager to any other professional who could defeat him in a head-to-head contest. *Golf* magazine reported that in 1889 he won his daring challenge by defeating Archie Simpson in a 144-hole match played over four courses: Carnoustie, St. Andrews, Musselburgh, and Prestwick. The match drew the attention of thousands of spectators over several weeks. Campbell later went on to be one of the first Scottish professionals to be hired in America at one of America's first golf clubs, The Country Club in Brookline, Massachusetts.

Willie Park, Jr. was another October competitor in Montrose that young Burgess and his fellow caddies followed with great interest. He was born in 1864 and was not much older than many of the caddies when he began his professional career in Musselburgh at the age of sixteen. By seventeen, he had won The Open at Prestwick. This golfing sensation and his father, Willie Park Sr., won the British Open six times between them, Junior winning twice, and Senior winning four times including the initial match in 1860.

Other former or future British Open winners playing in Montrose that day included Hugh Kirkcauldy, who would win in 1891, and Jack Burns, the reigning champion of 1888. Of course, the legendary white-bearded Old Tom Morris was there as well. Morris was the most prolific Open champion in Montrose at the time. His four Open wins prior to 1867 set a record that only his son Tom, Jr. could best by winning four *consecutive* times beginning in 1868! Old Tom had another less well-known son, J.O.F. "Jamie" Morris competing with him in Montrose that day. Not much was recorded about Jamie Morris's association with Montrose golf, but he finished eleventh in the tournament that day. Rounding out the competitors were several other professionals from St. Andrews and the host of the tournament, Bob Dow, the Montrose golf veteran who had been the Montrose professional for over twenty-five years at the time of the new circular course celebration.

• Fieldstones, Football, and Golf •

Charlie was passionate in his love for football and golf, but the sports remained only a pastime as he finished his masonry apprenticeship in 1891 and became a journeyman at age seventeen. He had a good trade and was insured of a stable future, as the demand for skilled tradesmen would continue well into the turn of the century. A vocation as a stonemason seemed to be his destiny.

For the last decade or so, the condition of the Scottish working class and the trade unions had been improving rapidly. The British Reform Act of 1832 enfranchising the middle class had been amended in 1868 and again in 1885 to strengthen the political power of all workers. A stronger middle class bolstered by an upwardly rising working class and an active trade union movement guaranteed young Charlie a prosperous future. By 1892 various trade unions including the newly formed Scottish Miners Federation would number hundreds of thousands of members. Although unsuccessful, the Scottish Labor Party became strong enough to call for Scottish home rule and the abolition of the House of Lords. Charlie's early exposure to the labor and trade union movement greatly influenced his life later on, as he became an influential leader in the professional golfer organizations of Scotland and in America. But at the time, it was an unimagined and far-flung notion.

The advances won by the trade unions and Charlie's promotion to journeyman allowed him more leisure time to pursue and enjoy his enduring passion for golf and football. At most of the seaside links in Scotland, golf was played year round. Although frequent blustery winds and rain in the spring made for some tough outings, summer months could be counted on for many rounds because of the long hours of daylight in this northern region. In mid-June, twilight came as late as ten o'clock at night. In the winter months, snow rarely fell in significant amounts or lasted very long because of the ocean influence. Hardy golfers could be seen almost any time of year and in any weather conditions in Montrose, but the long summer days meant equally long winter nights. For working-class golfers, their winter outings were primarily restricted to the weekends because of the early darkness. Care had to be observed when attempting to get in a round on a Sunday. Early church records reveal that golfers who missed church services in order to play golf ran the risk of some significant financial loss as their ministers could actually fine them for their transgressions!

Charlie's accelerated development as a championship-caliber golfer began to take hold in earnest in his early teens. He took to the links at every opportunity and at any time of year, and his passion for the sport was evident. His year-round pursuit of golf did, however, give way to his fondness for football during its late fall and winter season. As the seasons changed, Charlie was often seen playing casual pick-up soccer games with his friends until he was invited to join his older brother Jimmy on the local Montrose Football Club that played in both the Northern and the Forfarshire County League of the Scottish Football Association. At the time, the Montrose team was a highly organized and very popular amateur club, as were all of the association football teams of Great Britain. Professionalism was not legalized in Scotland until the early 1890's, and the Montrose Football Club did not pay its players until the beginning of 1900.

The Montrose Club was organized in 1879 and first played on a makeshift pitch or playing field, which originally encroached upon the northern end of the golf links. The team eventually moved its home site, Links Park, to its present location on Wellington Street—the very same street where Charlie Burgess was born. The team was nicknamed the Gable Endies, a name frequently given to anyone from Montrose at the time.

During the eighteenth century, the main thoroughfare of Montrose, High Street, featured a large open air marketplace. When the marketplace was no longer used as such, the town council gave permission for the adjacent homes to extend forward into the vacated land. The easiest way to expand the homes out to the street was to build a gable-ended extension out onto the main street. Thus, many houses and buildings in the center of the business district in Montrose were built gable-end out toward High Street, and the nickname Gable Enders or Gable Endies refers to Montrosians and the Montrose Football Club to this day.

Charlie was just fifteen years old, and still a mason's apprentice, during his first season with the Montrose Football Club in 1888–89. He was the youngest player ever chosen for the team that featured many outstanding players, including the famous Sandy Keillor—equally well known for his golfing prowess. Charlie played the position of "right back" for the team and the defensive position was a comfortable fit for him as he had matured into a big and powerful young man. Nearly six feet tall, he weighed 185 pounds and his stonemason trade provided him with all of the conditioning he needed. The teenager proved to be a phenomenon on the soccer field. He secured a regular position, playing against and alongside men five to ten years his senior, and was a member of the 1891–92 Forfarshire Cup Championship team. According to the official history of the Montrose Football Club published in 1948, Charlie joined a very elite group of athletes from Scotland chosen to play in international competition when he " . . . was capped for Scotland against Ireland" in 1892. Charlie remained with the local Montrose Club until he was twenty. During those years, he developed a characteristic style of play that saw him always trying to clear his lines at once by putting the ball out to a speedier wingman for the attack. He believed in lying back behind his own halfback and then used his size and strength to break up the advances of the opposing offense.

Throughout the six-year period when he was with the Montrose Football Club, Charlie continued to ply his trade as a stonemason and continued to improve his golf game. He entered many Montrose regional amateur and open tournaments that drew the area's finest golfers. In 1893, as a nineteen-year-old amateur, he played in a Montrose open tournament against veteran professional Davie Brown of Musselburgh, who had won the British Open seven years before. The experience of meeting and competing alongside an established and legendary professional like Brown was an epiphany for the young man. He played extremely well in the contest and was able to best the experienced pro on several tricky match play holes. He was of course very familiar with his home links. Using that to his advantage, he was able to challenge the ever-present ocean winds and take daring chances on recovery shots when he had to, tactics that soon became a trademark of his play.

Although he did not defeat Brown in the match, he saw that he had the potential to compete at the professional level against men like Brown and the other great Scottish golfers that he admired. He became attracted to the idea of earning a living from a game he loved to play. If his golf game was not yet up to the professional level, his football game certainly was. As an accomplished veteran of the local soccer club at only twenty, he came of age just at the time professional football was legalized in Scotland and throughout Great Britain. The opportunity to play for pay was as nearby as the city of Dundee where a relatively new team had indicated an interest in his service.

• Playing for Pay •

The summer of 1895 was a turning point in Charlie's athletic pursuits and career. It marked the end of three years as a journeyman mason, ten years as a serious student of Dow and Morris on the golf course, and six years of high-level organized football competition. The success of the Montrose Football Club and the contributions of the husky young fullback to the team became well known. As a result, Charlie's reputation had spread and the Dundee Football Club offered him a professional contract for the next season. His aspirations to become a professional golfer were put aside for the moment as he sampled life in pro football in the bustling industrial city of Dundee, which was a short thirty-mile train ride south of Montrose.

The Dundee Club, formed in 1893, was a new team looking for new talent. The managers were familiar with many local amateur teams and recruited players through a variety of innovative ways including even running help wanted advertisements in many of the region's newspapers. It is likely that Sandy Keillor, Charlie's former teammate from Montrose, influenced Charlie to join Dundee. Keillor was one of the very first players that the Dundee Club signed on in 1893 and was skilled at almost any position. Whether the highly regarded Keillor actually encouraged Charlie's signing is not known, but as they both shared a passion for golf and football, had been teammates before, and knew each other well, it seems likely that the strong connection between the two players might have had an influence. Charlie was signed for the 1895–96 season and played in 18 games as "west back number three." Playing for the Dundee Football Club was his first introduction to big-time sports and the life of a professional athlete. His skills were tested time and again as the season went on and he soon became regarded as a stalwart on defense for the club.

Because Dundee was relatively close to home, he still could maintain his trade and keep his ties to his community. During the football off-season, he kept up his play in local golf matches in Montrose and by summer was ready to challenge for the Montrose championship. At twenty-two he had improved to the point of qualifying for a bye, or automatic advancement to the second round of the tournament, in the most prestigious and competitive contest played for that year. Despite his advantageous seeding, Charlie did not capture the prize in his first major challenge against the golfers of Montrose but he did capture another prize that summer—his future wife.

Harriet Low was home one evening that summer waiting with her older sister Mary, who was expecting to be called on by the handsome and well-known Charlie Burgess. When he arrived, Mary, the daughter of a prosperous potato merchant, kept her suitor waiting in the parlor for quite some time as she dallied in the vanity. Harriet was sent down to entertain Charlie, while Mary primped, and had an unexpected chance to spend some time with her sister's suitor. Young "Hattie" with her turned up nose, deep blue eyes, and sweet personality enthralled Charlie. It was Harriet, not Mary, who won his heart that evening and they courted throughout the remainder of the year.

Charlie returned to Dundee in the late fall for his second season with the football club. It was a busy and productive season for the young man. At twenty-three, he played in 17 more professional games at his familiar west back number three position. He also found time during the season to marry his bonnie Hattie, age twenty-one, in the parish church of Montrose on January 26, 1897. Even though he had played in the Scottish professional football league for two years, the term professional did not mean that he could support a wife or even himself on his football earnings. Unlike contemporary athletes, the business of sports did not then provide, even in relative terms, a great amount of income to the players. He received about a one-pound salary for each match, received occasional performance bonuses, and was given travel compensation. So at the time of his marriage, he still considered himself a tradesman whose participation in professional sports was secondary to his vocation as a mason.

During the following spring, Charlie joined his father David as a committee member, or director, of the Mercantile Golf Club, where the entire Burgess family had become members. He continued to work on his game through the summer and early fall under the continued tutelage of both Bob Dow and Tom Morris, who had motivated Burgess often during their encounters in Montrose and St. Andrews. Morris was seventy-five and still competitive, though he had played his last British Open the year before in 1896, at Muirfield, near the capital city of Edinburgh.

Charlie and his young wife started a family right away. On a cold day in late November during a complicated birth, Charles Beattie Burgess, or Charles II, was born. The physician attending to Harriet concluded that her "stomach was upside down" and he advised that if she had another pregnancy, she would most likely die from it. There is no telling exactly what the complications were or what the actual diagnosis was from that rather unscientific explanation, but during the years that followed and until her death, Hattie suffered frequent rounds of intense intestinal pain and discomfort. That winter Charlie finished his final year with the Dundee Football Club. Throughout the season and into the spring, he endeavored to remain as close to home as possible while Harriet recovered.

• Life in Professional Football •

The Millwall Athletic Football Club, a well-known English team from London, approached Charlie the next summer. They were impressed by his performance in the Northern League and offered him a contract for the 1898–99 season. This was a big step. Playing for a major English football team meant a substantial increase in wages, to at least two more pounds per game, as well as board allowance and performance bonuses. The only negative aspect of the offer was that he would have to live away from Montrose during most of the winter football season.

The Millwall Club, once known as the Rovers, was formed a few years earlier, in 1885, by the workers at the Morton Jam factory in the hard-scrabble East End section of London known as the Isle of Dogs. The area was once a small island in the River Thames and was annexed to London by filling in a section of the river to form a small peninsula. The docks and factories of the area were home to rough and tumble neighborhoods of immigrants from all corners of the empire who lived in crowded tenements and inexpensive rooming houses. The Scottish influence on this young English Club was strong. The majority of the founding factory workers were of Scottish extraction, and eventually the blue-and-white of the Scottish flag became the team's colors. The trainer and later coach of the team was Bob Hunter from Montrose, who had been the Gable Endies trainer during Charlie's time with that team. Hunter had an eye for recruiting talented players from his home region and felt that the rugged and consistent play of Burgess would be an excellent addition to his current London team.

Charlie was only twenty-five at the start of the season and had taken to sporting a mustache, a fashion he would adopt and abandon quite frequently. London was hundreds of miles from his home, his still-ailing wife and his infant son would be alone, and he had never before lived outside of Montrose. But it was an unparalleled opportunity. A good showing in London could mean a wonderful future for his family. Charlie arrived for his rookie year in the English leagues with all the trepidation and uncertainty a young man could have. A London newspaper account of his much-heralded arrival was headlined *"Charlie Burgess' Trunk"* and recounted an amusing story of his arrival in the big city of London:

> "Charlie arrived at King's Cross railroad station in London from Montrose. He was met by Bob Hunter, the Millwall trainer. Burgess's trunk was so heavy that it took a couple of stout men to carry it. After much trouble and candid comment on the part of the carriers, the party reached the house in which Charlie was to live on the Isle of Dogs. Curious to know why the trunk was so heavy, Hunter waited until the lid was raised. Then it was revealed that Burgess had packed it with potatoes, turnips, and other vegetables because such eatables were believed in the far north to be very scarce in London!"

Charlie soon discovered that London had ample supplies of fresh produce and all of the other necessities of life. When he settled into life in the big city, the fans, coaches and players quickly accepted him, as he became the regular right back in every game while he was with the team. His play was consistent with his reputation from his days with Montrose and Dundee. A steady and reliable defender, he was known as a "tall, strong and resolute" player and one who was "invariably a prominent figure on the field of play." It was also noted that as a defender he "tackled with extreme determination." His rough-and-tumble play was extremely popular with this very pro-Scottish club located in the heart of London. He became one of the team's leading and most popular players. He played in 98 games for Millwall, including 50 Southern League and 12 English Cup appearances.

After his last season with Millwall, Charlie signed on with another English Club, Newcastle United, in May of 1900. United, like Millwall, was obtaining many players from Scotland and Charlie was one of numerous Scottish-born players signed for the 1900–01 season in the hopes of strengthening their lineup. Newcastle United was a club with a much greater following and much larger venue than his other teams. The stadium for Newcastle was a big wooden affair called St. James Park, set high upon a hill above the city and the Tyne River. The pitch could hold 30,000 spectators, including a large number of standees on the broad terraces or wide concrete steps of the stadium. The inexpensive terrace area was often home to each teams most vociferous and rowdy fans.

Famous for shipbuilding and its coal mining industry, Newcastle on the Tyne was the historic capital of northeast England. In the second century A.D., the occupying Romans built an incredibly extensive stone fortification, not unlike the ancient Great Wall of China, known as Hadrian's Wall, to keep out the fierce and warring Scottish tribes from invading England from the north. Over the ensuing centuries, however, the social, cultural, and economic ties between the Scots and this northern English city became so intertwined that even today, the city of Newcastle has the sound and feel of Scotland. In 1900, the ordinarily friendly and enthusiastic "Geordies," as the Newcastle residents were called, were somewhat unreceptive to Charlie's arrival, even though he played his usual strong and steady game throughout the season. For some unknown reason he was having a difficult time fitting into a club for the first time in his career. Contemporary club historians noted that: "Burgess was never a favorite of the Newcastle fans. It is recorded that he received some typical terrace abuse during his short stay at St. James Park."

Despite his inexplicable unpopularity among the English fans of Newcastle, Charlie played consistently and well at his fullback position in all 30 regular season games and in the only Football Association Cup match United had that season. He stayed with Newcastle only that one year. After three seasons in English football competition, he headed back south again to join the best team he would ever play for.

Notwithstanding his Newcastle experience, Charlie was very popular with the English football fans in Portsmouth. He signed on with the team on June 5, 1901 and played two seasons for this southernmost English club. His wages jumped to four pounds per week along with expense allowances and bonus money based upon performance. The Portsmouth Football Club was a powerful club from 1901 to 1903 featuring some very well-known athletes. During his tenure, nine international level players were on the squad. One was the team's captain, named C. B. Frye of England, the C. B. ironically standing for his Christian names, Charles Burgess! Frye was without question the biggest star on the team, and his opinions and comments concerning the game of football were well respected. Frye described Charlie as "solid and powerful" in the fullback position and throughout his career consistently hailed him as a great team player by virtue of his position on defense and his personal style.

Charlie's most unforgettable game for Portsmouth was his very first. On September 21, 1901, he made his debut against his old team from London, the Millwall Athletic F.C. When he was with Millwall, he was lauded as a hero but leaving the team for another was considered a form of heresy by the fans. Up until this time Charlie never had the occasion to return to play any of his former teams. But Portsmouth and Millwall were both in the Southern League and this first match of the season between them took on the complexion of a crusade for the riled-up London fans. In an incident that recalls the unruly behavior that unfortunately still sometimes occurs today, the Portsmouth newspapers reported the following:

> "The passion of the occasion marred the game. Former Millwall idol Burgess, making his debut for Portsmouth, was booed every time he touched the ball, with supporters regarding his signing for the south coast club [Portsmouth] . . . a gross act of desertion. Tempers continued to rise in the 6,000 crowd and when Portsmouth's Smith placed the ball for a corner kick close by the main stand, he was felled by a stone thrown at him by a spectator. The missile caused a dreadful gash to his forehead, rendering him virtually useless for the match . . . After the final whistle Portsmouth players were forced to run the gauntlet through incensed spectators."

Portsmouth survived the match 4–2 and Millwall had to appear before an inquiry of a special commission of the Football Association because of the hooligan behavior of the fans that day.

It saddened Charlie to return to London and his old club, a club where many of his old friends and teammates still played, and to have such an unpleasant homecoming. Still, this was professional football, and hostile fans were accepted as part of the game. Constant travel and often-difficult playing conditions were also part of the game. The Portsmouth Club played at least seven games per month during the season that ran from September through April, and sometimes to mid-May. Over half the games were away from home, necessitating long train trips and overnight stays in strange cities and towns. Many of the matches were played in the dead of the cold, damp, and dreary English winter. The players, clad only in their football kits—simple uniforms of shirt, shorts, and wool stockings—had to perform on frozen turf and in sleet and snow. Nonetheless, the team performed extremely well and Charlie and his defensive mates held the opposition to an average of less than one goal for every three Portsmouth scored.

His career at Portsmouth included 42 Southern League games, 25 Western League games, 11 non-league matches and seven FA Cup games. He was a regular on one of the strongest Portsmouth squads ever. The team finished as champions of the Western League in 1902 and 1903, champions of the Southern League in 1902, and won the Portsmouth Cup in 1902–03.

At the end of the 1903 season, Charlie was twenty-eight-years-old and had established himself as an accomplished performer at the highest levels of professional football. He was acknowledged as an internationally known star but the price of his success was costly. He had been away from home every winter for the past five years since signing on with Millwall in London and for three years before that in Dundee. Although he still loved the game, the constant travel, the wear and tear of the game and the months away from his home and family helped him make a decision that would shape the rest of his life. He chose to retire from major league football and return to Montrose to concentrate on becoming a professional in golf.

2 1903–1905

"In regard to lessons let me say one more thing. When it is considered feasible for a mother to give a child two lessons per week for two years in learning the rudiments of the piano, why become impatient at golf with only ten lessons? The secret of lessons in golf is to practice after each lesson and take more only when you have mastered those already taken."

—Charlie Burgess

• The Birth of American Golf •

Charlie's decision to return home and pursue a career in professional golf was a timely one. At the turn of the century there was a marked increase in the demand for the services of golf professionals because of the many new clubs and courses that were being built throughout Great Britain during the relatively prosperous time of rapid industrial development. During the same period, on the other side of the Atlantic, the long-established Scottish game had just begun to capture the interest of many well-to-do Americans and was getting a foothold in several regions of the United States. The need for experienced instructors and club managers would soon be great in America.

Although there is evidence to suggest that golf was played in America as early as the colonial period, most golf historians cite the often-repeated theory that the birth of the modern game of golf in the United States occurred in Yonkers, New York in February of 1888.

Scottish transplant and amateur golfer John Reid, along with several friends, were said to have laid out a primitive three-hole course on his farm just north of New York City during a mid-winter thaw. Shortly thereafter Reid moved his course to a larger site adjacent to the farm and some nearby apple orchards. Reid and his friends, later known as the Apple Tree Gang, were credited with establishing the first golf course in America, which became the St. Andrew's [sic] Golf Club, named after the venerable Scottish Mecca of golf. Reid's creation took root and became America's first permanently established golf club. The Country Club (Brookline, Massachusetts), Shinnecock Hills Golf Club (Southampton, New York), Newport Country Club in Rhode Island, and the Chicago Golf Club were also established at nearly the same time. These first five clubs formed the Amateur Golf Association of the United States, the forerunner of the United States Golf Association founded in 1894.

• Alex Findlay, American Golf Pioneer •

Alexander H. Findlay, a pioneering Scottish golfer from Charlie Burgess's hometown of Montrose, is clearly among the contenders for the honor of establishing, if not the original, certainly one of America's very first golf courses. Findlay had beaten the Apple Tree Gang to the punch by almost a year when he established a six-hole course in the unlikely locale of the Nebraska frontier on April 4, 1887. Because the course was of a transitory nature, only lasting a few years, Findlay's contribution to golf as the originator of the game in America and its first course architect has always been overshadowed by Reid's achievements in New York. But far more important than being the first person to lay out a course or play golf in America, Findlay became the first missionary of the sport in the New World. Throughout next five decades Alex was the "Johnny Appleseed" of American golf, sowing courses and golf's gospel as he traversed the country, tirelessly promoting the game that he learned as a boy in Montrose, as the game took root in the United States.

The adventurous Findlay left Scotland to seek his fortune in the American West in 1886 when he was in his early twenties. Eager to try his hand as a cowboy, he accepted a position on a cattle ranch that was owned by another recently transplanted Montrosian, Edward Millar, near the town of Fullerton, Nebraska. Findlay had brought along his golfing equipment to the New World only to be surprised to learn from his acquaintances that to their knowledge there were no golf links in existence anywhere in America at the time. The resourceful and tenacious Scotsman surveyed the landlocked rolling grass-covered sandhills of the Nebraska Plains and was reminded of the coastal dunes of his native Montrose. Inspired during the early spring of 1887, and before the prairie grass had grown too high, he created an adequate course by setting tin cans in the ground to make his six-hole layout. He and Millar enthusiastically introduced their cowboy and American Indian friends to the subtleties of golf. Imagine the unusual scene that the locals witnessed as they came upon Findlay in his full golfing attire, propelling his tiny white ball across the vast and empty plains where the great buffalo herds roamed just a few years before.

The romance of being a cowboy, even a golfing one, eventually wore off and Alex moved to Omaha in 1891 where he took a retail position in a dry goods emporium. There he had the opportunity to sell imported golfing equipment and to design his first major golf course on the 800-acre estate of wealthy rancher John Nelson Patrick. The course, which opened in 1895, became known as the Happy Hollow Country Club and is still in play today. Findlay thrived in his new role as a golf developer and in 1897 moved to the East Coast to join the Boston sporting goods company Wright and Ditson, which desired to establish a golf goods department in response to America's growing interest in the game. At Wright and Ditson he was selling imported clubs and equipment and even arranged to manufacture a line of clubs bearing his own name, the first such signature series ever produced. He made numerous trips back to Scotland and England for supplies and to recruit his fellow countrymen for the many golfing positions that were becoming increasingly available in America. Findlay continued his interest in golf course architecture and eventually built over one hundred courses across the land and up and down the East Coast.

• Willie Campbell, Donald Ross, George Wright, and Golf's Roots in Boston •

Alex Findlay's new residency in Massachusetts placed him in the center of what was perhaps the nation's most active region of golf development at the time, as evidenced by the continuous migration of Scottish professionals arriving there beginning with Willie Campbell. Campbell, originally from Musselburgh, was hired as the first golf professional in the Boston area when he came to The Country Club in Brookline in 1894. Another Scotsman, Donald Ross, from the far-northern Scottish coastal town of Dornoch, joined Findlay, Campbell, and a handful of other transplanted Scots in Boston in 1898 to became the professional at the newly formed Oakley Country Club, leaving behind his apprenticeship with Old Tom Morris in St. Andrews. During his time as a club and teaching professional, Ross began to establish himself as a part-time course designer as a great interest in establishing new clubs throughout America began to take hold. Ross soon began designing golf courses full-time as the game began to boom. Ross eventually became the most renowned and revered American golf course architect of all time.

Unlike the mysteries of *exactly* when and where the game of golf originated in Scotland and in the United States, the origins of the game in Massachusetts are fairly certain—to a degree. The events leading up to the establishment of the Boston area's first permanent golfing venue, The Country Club of Brookline, began with a young woman named Florence

Boit. Generally, the story goes that in 1892, Miss Boit had just returned home from a visit to France, where she had seen the game played, and had tried it herself. She brought a set of clubs and several balls back to America with her and used them on the grounds of her uncle Arthur Hunnewell's expansive estate in Wellesley, Massachusetts. Hunnewell was at the time a member of The Country Club, a well-established suburban retreat for the wealthy that offered up leisure activities such as polo, horse racing, lawn tennis, and fine dining to its members. Within a short period of time Hunnewell and his friends suggested that the club add golf to its many activities and in 1893 the first permanent golf course in Greater Boston was established.

There is, however, another sequence of events that may be correctly advanced as the start of golf in Boston and it concerns the first round of golf played in Boston—if not the establishment of the first permanent course.

George Wright, the founder of the Wright and Ditson sporting goods company, the same establishment that Alex Findlay came east to work for—was himself a pioneer in establishing the game of golf in Boston when he introduced the game in the 1890's. Even here there are conflicting versions about exactly how and when Wright first tried the sport, and each one was advanced by Wright himself! An account of the events he offered in a 1931 interview published in the *Pinehurst Outlook* is the version that Wright undoubtedly wanted to leave for posterity. It seems that Wright had seen some golf clubs advertised in an English catalogue from which he used to order other sporting goods supplies, mostly cricket equipment, as Wright was an avid cricket player and belonged to a cricket club in Boston. Out of curiosity he ordered a set of golf clubs and a few balls from the catalogue. After they arrived in Boston, Wright eventually put them on display in one of the store windows where they sat, apparently unnoticed, until one day in 1890 when a visiting Scotsman walked by.

The visitor entered the store, inquired of the clerk where the nearest golf course was, and the clerk promptly referred him to Mr. Wright because, in fact, there were no courses in Boston—or anywhere else in America—as far as the confused clerk knew. After conversing with the friendly stranger for a while about golf, Wright asked him if he would kindly send a copy of the game's rules back to the store when he returned to his native land. Soon afterward the rules arrived. Armed with the rules and a sketch of a course layout provided by the Scotsman, Wright set out to find some ground on which to play. He settled on a part of Boston's lovely Franklin Park, one of the gems of the "Emerald Necklace" of park lands that surround Boston, designed by Frederick Law Olmstead in the 1880s. After negotiating the fields of the park for use through the proper city government channels, Wright set out a golf course using twigs with red flannel flags as targets for each hole and played a round with several of his friends. So according to this version, the first game of golf was played on the wide-open and grassy plains of Boston's Franklin Park in 1890.

Linde Fowler, a Boston newspaper reporter who began writing about golf in 1900, wrote that the actual sequence of events differed slightly and in a most amusing way from the account that Mr. Wright provided for public consumption in that *Pinehurst Outlook* interview. According to Fowler, in a remembrance published in 1952, he recalled that Mr. Wright had told him a slightly different version of his first attempt at golf. The story is pretty much the same as above regarding the visit and conversation with the traveling Scotsman except for the part about Wright's first golf outing. Rather than waiting for the rules to arrive and then setting out to play, Wright was eager to get right out to try the game. He relied upon his fairly accurate recollection of the Scotsman's explanation of the basic rules and convinced a few of his friends to join him in an experimental round at a location that he thought would be an appropriate and suitable playing ground. His interpretation of what would be a proper playing ground for golf is where he made a slight mistake!

Fowler related that the party of pioneer golf pilgrims led by George Wright staged their initial game in the sand of a North Shore *beach* somewhere between Revere Beach and the Point of Pines section of that city in the year 1889! "Whether the Scotch visitor, in explaining something about golf and about golf courses in the British Isles, laid stress upon the sanded bunkers which were part of the better courses, or whether from something else that he heard or read, Mr. Wright labored under the delusion that sand was the primary feature of a links, hence his plan to give the game a try at a point along Revere Beach," noted Fowler. As Wright and his friends began hitting "lustily at the balls" on the compacted sand of low tide, there were a few "casualties" to the wooden shafted clubs that "were dried out and brittle" as the enthusiastic but novice golfers often hit the hard sand before they contacted the balls. Wright soon figured out that something had to be amiss and stopped the experiment before all the clubs were destroyed. He returned to his Boston shop to await the requested instructions from abroad before he ventured out to try the game again. When the instruction book finally arrived, it explained "that sand bunkers were only a hazard factor and not the fundamental feature of a golf course" as Wright had once thought.

It made little difference to golf history exactly where or when Wright actually played the first round, more important was his eventual demonstration that Franklin Park was a suitable location for the game, and that golf was a worthwhile recreational pursuit for the citizens of Boston. His outing led to the creation, in 1896, of one of America's earliest public golf courses, second only to the Van Cortlandt Golf Course in the Bronx, New York, which was established in 1895. Willie Campbell, golf professional at The Country Club in Brookline, had joined Wright in the effort to make Franklin Park the site for Boston's pioneer public course and was hired as its first professional when the club opened. Campbell thus became America's first municipally employed golf professional when he accepted the job at Franklin Park, as the New York course did not retain its first pro until 1899 when the City of New York hired noted course designer Thomas Bendelow as its "City Golf Instructor" in addition to having him supervise the further development of the course. The new golf facility at Franklin Park gave the common man, at least in Boston, affordable access to what was a then a game exclusively of the wealthy. The continued development of more and more public courses across America, and the latest evolution of one of the game's most expensive consumable items—golf balls—combined to foreshadow what soon would be a explosion in golf's popularity and growth in the United States and worldwide.

The latest innovation in the development of the game in both Scotland and America was the introduction of the rubber core golf ball in 1901. The ball was the latest evolution from the very expensive, handmade "feathery," and later the more easily produced "gutty" ball. The feathery was the first manufactured golf ball. It was a small round leather sack, stuffed tightly with a strictly proscribed amount of small feathers. In the process, the leather was thoroughly dampened and then stitched into a round ball shape as the equally wet feathers were stuffed tightly into the sack before it was sewn closed into a ball that hardened quite well after it dried. The feathery was used in the very early days of the game until around 1850 when the more durable, cheaper, and easier to make gutta percha ball replaced it. The gutty was made from a plastic-like resin produced by the gutta percha tree from tropical regions around India. The resin was tapped, collected and processed into thick chunks of material as the sticky substance dried out. Pieces were cut into sections, softened with hot water, and then the softened compound was pressed into round molds to harden. The hardened molded resin was then scored with lines for improved aerodynamic flight, painted, and became a golf ball.

In the 1900's the gutty gave way to the mass-produced rubber core ball, the immediate predecessor to the modern golf ball. The new rubber core balls dramatically increased the distance a ball could travel and the economic mass-production of them made the game more affordable. Thin strips of elastic rubber were wound under tension into a ball and then were covered with a thin layer of gutta percha to keep the wound rubber together. A series of developments and endorsements by leading players gave each new ball its own name and personality. There were "Bounding Billy's," "Haskells," and a host of other experimental balls that found their way on to the links.

• A Golf Pro at Twenty-Eight •

Continued improvements in the game's equipment, accessibility to playing venues, and interest in the exploits of the leading international players like England's Harry Vardon fueled a steadily growing interest in golf world wide, especially in America. Acutely aware of that ever-increasing growth, Charlie Burgess clearly saw that his love of golf might very well be able to provide him with a very good living, and in 1903 he accelerated his efforts to become one of Scotland's leading golfers, beginning in his hometown of Montrose.

For last several years Charlie had been able to reduce the amount of time he had to devote to construction work and was able to spend more time developing his golfing skills, thanks to the income he earned through football. His football career had been rewarding, but it was also a trade-off in the sense that in order to make more money he had to play for teams that were further and further away from his home in Montrose. However, as he made more money at football, he could afford to spend less time at his masonry trade and could concentrate more on golf to the point where he could develop his skills and turn professional. At twenty-eight, he was a veteran football player ready to leave that game behind and was just in his prime as a golfer. He astutely knew that golf was a game that could be rewarding for a lifetime, and he hoped to make his mark on the links over the next few years.

Montrose was home to one of the oldest golfing grounds in the world, but did not commission an official golf professional until 1863, when Bob Dow was employed as the clubkeeper of the Royal Albert. The Royal Albert, successor to the original Montrose Golf Club (formed in 1810 and documented as the seventh oldest golfing *society* in the world), employed Dow for over 35 years. Dow had turned seventy-one in 1903 and was ready for retirement. His personal choice for a successor was his young protégé, Charlie Burgess.

The members of the Royal Albert agreed and approached Charlie during the spring of 1903 to offer him Dow's position, making him just the second professional ever employed by the ancient golf club. Charlie's role as clubkeeper was varied, but in essence he supervised all of the affairs of the club and was afforded the benefit of a decent base salary and "fire and hearth," which was lodging and heat in private quarters attached to the clubhouse. He could now make his living exclusively from golf, but his duties were mixed, varied, and loosely defined. Like most of Scotland's early professionals, he had to manage all of the activities in the clubhouse ranging from overseeing the barkeep and liquor purchases, to the storage and repair of the members' golf clubs and equipment. He gave golfing lessons and could charge the members individually for his services, but only at a fee that the club strictly established. He made and sold golf clubs, oversaw all competitive tournaments, and occasionally pitched in to help maintain the course. He was a jack-of-all-trades at a time when the role of golf professional had not fully evolved and was not clearly defined. Clearly defined or not, Charlie Burgess enthusiastically accepted the position and was able to give up his masonry business and his faraway travels as a football player. He no longer had to travel away from home to earn a living from a sport he loved. Golf became his career, with football now just his pastime, as he agreed to play once again for his hometown team. Charlie was also elected to the Mercantile Golf Club governing board again, along with his younger cousin David and old football teammate Sandy Keillor.

Charlie also began a concerted effort to enhance his professional standing. He wanted to become a member of the world's first organization of professional golfers, The Professional Golfers' Association, established in Great Britain in 1901. Membership was desirable because for the first time British golf professionals had a measure of organization, protection, and governance for their continually growing numbers. Charlie's first step in that direction was to join the regional professional golfers' organization in Scotland so he could participate in tournament play and have a voice in the affairs of Scottish professional golf.

Charlie was a popular member of the Mercantile and was equally well regarded as the new professional at the Royal Albert. He quickly established a reputation as an excellent competitive player and able instructor. One facet of his personality that appealed to many people was the prankster sense of humor he had as a youth and still displayed as an adult. A spectator at many Montrose golf matches recalled that, "on one occasion Charlie was on the links in the foursome ahead of one of his co-workers, Old Geordie Croll, who was a clubmaker and prominent golfer, though a rather mediocre one. Geordie's foursome was playing a 'blind' hole behind Burgess' group and Charlie waited until Geordie played an iron shot at the par three hole—a wild shot it was, many yards from the green. Charlie quickly ran for the ball and placed it on the lip of the hole. 'Great Shot Geordie' was Charlie's remark when the players came over the brae (hill). For many years, in fact to his dying day, Geordie boasted of this great birdie shot, and neither Charlie nor his golfing cronies ever told the prank to spoil Geordie's elation."

When the matches were finished, Charlie, Geordie, and the others all retired to the clubhouse for cigars, drinks, and a private laugh over the trick on Geordie. Enjoying a lager or whiskey after a match at the "nineteenth hole" was a time-honored ritual of the game. While Charlie was not known to drink, he had a fondness for fine cigars and enjoyed a smoke during and after a good round. He was frequently seen on the links with a cigar or sometimes a pipe firmly clenched between his teeth as he approached and concentrated on a challenging shot.

The layout of the Montrose course in 1903 had been recently redesigned, or more accurately modified, by the local greenskeeper and skilled golfer, Andrew Simpson. The practice of regularly rearranging courses was very common at this time throughout Scotland, as conditions or events warranted frequent changes. New holes were laid out and then abandoned quite often. In October of 1903, the greens committee of Montrose once again decided to rework the layout of the links and this time turned to their counterparts in St. Andrews for recommendations regarding a suitable course architect to do the job. The St. Andreans recommended Willie Park, Jr., who had been Open Champion in 1887 and 1889 and had been active in course design and reconstruction in Britain, the United States, Canada, and in France, where he worked on LaBoulie—the French championship course. Park recommended that the course should be lengthened and that five holes be redesigned to take better advantage of the existing ground. Work commenced and most of the changes were made during the winter and early spring months so that the reconfigured course would be ready for the 1904 season.

As the golf links were being rearranged, the Montrose Football Club was having a very successful season. During the years when he was playing away from home, the Montrose team became professional and was able to lure Charlie as well as Sandy Keillor back to the team for encore performances. Charlie was able to get Saturday afternoons off from the Royal Albert as needed to play football for the Gable Endies and was happy to be home with Hattie and young Charles the Second during the winter for the first time in many years.

Many returning veterans from "first class" teams in Scotland and England bolstered the 1904 Montrose Football Club. The most famous were Keillor on offense and Burgess on defense. Their play together was described by local sports writers as "brilliant" with Burgess known for his consistently "smart, clever play . . . able to clear the ball in great fashion with his head." Further praise came as he and his defensive mates were hailed as "the heroes on many a field." The senior member of the team and perennial international star, Keillor, was the offensive spark "whose form at halfback was simply marvelous considering how long he has been disporting himself in the football arena." When the Montrose team ended their season in May their record was 26 wins, seven draws, and seven losses. They scored 91 goals and held their opponents to 55. The popular team led by the veteran duo of Keillor and Burgess broke all previous home game attendance records that year.

With football over, Charlie's attention was drawn back to golf full-time and to his duties at the Royal Albert. Of great concern to the members of the club was the rather shabby and inadequate facility that served as their clubhouse and its inconvenient location. The recent redesign of the Montrose course had abandoned several of the more southerly holes near the Royal Albert and the members had a good bit of a walk northward to get to the first tee. The club's governing committee began a concerted movement to address the need for a new clubhouse that spring.

Never far from Charlie's thoughts was his desire to gain supremacy of the Montrose Links. In June it was time for the Montrose Links Championship—the Boothby-Campbell Shield first played for in 1890. Charlie was at the top of his game and easily advanced through the first three rounds and into the semi-finals. There he was paired against the greenskeeper from the Royal Albert, Andrew Simpson. The weather that day was clear and favorable, but with gusty westerly winds blowing off of the sea ready to influence a careless shot. Simpson took an early lead with a great mashie shot that went in the hole after a very poor drive for a two on a difficult par three hole. As the match progressed, Burgess fell behind by three holes but then closed the gap back to one. On the following hole, he lost his chance to even the match by sending his approach shot only halfway to the green. He recovered but could only halve (tie) the hole and Simpson clinched the match a few holes later winning by two holes with one to play. Simpson went on to take the final and the shield was his. Although he was playing well, an errant shot or a bit of bad luck always seemed to plague Charlie in his attempts to win a major championship match.

Through the summer he continued to play competitively and won monthly prizes, local sweepstakes, and was generally regarded as one of the best golfers in the region. As a determined professional, he knew that he needed to bring his game to another level in order to join the ranks of Harry Vardon, James Henry Taylor, James Braid, and the other leading golfers of the day.

The opportunity for him came in September of that year when a major professional tournament in nearby Edzell was announced. All of the leading golfers in the Kingdom took part. The entries included previous Open Champions Vardon, Taylor, Braid, William Auchterlonie from St. Andrews, and the reigning British Open Champion Alexander Herd from Huddersfield. Many other top golfers including future British Open winners, Jack White, Jock Hutchinson, and Arnaud Massey were entrants as well. Entry into this Professional Golfers' Association event was his first test as a pro against internationally renowned competition but he was no stranger to many of the other entrants because of his fame as a former football player. During his football years in Scotland and England, Charlie often had the opportunity to get in a few rounds as he traveled with his teams. He met many of the resident golf professionals at clubs all over Great Britain and had been well known to them as an outstanding amateur.

The first rounds of the highly competitive PGA tournament consisted of 36 holes of stroke or medal play. Thirty entrants played in fair weather. During the initial rounds Charlie was poised to finish among the leaders and get a crack at a major championship prize at last. Although understandably nervous to be pitted against such august competition he was at the top of the pack after the first 27 holes, along with leaders Vardon and Massey, until he misplayed several crucial shots. Normally he was known for his power of recovery, but his ability to make up for a poor shot abandoned him during the qualifying round. Harry Vardon and Arnaud Massey tied for the first place medal followed by Ben Sayers, Herd, Braid, Taylor, T.G. Renoof, and Jack White, all qualifying for the match play rounds. Charlie finished tied for thirteenth place in the all-important medal round, nine strokes behind the last qualifier. Disappointed but not discouraged by his performance, Charlie watched the rest of the tournament from the sidelines. In the next round Herd, Braid, and Taylor all advanced as did Harry Vardon who defeated Jack White in a driving rainstorm. Typical of the often-uncertain Scottish weather, sunshine could give way to monsoon-like conditions within minutes. All British professionals had ample foul weather experience so the match was never interrupted. James Braid emerged as the eventual winner beating the great Vardon by four holes with three to play in the final match play round.

At the conclusion of play, Charlie and the other Scottish professionals at the match remained in Edzell for an important meeting of the Scottish section of the PGA. Charlie had joined the association immediately after his appointment as clubkeeper at the Royal Albert and with his background in the trades, he was understandably a strong believer in a union-like movement for the professional golfer. Ben Sayers of North Berwick presided over the meeting after he was elected Captain of the section. Bob Simpson of Carnoustie was chosen vice-captain, and Charlie was elected to sit on the six-man governing committee. One of the first orders of business was a decision to play the next year's PGA Championship qualifying tournament at Montrose. The committee gave Charlie the responsibility of hosting the event and he was asked to bring the request back to the Greens Committee in Montrose for approval. The assignment was an indication of the respect his fellow professionals had for his organizational and leadership abilities and it marked Charlie's quick ascension into a leadership role in the Scottish PGA.

• A New "Merky" Clubhouse •

One of the first affairs that Charlie attended to upon his return to Montrose from Edzell was to participate in the pleasant celebration surrounding the greatly anticipated dedication of the new Mercantile Golf Clubhouse. The building was the philanthropic gift and the fulfillment of a promise from William Jameson Paton, one of Montrose's leading industrial manufacturers, to the working-class golfers of Montrose who formed the bulk of the membership at the Mercantile Club.

Two years before, in 1902, a large silver tankard was presented to the Mercantile Club to commemorate the June 26 Coronation of King Edward VII. The day was to be a public holiday and the tankard and prize money would be played for that day. However, a large number of Mercantile members worked for Mr. Paton at his mill. Paton's Mill was the largest single employer in town and for some unknown reason—perhaps the need to meet a production quota—Mr. Paton decided not to grant his employees the day off for the national holiday. With so many "Merky" members stuck at work, the tournament festivities had to be postponed until later in August.

Several weeks after the golfer's disappointing Coronation Day, the members met in their small and rather derelict clubhouse for the monthly Club Committee meeting where a surprising letter from Mr. Paton, addressed to Charlie and the directors, was read. Astonished members heard that Paton, in a magnanimous and totally unexpected civic gesture, was presenting the Mercantile members with the funds required for the construction of a new clubhouse! Montrose golf historian William Coull noted that,

> "In regard to the turn of events, it may be that the Merky members who worked in the mill may have lost a holiday, but gained a clubhouse."

A modern and very spacious lodge was designed and completed by the beginning of September of 1904 and most of Montrose's dignitaries were on hand for the dedication including the local provost, town councilors, representatives from nearby clubs, and the Mercantile officers. The building was magnificent and no expense was spared by Mr. Paton to provide a first-class facility. In fact, the clubhouse was far superior to the dowdy, run-down clubhouse that was being used by the much more affluent Royal Albert Club.

Mr. Paton was enjoying the evening of ceremony and was pleased to share his thoughts with the assembled quests. He thanked the provost and other invited dignitaries remarking that "their presence showed they were taking an interest in everything in the way of promoting the welfare of the working classes." The rest of his remarks and the audience's eager reactions as recorded by the local press provide an interesting insight regarding the relationship between the classes around the turn of the century. Paton demonstrated a notable example of noblesse oblige as he remarked in a sincere and well received speech to the Mercantile members:

> "I have very great pleasure, indeed, in handing over to you this clubhouse, for the exclusive use of the artisan classes of the town of Montrose. And I hand the house over to you without any restrictions or condition whatever. (Applause) I

have been actuated in making this presentation to you from three chief reasons. The first is that I thought your old clubhouse was too small for your large and constantly increasing membership. (Applause) In the second place, to show my esteem for the working classes of Montrose, a more respectable, intelligent, or refined lot of people you will not meet within any of the other towns in the county. (Applause) My third reason is a wish to promote and foster the enjoyable and healthful game of golf amongst them. (Applause) This clubhouse can be formed into a social rendezvous where members can drop in at their leisure, meet their friends, have a game at bagatelle, chess, drafts, dominoes, backgammon, cards, and have a look at the daily paper and a few of the monthly magazines. Members may partake of most excellent refreshments, which are served to you at most moderate terms (Hear, hear, and applause). You will find this a far more sensible way of spending your leisure time than frequenting public houses, sitting in stuffy rooms, meeting objectionable company and partaking of refreshments which are neither agreeable to the palate nor conductive to your health. (Laughter and applause) . . . I have done my best to make the house as comfortable as I possibly could for you. (Applause) . . . You are now entirely masters of the situation and you can alter anything and everything to suit your own views and your own convenience . . . I hope the present members are long spared to glean any little comfort from the house which I present to you tonight. (Loud applause)."

• Election to The PGA •

With the busy summer behind him, Charlie joined several other renowned Scottish professionals on October 10, 1904 as they were elected to full membership in the new (British) Professional Golfers' Association—*The* PGA—the parent body of the Scottish section as well as the English, Welsh, and Irish regional associations. The 1904 PGA inductees formed a very distinguished class and included Rob Simpson of Carnoustie, Jack Kirkaldy and Jock Hutchison of St. Andrews, and Willie Fernie of Glamorgan as well as Burgess. Charlie was doing all that he could to develop his skills and expert standing during these early years of growth and change for the professional golfer. He was joining the newly formed associations, serving on their committees, playing in sponsored tournaments with the most famous and strongest players of the times, while still attending to his many professional duties at the Royal Albert and serving in a leadership position at the Mercantile.

As autumn waned and winter approached, he signed on once again for what would be his final season of football with the local Montrose team. His role for the next season would be somewhat of an insurance policy for the club. In the event that some of the younger newly acquired backs failed to perform, the club could be sure of having a seasoned veteran who had seen a lot of duty with the excellent clubs of the English leagues ready to step in. Charlie may have been near the end of his most productive football years, but he was just at the beginning of a most promising career in professional golf.

3 1905–1908

"At least fifty percent of the game is concentration, mental distortion has ruined many hopeful golfers. A perfectly simple mashie shot to the green is often upset because a trap or a bunker is in sight. The shot is really no different because of the hazard, but some golfers become fearful. When that needed confidence is shaken mentally, what happens? He tightens, contracts, and something goes wrong. The hazard shot becomes a needless reality, for without the tightening or contraction, the shot would have been an easy affair. Again if a golfer is afraid he will not drive far enough and presses for distance. Opening the door for trouble again."

—Charlie Burgess

• The International Links of Montrose •

1905 proved to be a very eventful and busy year in golf for Charlie Burgess. He was called upon to organize and coordinate several major national and international tournaments, and by the end of the year had competed against the most renowned golfers in the world. Very quickly, Charlie became known as an expert on organizing important golf events and became an intimate associate of golf's greatest celebrities.

In January, Charlie was once again re-elected to the Mercantile Golf Club's governing body and the committee discussed the upcoming year's schedule of matches against other clubs at Carnoustie, Monfieth, St. Andrews, Aberdeen, and Dundee. Also on the agenda was the request Charlie brought from The Professional Golfers' Association asking the members for support in hosting the Scottish qualifying rounds of the *News of the World* prize competition in Montrose in June. The popular British newspaper had sponsored this professional golf tournament since 1903. It was the forerunner of the current British Professional Golfers' Association Championship and in 1946 officially became The PGA Match Play Championship. Charlie received unanimous permission of the Mercantile Club Committee to allow the large contingent of famous visiting professionals the use of the clubhouse and facilities of the friendly Merky.

Despite the fact that Charlie was highly regarded by his employers at the exclusive Royal Albert, they would certainly not have consented to let the professionals use their club during the matches. Even though all Montrose golf clubs had equal access to the links, equality among the clubs themselves was something else again. The Albert was the club of the gentry and as such held the amateur golfer in high esteem as a gentlemen sportsman. Professionals—golfers who sought prize money or were paid for their instructional services—were deemed a different and lower class of golfer by the aristocracy that had governed golf since long before its formalization at St. Andrews. Over the years this attitude was tempered by a begrudging admiration for the skills displayed by the pros and hence a certain degree of acceptance for them as they mingled on most of Scotland's links. But the reluctant tolerance of the pros did not extend to the clubhouses or in society at large. This attitude of superiority and classism was even more pronounced in the United States as golf took root there at the turn of the century because of the nature of the way the game developed in the United States. Unlike Scotland where the game evolved on the linkslands that were accessible to all, American golf was initially rooted and permanently established on the private estates and exclusive preserves of the wealthy class. The great divide between the working-class professionals and the wealthy amateurs who controlled the sport was one of the most difficult obstacles that the early professionals faced—on both sides of the Atlantic.

In addition to the *News of the World* sponsored championship on tap for 1905, the *Dundee Telegraph* newspaper also sponsored a tournament open to both amateur and professional golfers, at various locations in Scotland since 1895. In 1905 it was held in Montrose and it was the second major tournament of the season that drew an international field.

As spring approached, Charlie arranged for still a third major tournament in late August. This match, designed to accommodate "All Professionals," was an exhibition held after The Open was played in nearby St. Andrews that summer. Players participating in The Open would often tour the hosting region before and after the championship and Montrose figured as a major destination because of the full schedule of professional events it offered.

The three tournaments drew some of the most famous golfers in the world to the links at Montrose. But before the international stars came to Charlie's home course, he had a lot of work to do. In March he began to prepare the links for the play. As noted, in the early 1900's a professional would often be required to perform a multitude of tasks in the fulfillment of his duties. On this occasion, Charlie and a crew of helpers brought out surveying equipment, stakes, twine, shovels and rakes, and prepared the realignment of several holes to better challenge the visiting elite contingents of professionals. In addition to his other duties, he became a part-time golf course architect.

Charlie's continuing development as a professional and his efforts at making sure Montrose would be a suitable host to its illustrious guests did not go unrecognized. In May, he was offered and accepted the position of "Superintendent" or head professional of the Montrose links by the Town Council. He replaced his friend Sandy Keillor in the job that was first held by Bob Dow. This promotion to the top supervisory position at one of Scotland's oldest and most prestigious courses represented a great degree of respect from the town governors as it included a decent stipend that augmented his salary from the Royal Albert. He now had managerial responsibility for the links and supervisory duties in regard to other golfing concerns in Montrose.

The Royal Albert Golf Club was a golfing fraternity whose members came from the upper classes and gentry of the community. Ironically, due to the patronage of one of the Royal Albert's most prominent members, Alan Paton, the working-class members of the Mercantile Club now had a much grander and newer clubhouse than did the members of the Royal Albert. Not only did the Mercantile members have the better clubhouse but it was also much more conveniently located since the recent reconfiguration of the Montrose course left the Royal Albert a considerable distance away from the starting tee. Mr. John Sim, the civil engineer and noted architect who designed the new Mercantile Clubhouse, was hired to build a new Royal Albert. The result was a large two-story stone building situated in a very advantageous location with many large and ornate windows that captured spectacular views of the links and the distant sea. One entered the clubroom from a grand vestibule into a main hall with a fireplace and a broad stairway to the second floor. The clubhouse also featured a spacious ground-floor apartment for the professional, a large dining hall, locker rooms, and lavatories for the members. The upper floors contained six bedrooms, with fine views, that were leased out to visiting guests. This new clubhouse was opened in the late spring of 1905 and Chay, Hattie and seven-year-old Charlie moved into their new quarters provided by the club.

• "The Great Triumvirate" Taylor, Vardon, and Braid •

During that spring, famous English professional John Henry Taylor, more commonly known as J. H. Taylor, resided temporarily in Montrose and joined the Mercantile Golf Club. Taylor was recognized as one of the greatest golfers in the world at the time, part of the "Great Triumvirate" of British golfers along with James Braid and Harry Vardon. Oftentimes, visiting professionals such as Taylor were extended guest memberships in local clubs when they were visiting or touring various regions. It is speculated that Taylor was using Montrose and the Mercantile as a local base during the late spring in preparation for The Open at nearby St. Andrews in June. Certainly the schedule of Montrose events would have served as an incentive to settle temporarily in the region as Taylor sought out top-level competition.

Taylor was from Devon, England and during his career won The Open five times and was runner up to Vardon in the United States Open Championship held in Chicago in 1900. He was also a founding member of The Professional Golfers' Association. Taylor's fellow triumvirate partner, James Braid from the Scottish village of Guardbridge in Fife, also won the British Open five times from 1901 to 1910 and finished second three times. He too was a founder of the British PGA. His professional career spanned an incredible 45 years as head professional at Walton Heath in England. The third member of the Great Triumvirate, Harry Vardon, came from the English Channel Island of Jersey. He won six British Open Championships in addition to the United States Open in 1900. This trio of golfers was the greatest in the world at the time and each still rank highly among the all-time great players of the game. Their incredible accomplishments in the era of gutta percha balls and hickory shaft clubs clearly made them the superstars of their day.

Taylor's arrival in Montrose and membership in the Mercantile Club during the 1905 season posed an interesting challenge to Burgess. On the same day that Charlie accepted the superintendent's position, he played against Taylor and the other Merky members in the season's first monthly club tournament. Charlie won the tournament with a lowest on the green score of 75. The term "lowest on the green" referred to the fact that he was a "scratch" golfer, having no handicap adjustment to his score and the actual stroke count of 75 was the best among all of the other members that day, including Taylor, the triumvirate representative. It may have been just another round of golf for Taylor, but for Charlie it must have been a major accomplishment as he looked forward to a season that would often test him against the world's best golfers.

• Charlie's First Open •

Top-level competition continued as Charlie joined his fellow Mercantile members for the start of interclub competitions. The season's first match was against their southern neighbors from the well-known course at Carnoustie, located about 20 miles south of Montrose along the East Coast of Scotland. It too was a links course and has subsequently served as the site of numerous British Open Championships and other prestigious golf events. Charlie's status and importance to the team was reflected in the Mercantile Club Committee's efforts to insure his availability for the season's first interclub match. Aware that he was under the employment of the highly demanding members of the Royal Albert, the Mercantile members wrote a letter to the Royal Albert Club Committee requesting that Burgess be allowed to have the day off to represent the Mercantile against Carnoustie. In a gesture of good will and interclub cooperation, the Royal Albert gave Charlie the day off. The interclub matches continued throughout the season against other cities and clubs, sometimes as many as 30 Montrose players at a time would travel by coach or train all over Scotland for these matches.

On June 8, 1905, Montrose turned its attention to its neighbor St. Andrews where the forty-fifth British Open, the oldest golf tournament in the world, was being held. A record 152 golfers registered with the Royal and Ancient Golf Club. The weather was bright and favorable from the spectator's point of view but a strong ocean wind proved extremely troublesome to the competitors. In the morning of the first day of play a gale blew across the links from the northeast interfering with play from the first hole to the seventh and later holes as the players returned to the clubhouse. The first two days of play consisted of medal play (total strokes taken), 18 holes each day, and a qualification score was needed to advance to the match play (head to head competition between two players based upon how many holes were won by each) elimination rounds.

The players went off in foursomes and Charlie was grouped with the defending champion, Jack White of Sandwich, England. No doubt it must have been quite an unnerving experience for the relatively new professional from Montrose. As the day wore on, high scores were the rule for most of the players although Taylor, Herd, Vardon, and Walter Toogood led the field tied at 80. The qualification score for the first round was 87 and defending champion White just squeaked in with an 86. Burgess and his amateur friend from Montrose, Fred Findlay, Alex's brother, finished next to the bottom of the 118 players competing that day with scores of 93. It was a disconcerting experience for the two Montrosians who were very well respected in their local circles but did not make the cut at St. Andrews. Defending champion Jack White, Charlie's playing partner in the first round, went on to shoot an 83 the next day and qualified for the final match rounds, but James Braid emerged as the eventual winner and J. H. Taylor was the runner-up. After watching the finals, Charlie headed directly back to Montrose to regroup and prepare for the Scottish qualifying round of The Professional Golfers' Association Championship.

• News of the World •

On June 21, the starting draw for the Scottish qualifying rounds of the *News of the World* tournament was made in Montrose's Central Hotel. The top contestants in this tournament were rewarded with substantial prize money and the first three finishers represented Scotland at Walton Heath, England, for the international finals of the forerunner of The PGA Championship of today. Play began on June 22 and consisted of 36 holes of stroke play. The Montrose course was reported to be in "excellent order," as an overnight rain had made the normally fast putting greens improve their hold. But the ever-present winds of Montrose, this time blowing strongly from the Northwest, "mitigated against low scoring."

Andrew Kirkcaldy (sometimes spelled Kirkaldy) of St. Andrews, shot rounds of 80 and 79 for first place. Kirkcaldy had been runner-up three times in the British Open and was rated among the best of the Scottish professionals of the era. Frenchman Arnaud Massey, representing the Scottish Club of North Berwick at the time, shot 81 and 77 for second place. The third qualifier was Jock Hutchison of St. Andrews. All three Montrose qualifiers received a prize of ten pounds and went on to the fall finals in England.

Charlie, representing the Royal Albert Club, finished tied for fifth place with a score of 169, just four strokes shy of the top cut, and shared in the prize money getting a little over three pounds for his efforts. It was his best finish against premier competitors so far. *Golf Illustrated*, one of the world's oldest golf magazines, had dispatched a correspondent to the important match. He reported that Charlie played a good long game and his ability to cheat the wind on his approach shots, by keeping the ball low in a pitch-and-run style, no doubt helped him. He suffered from weak putting during the morning round that cost him strokes; otherwise "he would very likely have qualified" for the finals in England. Given the competition, it was his best and a very impressive finish for the thirty-year-old golfer who had only competed professionally for two years.

• Coronation Tankard •

Charlie quickly had the opportunity to go after still another prize. On June 26, he entered the Coronation Tankard Competition. This was the annual competition held to celebrate the coronation of King Edward in 1902. Mr. John Reid of London donated the silver tankard to the Mercantile Golf Club, and it was awarded as the Club Championship prize along with a cash award to the winner. As has been noted, play for the Coronation Tankard did not commence as planned in 1902 due to the strange turn of events that eventually rewarded the Mercantile members with the gift of their new clubhouse. Thus the Coronation Tankard challenge was first played for in 1903 and has remained a fixture on the Mercantile Club's calendar of events ever since.

The 1905 challenge found Charlie in the final round dueling with an amateur, Mr. James Stuart. The match was evenly divided through regulation and ended in a tie for the cup with Charlie emerging as the winner after an elimination play-off. But he faced an unexpected challenge off the course after the match and was nearly stripped of his claim for the Tankard. It seems that one of the club committee members raised an objection to his win due to the fact that he had entered his name on the sign-up sheet "sometime after the draw." The protester was Sandy Keillor, Charlie's long time teammate on the Montrose football club and friendly rival on the links. To add insult to injury, the motion to disqualify Charlie was seconded by his own cousin David Burgess! It is not clear whether Sandy and David were serious or were just setting up Charlie with a rather elaborate prank. The other club members came to Charlie's defense at once and overwhelmingly voted that Charlie's score stand. Charlie remained champion of the Mercantile Club and winner of the Coronation Tankard Challenge. What he said to his two antagonists after the meeting was not recorded.

• Links Championship •

If Charlie was offended or even upset at the protest of his Coronation Tankard victory, it never showed. He had business to attend to, preparing himself and the Montrose course for the next major event of this busy year—the annual Montrose Links Championship. The contest for the coveted Boothby-Campbell Shield began as usual with a large field of entrants in a medal round to determine who would go on to the several rounds of match play.

Charlie easily progressed through the first three rounds of the elimination tournament and had a chance to score a measure of retribution against Keillor as he drew him as his opponent in the fourth round. A brisk westerly breeze was blowing and the dry, fast, and ticklish greens militated against low scoring. The first few holes were give-and-take between the two men with Burgess first falling behind, then rallying to catch up, and then finally taking the lead by one hole with three holes left to play. On the next hole, Keillor had a poor tee shot, duffed his second shot, and sent his third shot into the impossible Montrose rough of broom plants and gorse bushes. He gave up the hole and Burgess was ahead—two holes up with two to play. The next hole decided the match. They tied the hole and Burgess won the contest by two holes with one to play.

In the other fourth-round bracket, relatively unknown Alex Wheatley eliminated the famed J. H. Taylor, and it was Wheatley vs. Burgess in the semi-finals. The match against Wheatley was another very close one but Charlie escaped by a score of two holes with one to play again. He was now just one round away from his second championship of the season.

The final round featured Burgess and John "Jock" Douglas, the Montrose Links greenskeeper, both in the finals for the first time. The championship boiled down to a 36-hole match play affair between the men, resulting in a dramatic tie, going down to the very last hole where

Douglas pulled up short on a putt that would have won it for him. It was reported that when Jock missed, Charlie was so excited that he flung his cap up into the air. Charlie was confident he would win the playoff and he did, on the very first extra hole of the "sudden death" round.

• Vardon, Burgess, and Braid •

Next up on the crowded 1905 Montrose calendar was the Dundee Telegraph Cup. Sponsored by the *Dundee Telegraph* newspaper since 1895 and played at various locations throughout Scotland, it was won by the defending champion and reigning Scottish amateur champion Frank H. Scroggie from Carnoustie with Rob Simpson of Carnoustie as the runner up. Simpson had been one of the players who had tied with Charlie in the *News of the World* Match earlier in June.

In August, the last major tournament of the season, the All-Professional Tournament of Montrose, was held and Charlie was up against what is now termed world-class competition after a rather mediocre, middle-of-the-pack finish in the Dundee Cup match.

Kirkcaldy and Hutchison from St. Andrews were back again for the special Montrose event. Alexander Herd, The Open winner of 1902, made his first appearance of the summer in Montrose as did Jack White, the 1904 Open winner and Charlie's playing partner in the first qualifying round of the 1905 Open. In all, six previous or future British Open Champions and two of the three Scottish qualifiers for the PGA finals joined the top Montrose and regional professionals for the three-day event.

Play began on August 24 and the pros played 72 holes in three days. The favorite to win was the new British Open Champion James Braid. But both Vardon and Taylor were considered overdue for a victory and the betting was heavily in their favor as well. At the end of the first two days of play, it was Jack White who led the field with a 152. Braid was next with a 153, followed by Taylor's 154, and Herd's 155. Kirkcaldy tied Perth professional Edward Colthard for fifth at 156. Willie Hunter from Richmond was next at 157, tied with Harry Vardon, five shots behind the leader. After being as high as in sixth place during the first round,

Charlie Burgess slipped in just behind Vardon with a two-day score of 165. Tied with Burgess on the leader card was Jock Hutchison.

Harry Vardon had recently been employing a new way to grip his golf clubs. Rather than holding the clubs one hand over the other in a "baseball" grip, or the interlocking grip in which the index finger of the left hand interlocked with the little finger of the right hand, Vardon employed a variation of the interlocking grip. Vardon modified the grip by placing the little finger of his right hand on top of the knuckle of the forefinger of the left hand, instead of interlocking his fingers. Its advantage was to keep the hands from slipping on the club shaft, yet allow the wrists to flex freely during the swing. This technique was popularized, although not invented by Vardon, and it became known to golfers everywhere as the Vardon Grip.

It was reported that Vardon's new grip might have been giving him some problems during the first two days of the match. The unpredictable winds and the unforgiving rough on the seaside course were also giving him much difficulty. Even so, for the talented Vardon, his five-stroke deficit was not impossible to overcome in the final round. On August 26, the final day of competition, Vardon apparently managed to get control of his game and slowly climbed hole by hole to claim the first prize. Braid and Taylor dropped to fifth and sixth and Charlie finished just out of the top ten.

At the conclusion of the tournament, Burgess, Vardon, and Braid posed for a photograph in front of the Mercantile clubhouse. Knowing Charlie's mischievous sense of humor, he may have laid claim to a portion of the famed triumvirate designation that summer as he literally stood shoulder to shoulder with the two giants of the game. After all, on the afternoon of August 26, the three men in the photo all were 1905 champions. Vardon had just won the Montrose All Professional Tournament that day, Burgess was the reigning Mercantile and Montrose Links Champion, and Braid was the latest British Open Champion. Triumvirate member Taylor had not picked up a significant victory that summer but before he left to return to Devon, he entered one more Mercantile monthly match and on September 25, he took the Autumn Holiday Competition trophy with a lowest on the green score of 76.

In October the qualifiers for the News of the World Tournament assembled at Walton Heath for the final rounds. The Scottish qualifiers

Kirkcaldy, Massey, and Hutchison joined others from all over the British Empire vying for the professional championship. On October 5, after three days of match play, Burgess's photo mates from Montrose took all the honors. James Braid won first prize and a gold medal as champion, and Harry Vardon took the silver runner-up medal for second place.

The 1905 golf season was a benchmark one for Charlie Burgess. His continuing professional development had elevated him to a position of national recognition as his career represented the diverse nature of a turn-of-the-century British golf professional. Charlie experienced all of the facets of life as golf professional—greenskeeper, clubmaker, clubhouse manager, instructor, tournament organizer, and competitor against the touring pros. He had competed well against the leading players of the game, won their respect, and had good reason to be optimistic about the direction his career might take.

• Becoming a Teacher •

During the winter hiatus between the 1905 and 1906 golf seasons, Charlie had time to reflect upon the events of the previous summer and how they might impact his future. Having finally given up his commitment to professional football, Charlie spent the winter attending to the Royal Albert clubhouse, mending and making golf clubs, giving a lesson now and then, and spending more time with his family. His performance during the previous season made him realize that although he was a very good golfer and could often play as well as the elite pros, he had not been able to break into the winner's circle at that level. Much like his mentor Old Bob Dow, he had all of the skills, certainly the potential but not yet the fortune to win or even finish in the money in a national championship. Regardless, 1906 found him to be widely recognized as one of the premier golfers in Montrose and Northeast Scotland. As the new season opened, his game seemed as good as it could be. He was active in all of the fixtures on the Montrose golfing calendar and often partnered successfully with his good friend Fred Findlay in many fourball matches. As a professional, he would often have a money stake of one or two pounds on each match and was most appreciative of the consistently fine performances of his skilled amateur partner. His game was so good that in early May he established a new course record for the Montrose Links, a remarkable 68. It was said that he did so in brilliant fashion throughout even though he slipped once and shot a 6 on the thirteenth hole. Once again he ventured into international competition at The Open held at the Muirfield course outside of Edinburgh, and once again was frustrated by the experience as he failed to qualify for the second time in two years.

It was back in Montrose that year that Charlie Burgess found his place in the expanding world of professional golf. He began to develop a reputation as a skilled teacher who could instruct with humor and who possessed a natural ability to pass on his knowledge of the game. It was said that he could take an absolute novice and have the beginner making respectable shots within a matter of weeks. He taught a pendulum swing featuring a short backstroke and had his pupils envision the motion of a grandfather clock until they gained confidence. A stiff left arm as an extension of the club shaft was another bit of his technique, long before it came into general use.

Soon the demand for an instructional outing on the links with Charlie was so great that most of his time was spent giving golf lessons. Most often the lessons were given on the links themselves, playing lessons, as the concept of an extensive separate practice area for instruction was not then established. Charlie would walk the course with his pupils as he instructed them shot by shot. A round of golf could be agonizingly long for the professional if his student proved inept, uncoordinated, or difficult. A slow round or two would reduce the professional's income for the day or week considerably. It was all the more important for him to be effective in his techniques, preparing students with some fundamentals off the course and clearly communicating to them any deficiencies in their game without putting undue pressure on them to perform. Charlie was very good at recognizing the talents of his pupils and never had to rush a player off the course. In fact, his generosity at giving extra time to anyone who required it, without additional compensation, was often noted.

Although most of his time and energy was focused on teaching, he still continued to venture into many local and regional competitive matches. He was reported to have maintained an advantage there by avoiding the popular hammering hit-or-miss type of game and would focus on three factors that marked his play. The first was that he had an uncanny ability to conquer the wind by playing his approach shots low, a pitch-and-run style on his blustery seaside course. The next major aspect of his game was to take great care in his consistent putting. He never failed to remember his constant reminder to his students, the obvious but often-forgotten fact that, "a good putt of a few feet counts the same as a powerful drive or long fairway shot one stroke for each, so they are all important." Finally, he had a remarkable power of recovery from poor shots or misses, and did not let the frustration of a bad shot carry over to the next. He was practicing and mastering the psychology of golf long before that term was coined.

There is an amusing tale about how Charlie's trademark power of recovery was once severely put to test, during a charity tournament held in England at Walton Heath, the home club of his good friend James Braid. In a weak moment he consented to play in the annual mixed tournament that featured alternating shots between the visiting professionals and their amateur partners. Charlie was drawn to play with a very charming woman, but one whose talent did not happen to be golf. Time and time again his fair partner placed him in difficulties but on every occasion he recovered brilliantly, until eventually she hit the ball into the roots of a small bush, where it wedged solidly. Without any other options Charlie took his heaviest club, demolished the bush and sent both it and the ball flying nearly ten feet back onto the fairway! To his surprise and amazement, his partner turned to him after the shot and said, "It is a comfort to see that even *you*, Mr. Burgess, can miss a shot sometimes."

• Surprising Setback •

Charlie's new situation as a sought-after instructor brought increased financial reward and enabled him to provide his family with many of the finer things of life. Young Charlie the Second was almost nine years old now and, while not exactly raised with the proverbial silver spoon in his mouth, he was, as an only child, never wanting for much. The fact and circumstances of his birth ensured that he would always be doted upon and was surely a little spoiled as a youth. Even though he had no siblings, Young Charlie, big for his age, had a platoon of cousins to play with. The many Nicoll brothers, the children of Chay's sister Jeannie, were close to him in age and shared his interests in emulating their uncle. Uncle Charlie took his sister's boys under his wing and instructed them and his own son in the finer points of the game. With cut-down clubs under their arms, the youngsters would often tag along after the adults, another generation of Scottish golfers learning their craft on the ancient links of coastal Montrose.

When the 1907 golf season got under way, Charlie's good friend, highly skilled amateur golfer Fred Findlay, won back the Links Championship for the second time while Sandy Keillor won the Mercantile Club Championship for the third time. The Royal Albert Club elected a new captain, the Earl of South Esk, and under his aristocratic leadership, some dramatic and unforeseen changes were about to be made at the venerable old club.

Today golf enthusiasts look back upon the ancient history of the game with great fondness and admiration for the early professional pioneers like Old Tom Morris, Willie Park, Vardon, Taylor, and Braid. But those pioneers often encountered considerable disdain and snobbery from the polite society of the time. Before the turn of the century, traveling golf professionals were frequently considered only slightly less repugnant than tramps, vagabonds, or gypsies as they went from place to place in search of the prize money they depended on. Even the more rooted club pros, well respected within their own communities, were commonly treated as mere servants by many of the exclusive upper-class clubs that employed them. Trying to earn respect from the gentry while serving as the steward of their club was a difficult and demanding position to be in. It was one that Charlie Burgess had been experiencing for the last several years.

Charlie's position at the Royal Albert and his activities in the greater golfing community had evolved into distinct and perhaps conflicting roles. As a professional golfer and member of The PGA he could be, if he wanted, somewhat autonomous. As the links themselves were common land, Burgess could arrange and give lessons for hire. He could also engage in wagering on his matches and could compete in any number of competitions and sweepstake events. These activities produced significant additional income and a moderate degree of independence for him. But his agreement with the Royal Albert providing him with his base salary and "free house, fire and light" required certain obligations from Charlie that had to come before any outside activities. For example, it was expected that he would schedule and provide lessons for the club members before outsiders and at a fee determined by the club, not himself. As the clubkeeper or steward, he was also expected to attend to many matters often unrelated to the game itself. Respected Montrose golf historian Willie Coull has noted that the early club professional "was expected to do everything required in the running of the club; the cleaning, lighting and keeping the coal fires going; the tidying of the garden and even, on occasion, the painting and decorating. The attitude of certain members could make their lives a misery."

Of course every club's relation to its clubkeeper was a bit different and, as it evolved, Charlie's position was perhaps more advantageous to him than it was to the club. Charlie was more or less free to make his own schedule and the club had always been most generous in allowing him days off over the years for his many football and golf matches. By virtue of his long-established good standing in the community and value to the club, he was paid very well. His base salary alone was nearly sixty pounds per year—by the standards of the day well above the wages of the average working man. As the wife of the professional, Hattie was expected by the members to contribute her efforts to the needs of the club. But she would have little to do with that, in fact actually demanding and receiving the help of a maid around the clubhouse.

The year passed uneventfully but things were about to change in a most dramatic and unexpected manner in the early spring. On April 23, 1908, while attending to his duties at the Royal Albert, Charlie received two shocking and devastating bits of news. The first was that his friend and mentor Bob Dow had passed away at age seventy-seven. The second was that the Royal Albert was voting to fire him!

As recorded in the hand-written minutes of the first annual meeting of the year, Lord Esk, the new chairman of the Royal Albert Club Committee, "brought forward for consideration the question as to whether the position of the clubkeeper was in all respects satisfactory." He cryptically remarked that the circumstances were "so well-known that it was hardly necessary to enter into details." After considerable discussion, the feeling of the members appeared to be that it would be desirable to procure a new clubkeeper and it was left to the committee "to arrange accordingly." The deliberately circumspect wording of the resolution by the members of the committee makes it impossible to tell exactly why Charlie was suddenly "unsatisfactory" after five years of successful tenure and good relations with the club. One can only guess as to what the "well-known circumstances" might have been. Perhaps the gentlemen of the committee, led by Lord Esk, were alluding to Charlie's trade unionist roots that inevitably led to his increasing involvement with matters of The Professional Golfers' Association. They may have also felt that his many outside activities—participation in numerous competitions, governing the Mercantile, and scheduling private lessons for non-Royal Albert members—were not consistent with the expectations of the club's managing committee. Hattie's demands for household help and Charlie's independent nature may have combined to contradict the image the wealthy members had of a properly dutiful club employee and wife. Charlie may have been thought to have forgotten his place in regard to his station and to the club.

The terms of employment that the Royal Albert committee members proposed for the new clubkeeper that followed Charlie offer up some likely clues about what probably led to Charlie's removal. A firm condition proposed for his replacement was that "the clubkeeper was not to go away for a day without the secretary's consult." The new clubkeeper also would have to "keep himself free till 5 p.m. for engagements with members of the club." Finally the club limited the fees the pro could charge for lessons setting the rate at "two shillings and six pence to be the charge for one round with the clubkeeper and four shillings for two rounds." The inclusion and the tone of these conditions in the new contract seem to indicate that Charlie may indeed have, in the opinion of Lord Esk and the new club committee, been putting his own interests ahead of the club. No matter what the actual cause of the dismissal was, not all of the club members agreed with the decision, and the motion did not pass without a long and charged debate amongst the committee. Charlie had many loyalists on the board who highly valued him and the service he had given and were not at all pleased by the verdict to let him go.

Characteristically, Charlie put his concern for others ahead of himself. His reaction to the disturbing events of April 23 was to first attend and participate in the memorial services for Bob Dow and then tender his letter of resignation to the Royal Albert. On April 27 the club's secretary read his simple declaration, "For certain reasons I tender my resignation as clubkeeper and professional for the Royal Albert Golf Club and as arranged will leave one month from this date. Yours truly, Charles Burgess." Charlie also stepped down as Links Superintendent as well.

The committee then instructed the secretary to speak to none other than Charlie's good friend Fred Findlay, "with a view to him becoming the professional of the club." Fred was offered "free house, fire and light, and twenty-five pounds a year"—less than half of the salary the club had paid Burgess. Findlay accepted the job after negotiating a raise to thirty pounds per year as his base pay. Charlie sincerely wished his old friend well and promptly moved out of the clubhouse and back to one of the Burgess family dwellings on Victoria Street. He immediately hung up his shingle declaring that once again his occupation was that of a stonemason.

Charlie's departure from the Royal Albert did not preclude him from remaining one of Montrose's leading golfers, however. In fact, he won the First Class Sweepstakes in the competition for the Mercantile's Findlay Medal, a prize donated by Alex Findlay some years previous. He did this on April 24, the day after the Albert sacked him. Within a week of losing his job and the passing of Bob Dow, Burgess was hit with more bad news. His other boyhood hero, friend, and mentor Old Tom Morris fell down the stairs at the St. Andrews Clubhouse and, as a result of his injuries, died at the age of eighty-seven.

Charlie managed to hold on to a preeminent position in the Montrose golfing establishment despite his severed relationships with the Royal Albert. His old football teammate and golfing rival Sandy Keillor was aiming to take the Mercantile Club Championship, the Coronation Tankard, for an unprecedented third consecutive year that summer. After Charlie won the Tankard in 1905, Sandy recaptured it in 1906 and kept it in 1907. Charlie's sweep of both the Montrose Cup and the Links Championship in 1905 had eluded a repeat. Keillor was the man to beat once again and Charlie's steady play and power of recovery came together to reclaim the 1908 Tankard. He did not know at the time that it would be his last major victory in Montrose.

Burgess continued playing excellent golf all summer, almost as a kind of rebuke to the poor treatment the Royal Albert Committee handed him. His fine play continued into the autumn when on October 2, 1908, he set a new course record of 71. The score was the best ever recorded since the often-changed links were reconfigured from the layout where Burgess shot his record 68. A little later in the month, Fred Findlay, now the Royal Albert pro, also shot a round in 71 and he and Charlie both held the record, Findlay as a professional, and Burgess as recently reinstated amateur! Charlie Burgess would not remain an amateur for long, however, thanks to a most intriguing proposal from Fred's enterprising older brother Alex.

4

1908–1909

"If all golfers worked for form, rhythm, and timing, they would find distance and accuracy without physical or muscular application. It's not the strength of a man that sweeps the ball afar but the perfection of the swing."

—Charlie Burgess

• Findlay Returns •

Montrose native Alexander H. Findlay had traveled back to Scotland in the early fall of 1908 to meet with Charlie after learning about his surprising dismissal from the Royal Albert. He wanted to discuss the possibility of Burgess going to America as the professional for a relatively new golf club near Boston. Alex knew if golf were to prosper in America, it would require the guidance of experienced Scottish pros. He also knew that Charlie Burgess was just the kind of professional that America needed. He would do his best to bring the talented teacher to the States to join the growing number of other Scottish pioneers who had already made the journey.

Findlay was a tireless advocate of the game in America and by 1908 was well known as a course architect, competitive player, and as a great promoter of the sport. After he moved to the East Coast from Nebraska to work for the Wright and Ditson Company, Findlay continued to design golf courses. Findlay designed or redesigned more than 100 golf courses in America during this period of rapid golf development and, along with his fellow Scotsman Donald Ross, had a major impact on the growth of golf in the United States. Findlay's regulation courses can still be found in Arkansas, Florida, Maine, Maryland, Massachusetts, Montana, New Hampshire, New Jersey, New York, North Carolina, Oklahoma, Pennsylvania, Tennessee, Texas, Virginia, and also Nassau in the Bahamas. In addition to his golf promotions and course construction, he even was the Mexican Open champion at one point. Perhaps one of the most interesting facets of Findlay's career was his association with Florida Railroad tycoon and resort developer, Henry Flagler. Flagler opened up Florida as a tourist destination at the turn of the century by converting the mangrove swamps and palmetto covered wastelands along the Atlantic Coast into warm weather destinations for winter-weary northerners. As Flagler's railroad expanded southward, he erected luxurious landmark resort hotels and golf courses along the way. Alex Findlay was his "golfer in chief." The elegant Ponce de Leon Hotel in St. Augustine featured Findlay's St. Augustine Country Club and Ponce de Leon Golf Club. Further down the coast at Ormond Beach, near Daytona, Findlay designed the Ormond Country Club. Findlay also designed The Breakers Golf Course in Palm Beach (then called the Palm Beach Golf Links), the Miami Golf Links, and—just a short boat ride away—the Nassau Golf Links in the Bahamas, as the East Coast Railway tracks were laid all the way down to the end of the Sunshine State.

Findlay's golf promotion activities extended to arranging for many of the greatest British players to come to America for promotional tours and exhibitions. Findlay often participated in those matches, particularly against Harry Vardon, who barnstormed the world several times on behalf of the game. One such promotional tour occurred in 1900 on the occasion of the seventh playing of the United States Open, when the game was not very well established in the country and still remained only a rich man's sport.

Findlay organized the tour along with fellow promoter Julian W. Curtis, who had also been re-selling golf equipment in America that he had purchased while abroad. Curtis was a director of the Spalding Sporting Equipment Company founded by former baseball player Albert Goodwill Spalding. Spalding had been a pitcher for the Boston Red Stockings in the 1870's, and upon his retirement, founded his sports equipment company in New York. Interestingly, the Spalding and the Wright and Ditson companies had entered into a subtle, if not secret agreement, to join forces in the delivery of recreational goods. Many of the items carrying a Wright and Ditson label were identical to the Spalding brand. The Spalding Company was among the first American manufacturers and distributors of golfing equipment after the rest of the directors realized that Curtis' venture in selling golf equipment was successful. The Spalding Company also entered the sports publishing business at the turn of the century producing authoritative annual guides through a series known as the Spalding Athletic Library. An annual "Golf Guide" containing news, rules and related information (edited by Grantland Rice) soon joined guides to baseball, football, ice hockey, track and field, tennis, and other leisure time interests enjoyed by the American public.

In 1899, Curtis saw Harry Vardon win his third British Open title and offered him a contract to endorse Spalding's new golf ball, which they dubbed the Vardon Flyer. Ironically the Flyer was one of the last gutta percha balls manufactured as the rubber-cored ball was introduced the very next year. Vardon's extensive golfing tour to promote the new golf ball began in February of 1900 and was a great success. His exploits were followed closely by an American press enthusiastic about the new sport that was being widely demonstrated. Although the game was primarily of interest to the members of American society wealthy enough to afford it, many average citizens were attracted to the tours and publicity surrounding the famous players. Soon they would have a chance to play the game themselves on new municipal or public links that were beginning to be built in most metropolitan areas of the nation.

Hundreds of youngsters who had taken to golf as caddies at the exclusive American county clubs also eagerly followed the exploits of the great Vardon as he toured the nation. One eight-year-old working-class youngster from Boston convinced his mother to take him to a downtown department store to see his idol Vardon first-hand. The boy had read everything he could about the great English golfer and dreamt of become a champion himself some day. In just a few more years that young boy, named Francis Ouimet, would meet Scotland's Charlie Burgess, the man who was destined to help him realize his dream.

Vardon was undefeated on the tour except for one match against transplanted Scotsman Bernard Nicholls who won the contest decisively 5 and 4. Bernard was the younger brother of Gilbert Nicholls, a nomadic professional in both Great Britain and America. Both men were good friends of Findlay. Gil Nicholls later was engaged for a very short time as the first professional at the Woodland Golf Club in the Boston suburb of Newton, Massachusetts. In 1908 Findlay was keen on persuading Charlie Burgess to succeed Nicholls at that very same club.

As Vardon's 1900 tour continued, he met up with Findlay in a head-to-head match in Palm Beach, at a course that Findlay had just designed. Vardon nearly lost his second match of the tour as the contest went down to the final hole, Vardon winning by a stroke.

Findlay remained based on the East Coast of the United States after the tour because of his association with Wright and Ditson of Boston. Wright and Ditson, like the Spalding Company, was among the first American sporting goods companies to import, re-sell, and later to manufacture golf equipment. A complete set of clubs advertised under the Findlay signature line consisted of a putter, niblick (seven/nine iron), mashie (five iron), mid iron (two iron), cleek (four wood), brassy (two wood), and a driver. A dozen Wright and Ditson Silver Queen golf balls completed the turn of the century outfit. Findlay would later be associated with the famous Philadelphia department store Wanamakers, in a similar capacity to his job at Wright and Ditson.

• America Beckons •

During Findlay's 1908 trip to Scotland, he approached Charlie Burgess with an offer from the Woodland Golf Club to become the head professional there. It is not known exactly how Findlay became the agent for the club, but his offer was a bona fide one apparently agreed upon by the club's board of directors before his departure. Woodland was one of America's first golf clubs when it formed in the late 1890's. It had started modestly on leased land and made use of a neighboring hotel as its clubhouse. In the fall of 1897, Woodland applied to the newly formed United States Golf Association for membership and along with 47 other clubs, was elected to that body as an allied club at the annual meeting held in January 1898. Prior to 1897, the USGA had only 31 officially recognized members. The relatively large number of new clubs accepted into the 1898 membership class reflected the expanding popularity of American golf and foreshadowed the increasing need for the importation of skilled Scottish professionals. In 1902, Woodland formed itself into a corporation and continued its growth as an active golfing society in the greater Boston area. By 1907, American interest in the game had continued to grow and so did Woodland. The course expanded from 12 to 18 holes and the club was ready to employ its first professional, Gil Nicholls. Nicholls only stayed at the club through the 1908 season, however, as he wanted to pursue prize money by playing in exhibitions and competitive tournaments on the fledgling American professional circuit.

Charlie could not take Findlay's employment proposition lightly. Findlay's reputation and golfing credentials were world renowned. Besides that, the Burgess and Findlay families were longtime Gable Enders and close friends. Charlie and Alex had been friends as teenagers and Fred Findlay was also a close personal friend and golfing companion. Most all of the Burgess and Findlay family members had also been members of the same church and choir for years as well. Charlie trusted Alex's judgment and sincerity, but needed some time to think it over. He had to think of his family and the effect a move like this would have on them. Even without a professional position at the moment, a man with his skills surely could find employment on the links nearby if he chose to. His ties to his community, family, and Scotland were very strong and it would be hard to leave. On the other hand, America was a land of unparalleled opportunity and excitement. Interest in golf was starting to boom and the economic fortunes of the States were creating a wealth that could afford an outlet in sports, recreation and leisure-time pursuits.

Scotland's teaching professionals were in demand in America because of their obvious expertise. Skillful sportsmen could achieve unprecedented prosperity as their reward for bringing the game to the States. It was an attractive proposition for Charlie and the other golf professionals who left their homeland in what was called "The Scottish Invasion" of the United States during the first two decades of the twentieth century. While St. Andrews and Musselburgh produced the largest number of new American professionals during this time, Montrose also exported a considerable number of talented golfers. By 1900, the first Montrose golfers to leave for the States beside Findlay were the Clark brothers—John, Thomas, and Walter. As Charlie was contemplating his relocation to America, the Clarks were already settled in the western part of Massachusetts, about a 90-mile train ride away from Woodland, where Charlie would be. Walter Clark was the pro at the Springfield Country Club, Tom was at the Tekoa Golf Club in Westfield, and John was located a bit further west in Pittsfield. Montrose continued to provide America with a dozen more teachers of the game through the 1920's.

The Boston area was one of the major centers of the American golf movement beginning with George Wright's experimental round at Franklin Park and the introduction of golf at Brookline's Country Club. Certainly the prospect of being in close proximity to some of the other Scottish golfers who had already taken up residency in the Boston area would give Charlie an established network of friends and colleagues. Alex Ross, who won the U.S. Open in 1907, was the pro at the Brae Burn Country Club, located in the same city as Woodland. In fact the Brae Burn and Woodland courses were within a short walk or a long mid-iron shot of each other, separated only by a small wooded area beyond the main thoroughfare in front of the Woodland clubhouse. Alex had joined his brother Donald, a professional at the Oakley Golf Club in the adjacent community of Watertown, Massachusetts, around 1902. Boston and its suburbs already had more than a dozen clubs and most of them featured Scottish transplanted pros that were well known to Charlie.

Findlay also reassured Burgess about the community to which he would be bringing his family. He told him of a nearby Episcopal church and its exceptional choir, which would welcome another fine baritone voice such as his. He even had some thoughts about Charlie's reputation as an expert in football. A well-known and distinguished university located in Cambridge, another city next to Newton, had been looking to better organize the association football team there. Although not as popular as the American version of football, an association football (soccer) team had been formed and had played for several years as a club team with students managing the practices. Charlie would be just the man to take charge of this minor sport, which was played in the winter and early spring months during golf's off season. He could become the first professional soccer coach at Harvard University.

After much consideration he accepted Findlay's offer, but on one condition. He would go to America with Findlay that autumn to try it for a while. If he found it satisfactory, he would return to Montrose for Hattie and young Charlie. With a handshake and gentleman's agreement, the deal was made. True to his word, Charlie came to the States and resided at the Woodland Park Hotel, which had once served both as a hotel and the golf club headquarters, and from which the club derived its name. He spent the late fall and early winter months of 1908 considering the situation in America. He consulted departing professional Gilbert Nicholls about the various business aspects of the game beyond teaching. He spoke with Donald and Alex Ross and many of the other American-based professionals about the status of the sport in America. He inquired about housing, schooling for his son, and all of the other things anyone relocating would do. He was concerned about the impact the move would have on his wife and son, but decided that coming to America would offer them opportunities that could not be equaled in Montrose. As soon as he was satisfied that he had seen enough, he returned to Scotland for Hat and young Charles.

Charlie was still a member of the Montrose Mercantile Golf Club and the holder of the recognized course record in the early part of 1909. His membership card for the Merky showed that several important events or "fixtures" were on tap for the season even as early as February. The first monthly badge was set for March third, and in May the St. Andrews team was scheduled to visit Montrose. Charlie would not finish out the season in Montrose. After learning of his impending departure for the United States, the *Montrose Review* lamented that the community was losing "one of its most familiar and popular players on the Links" and "one of golf's most enthusiastic and successful devotees." In March, Chay, Harriet, and eleven-year-old Charlie bid farewell to their family, friends, and Scotland. They packed their steamer trunks and traveled south by rail to Liverpool to board the Cunard Line steamship *Ivernia* for the journey to America.

• The Crossing and Arrival •

The famous Cunard Line featured the "largest, fastest, finest steamships afloat" in 1909. The *Mauretania* and the *Lusitania* serviced New York City, and the *Saxonia* and the *Ivernia* sailed directly from Liverpool to Boston. According to an advertisement of the company, all of the vessels were fitted with the new system of "wireless telegraphy by Marconi," carried "orchestras of trained musicians," and were equipped with the latest "submarine signaling apparatus."

It was both an exciting and apprehensive journey for the Scottish golf professional and his family. Anticipation of what they would find on the other shore excited them. Anxiety about what they were leaving behind gave them pause. They sailed across the Atlantic on the *Ivernia* because of her direct route to Boston. Although a slightly smaller ship than the line's flagship *Lusitania* or the speedy *Mauretania*, it was nonetheless a fine example of the luxurious seagoing vessels of the era. Even the second-class accommodations of the Burgess family featured some of the most comfortable staterooms, dining facilities, and entertainment afloat. The competition for transatlantic passenger service between America and Europe was keen. The British-based Cunard and the White Star Line, purchased in 1902 by American millionaire J. P. Morgan, were rivals for the supremacy of the North Atlantic sea routes. Each line was vying to have the biggest, fastest, and most luxurious ships on the oceans. During the very same month that the Burgesses sailed on the *Ivernia*, the White Star Lines laid down the keel of what would be the largest, most extravagant transatlantic steamer ever built—the *Titanic*.

No matter what line or what ship was sailed on, the most comfortable and lavish accommodations were reserved for the first class passengers. Premier passenger travel included luxurious staterooms, modern up-to-date libraries, private parlors, lounges, marvelously ornate dining facilities, and opulent ballrooms. The cost of a first-class passage was about two hundred British pounds. Second-class passengers saw more modest yet still very lovely surroundings for a fare nearly half the first-class price. For example, the bathroom fixtures in second class were chrome-plated instead of silver-plated, staterooms were smaller and the lounges a bit less luxurious. But on all of the ships, the combined total of first- and second-class passengers was nowhere near the total number of third-class or steerage passengers on board. The steerage-class travelers were crammed into tiny rooms, far down in the lower levels of the ship and away from the fresh air and light enjoyed by the upper classes. Little attention was given to the aesthetics of the third-class accommodations, yet the twenty-pound fare from thousands of impoverished immigrants heading to America provided a lucrative business and was the financial backbone of the steamship lines.

The Burgess family disembarked from the *Ivernia* in Boston after a week-long crossing and passed through the U. S. Customs building on the waterfront at State Street. There they were met by representatives of Woodland and were escorted to their new home. A branch of the Boston and Albany Railroad served the Woodland Golf Club. The Newton Circuit Steam Line of the railroad system began in Boston and ran eight miles west through the communities of Brookline and Newton with a stop right at Woodland. The population of Boston was about 600,000 people; by comparison the city of Newton had a population of approximately 37,000 people spread out among many small villages that comprised the city.

Newton was one of several cities and towns that were adjacent to and ringed the hub of Boston. To the city's east was Boston Harbor and Cape Cod Bay. Southward was the city of Quincy. The towns of Milton and Dedham were south-southwest of Boston. Newton occupied the western and southwestern position around Boston. Brookline, Watertown, and Cambridge bordered the west-northwest side of Boston, while Somerville, Everett, Chelsea, Revere and Winthrop completed the rim of communities north around the central city. In and around these communities, a great number of golf clubs emerged as the explosion of interest and participation in the game rapidly developed during the next two decades.

Charlie's arrival at Woodland marked the beginning of a remarkable stay that was unprecedented and unrivaled by any other American professional of the era. He faithfully remained at his new club for over 35 years despite many flattering offers from other clubs, becoming Woodland's longest serving pro. Many of the other local clubs had been recruiting and employing British, if not exclusively Scottish, talent for several years. Alex Ross began his career at Brae Burn in 1902. Donald Ross came to America in 1899 and was still working as a teaching professional at Watertown's Oakley Country Club when Charlie arrived. The Wollaston Golf Club in Quincy, Massachusetts had hired St. Andrews transplant Bob MacAndrew in 1906. MacAndrew followed the legendary David "Deacon" Brown, the 1886 British Open Champion from Musselburgh who arrived in America around 1903 (Brown was also an acquaintance of Charlie in the old country where they met each other for the first time on the links of Montrose in 1893). Willie Campbell, also from Musselburgh as previously mentioned, had been hired by The Country Club in Brookline in 1894 and later became the first professional at Boston's municipal course at Franklin Park. Campbell was well known to Charlie as the runner-up to Brown in the 1886 British Open and also as the runner-up to fellow Scotsman Willie Dunn in the very first, but unofficial U.S. Open in 1894. Campbell died in 1900 at age thirty-eight, but was succeeded at the Franklin Park club by his wife, Georgina Stewart Campbell, who became the first woman professional golfer in the United States and was part of the Scottish alliance of golf professionals Charlie would join. Meanwhile Alex Campbell from Troon was the current Scottish professional in residence at The Country Club. All of these Boston area Scottish pros formed a natural network of friendship and support for each other. Each in his own way made significant contributions to the early evolution of golf in America. Charlie Burgess was the newest member of a small and very exclusive fraternity.

Charlie and his family settled into a simple but adequate clapboard cottage provided by the golf club on the western side of the course. Washington Street bordered the golf course on its eastern end and Grove

Street to the west. The Washington Street side of the course served as the main entrance to Woodland and besides being one of Newton's main arteries, was also one of the roads used for the route of the famous Boston Marathon. Grove Street was on the backside of the course, and the little house at 368 Grove Street, where the Burgesses lived became known as the Knickerbocker. The nickname derived from the fashionable knickerbockers or "plus-four" golf trousers of the era.

The contract that began the relationship between Burgess and Woodland was based upon goodwill and mutual trust, and was sealed with a handshake. Although the early Scottish professionals in America had no governing body to protect their interests, the best of them were able to establish equitable and beneficial contracts with their new employers based upon their legitimate credentials and good performance on the job. Unfortunately, many others found themselves in far less favorable situations. Because the sport was restricted to America's wealthiest members of society, a class distinction often even more pronounced than was experienced in Great Britain greeted the transplanted pros. America's gentry, landed or self-made, took great care to insulate themselves from the working class. The early American golf pro entered the country clubs from the back door, worked out of the basement, and ate his meals in the club's kitchen with the servants.

Acquiring a Scottish professional was in many ways a considerable achievement for an American country club and conferred status upon a club eager to show its faithfulness to the ancient game by having a real Scotsman in its employment. But sometimes during this period of great demand for experienced golf experts, the clubs picked a candidate that was unskilled or had little training. At one point during the height of the "Scottish invasion," it was said that getting off of a transatlantic ship with a Scottish brogue and a bag of clubs were often credentials enough to find a job regardless of ability. This rush to hire often created a situation that was detrimental to both the club and to the efforts of legitimate professionals as they sought to establish better working conditions and respect from their employers, many of whom might have been stung at some time by an incompetent so-called professional.

Thus, for a variety of reasons, not all of the new American golf professionals of the era enjoyed the same agreeable situation as Charlie. Most of the transplanted pros had to struggle mightily for financial security and respect for their profession. As time went on, Charlie's gentlemanly conduct and his integrity in business dealings proved to do more to raise the level of regard for the professional golfer in America than any tournament championships he could have ever won. His managerial ability and experience as a leader in the professional golfers' organizations of his native land fated him to be deeply concerned with the well-being and union of his fellow pros in America during the 1920's.

His lifelong experience in golf and his ability to transfer his knowledge to others made him the prototype of the new club professionals recruited to the United States—men whose influence on the game was not through their own championship records but through their ability to teach the game.

The first American golf professionals were responsible for the rapid development of a new generation of young "homebred" American champions. These were champions who eventually shifted the center of the golfing world from Great Britain to the United States during the early 1920s, a shift that came about soon after the revolutionary outcome of the 1913 United States Open. Charlie Burgess's very first American student was single-handedly responsible for that revolution.

5 1909–1913

> "An important factor in rhythm and timing is relaxation. Without that a contraction occurs deviating the club from the pendulum arc swing of a grandfather's clock. The motion that should be emulated in a good golf swing."
>
> —Charlie Burgess

• American Professionals and the USGA •

The transition from being a golf professional in Scotland to being one in America involved several notable and important differences for Charlie and his contemporaries. As in Scotland, Charlie would receive a base salary, augmented by the income from his golf shop and by fees earned from giving lessons. The first noticeable difference was in the degree of skills with which his students came to him. Unlike Scotland, where almost everyone near a golfing community was somewhat skilled at golf or at least familiar with the pastime, Americans were woefully behind their British counterparts. To most Americans, golf, along with polo and yachting, was a privileged pastime for the very rich and was not considered a mainstream activity for the average person. At the time, they were correct.

Because the game was so new to so many Americans, Charlie estimated that in order for even the best American amateur golfers to be competitive with the Europeans, it would take nearly a generation for them to catch up. Many of his new students were completely unfamiliar with the sport and had often never even held a club in their hands before. However, most of his new pupils made up in their enthusiasm for what they lacked in their initial golfing skills. Charlie's genial personality, relaxed style, and obvious abilities provided a comfortable learning environment for his new pupils. It was not unusual for him to be out on the course from dawn to dusk during the initial years of his employment in the United States.

The second most obvious departure from life in Scotland required the professionals to make some significant adjustments in their social lives. The first American professionals had very little chance to associate with their fellow golfers on or off the links. While most all of the early American professionals were admired for their skills on the golf courses, fraternizing in the clubhouses after a match was restricted to the amateur members of each club. Most clubs considered the club professional merely as another employee, on par with the domestic help. Social interaction between the pro and the club members was generally limited to a formal employer-employee relationship. Back in the professional's native land, even if one club employed him, he could always maintain a membership at another club of his choosing, due to the large numbers of golf societies that existed, and he had almost unrestricted access to the many courses held in public trust. In the United States, country clubs were located on private lands, relatively isolated, and were the social equivalent of the Royal Albert, governed by America's aristocracy for the recreation of upper-class amateur golfers. American golf provided no opportunity for the early professionals to belong to a club for their own recreation. Besides, the demanding job of the new American professionals left little time for recreational rounds of golf or to keep up their competitive skills, as they often worked very long hours and six days a week. It was only the force of personality and the individual relationships between the professional and his club that determined exactly where he fit into the club's social hierarchy. Generally, most clubs offered great latitude and respect for the professional on matters regarding the game itself, but were less magnanimous when it came to including him in affairs inside the clubhouse.

Thirdly, the early professional golfers in America had no governing body, union, or anyone to look out for their interests. In their native lands, the most recently transplanted British professionals like Charlie had benefited from membership in local and national professional organizations, established to reflect the needs and concerns of the professional golfer. Britain's Professional Golfers' Association, The PGA, formed in 1901 by the leading figures in British professional golf, was the world's first such organization. At the time of Charlie's arrival in 1909, American professionals had no voice in the management of the game that they depended upon for their livelihoods. Since 1894, when the modern game of golf finally became permanently established in America after the founding of America's first five golf clubs, the sole governing body and guardian of all aspects of the game was the United States Golf Association. Created and administered by the amateur golf establishment, the USGA reflected the attitude of its member clubs toward the position of the professional golfer in America. The clubs in need of their services tolerated the pros, but every effort was made to insure that they did not taint what was considered the gentlemanly game of golf. The charter and rules administered by the USGA insured that such a situation would not occur.

The USGA even began to see itself as the gatekeeper for the British professionals coming into America to work at any of its member clubs. *The American Golfer* reported that, in 1911, USGA Secretary Robert Watson sent a letter to all member clubs declaring in essence that from then on the USGA was to be the official clearinghouse regarding the employment of professional golfers. Watson then sent out a survey form to all the USGA clubs to monitor the dismissals or resignations of their pros, "giving the exact cause." When all the clubs complied, the USGA would then maintain "an accurate file of the whereabouts of all the professional golfers and greenskeepers in this country employed by clubs." Watson declared that he was sending the same surveys abroad "to get a line on professionals . . . coming to the United States looking for a position." One view of this new policy could be that the USGA was trying to help both the clubs and the pros find mutually beneficial match-ups and to maintain high standards for the game as it evolved in the United States. On the other hand, if a club for any reason dismissed a professional, deservedly or not, he was assured that the USGA would be in control of his future employment, if any.

The USGA's constitution explained that the association "exists for the purpose of promoting and conserving throughout the United States, the best interest and true spirit of the game of golf as embodied in its ancient and honorable traditions." Its four major charges included: the regulation of amateur standing; the enforcement and interpretation of the rules of golf; holding an Amateur, an Open, and a Women's Championship; and in general, acting as an arbitrator and final determiner of all questions relating to the game in America in the same way as the Royal and Ancient Golf Club governed British golf.

As the governing body of the American game, the USGA was most specific in the distinction between the professional and amateur in America. "A professional golfer is any player who has played for a money prize or has received payment for playing or teaching the game." This definition of professionalism was an element of the group's charter that came under criticism often, as the enforcement of the rules against professionalism seemed to be unevenly and often arbitrarily enforced in many cases.

The USGA also had the right "of declaring ineligible to compete in the Open Tournaments under its jurisdiction, anyone who, in its opinion has acted in a manner detrimental to the best interests or to the spirit of the game." This authority gave them great power over the one and only national tournament American professionals could play in at the time. The USGA was primarily concerned with, and most protective of, the amateur game. The transplanted Scottish professionals and the handful of American "homebred" pros were out on their own, subject to the rules and regulation of their clubs and the USGA as they went about their livelihoods. Fortunately, Charlie Burgess was to become one of the better-situated professionals of the period, having a fair contract, decent working conditions, and the genuine respect of his employers as he began his tenure in America.

• Setting Up Shop •

The original meeting place and clubhouse for the Woodland golfers was in the basement of the well-known Woodland Park Hotel adjacent to the tract of land that they leased for their course. The Woodland Park Hotel was an elaborate Victorian resort accommodating 150 guests and advertising itself as "an ideal spot for the country-loving." Its promotional brochure described its amenities as "charming in all seasons" with walks and drives that were delightful. Safe riding horses and grooms were obtainable at reasonable prices and Thursday dinner-dances were a popular feature. The cuisine was "of unvarying excellence." The resort had bowling alleys, a poolroom, elevators, steam heat, electric lights, and a spacious steam-heated sun parlor. The hotel was also advertised as very accessible to Boston as the Boston and Albany Railroad trolleys ran past the grounds many times daily. Clearly, it was a very grand turn of the century retreat and a very suitable location for the establishment of one of America's earliest golf clubs.

Although the Woodland Park Hotel was a lovely and genteel location for the golfers, the growing legion of Woodland members soon outgrew their basement quarters. In 1902, they voted to incorporate and lease the nearby mansion and the adjacent property of Mr. William H. Monroe for their new clubhouse and golfing grounds. The course itself originally consisted of nine holes, until it was expanded to twelve, then eighteen holes in 1907. At that time the Monroe mansion was renovated and as part of the renovation an annex housing the professional's quarters and members' locker room was constructed. The professional's accommodations were hailed as one of the finest professional facilities in the country.

Most clubs rarely planned the pro shop, as it is now called, as a consideration for the club proper. It was usually the last inch of space that was given up without conflicting with anyone else. The professional was usually crowded into an old out-building, a rebuilt shack, or a corner of the basement. Since much of the early professional's income was derived from his shop, the inattention of the clubs in regard to their professional's needs in this area caused a hardship and loss of income for many early pros. Charlie was in an enviable position because of the consideration given to his facility at Woodland. The newly constructed clubhouse addition was about sixty feet long and thirty feet wide. It had a massive fieldstone fireplace at the narrow end that serviced both the pro shop and adjacent men's locker room. Inside the shop were glass display cabinets for golf balls, various early handmade types of tees, (mass produced wooden tees were not yet manufactured), and sundry golf-related items. Individual golf clubs, sets of clubs, and golf bags could be purchased from the professional here as well. The heart and soul of the shop was the workbench and club-making area located behind the retail area. The only restriction placed upon Charlie by the club was in regard to the selling of golf balls. Here the club reserved the right to be the sole supplier of that important item to its members. It has been estimated that ball sales accounted for nearly half of the average pro shop revenue. Frequently lost or damaged golf balls insured that new balls were very profitable items, so that this was one area where Charlie was put at a considerable disadvantage in his otherwise decent contract with Woodland.

When Charlie arrived from Scotland, he brought several trunks of golf club parts and club-making equipment with him. He maintained relationships with many of the well-known British golf equipment companies, particularly the Winton Brothers shop in Montrose, and imported many high quality items for sale to the Woodland members through his shop. He also established working relationships with the new American golf suppliers, particularly Wright and Ditson, Spalding, and later the Kroydon Company. Charlie would order club heads, shafts, and leather for grips, and then assemble the parts in his workshop or would re-sell the factory made clubs of the top manufacturers. However, at the time of his arrival, American suppliers still did not make golf clubs in great numbers and the handcrafted clubs assembled at the club and fitted to each member by Charlie and his assistants were prized.

A look around his workshop would reveal dozens of pre-shaped, partially carved blocks of hardwoods like maple or exotic persimmon resting along the shelves next to pre-cast iron club heads. Hundreds of hickory shafts and rolls of tanned leather for the grips lay alongside. The lathe used for turning the ends of the shafts down to fit into the club heads occupied a prominent spot in the shop. A small gas-fired forge was used to heat and expand the iron club heads so that the turned-down hickory shafts could be inserted. Fitting neatly in one corner was a hot glue pot needed to secure the shafts into the wooden club heads that were then wrapped with yards of thin, strong, twine called whipping.

A skilled clubmaker like Charlie could fine-tune a set of hickory clubs and provide a varying amount of shaft flexibility in each club much like the difference between a modern steel shafted club and a graphite one. For example, the amount of spring in a hickory-shafted wood could be subtly adjusted by the amount of whipping wound around it. Oversized clubs, very popular today, are not a new development. Charlie and other clubmakers were using various sizes of club heads and his former Scottish colleague Ben Sayers was known to use a very large-headed, commercially manufactured club called the Dreadnought Driver in competition at the time.

A wide array of wooden-handled rasps, files, and other specialty tools were lined up, ready to finish off the woods and also for the fitting of brass or other metal inserts that went into the business end of the club. Metal stamps, used by the early club makers to emboss the club head with their name or "cleek mark" which identified them as the maker, completed the equipping of the shop. Charlie's simple cleek mark read "Cha" Burgess Special and occasionally featured the profile of an American Indian wearing a feather headdress. That symbol adorned only the clubs he fashioned in the United States.

Besides his retail shop and club-making business, another important adjunct to the professional's non-teaching livelihood was the cleaning and storage of the members' equipment. The professional could charge each member a monthly fee for this service, usually 50 cents, and a club with a hundred or more members translated into a considerable extra income for the pro.

In order to make clubs, run the shop, manage the clubhouse, supervise tournaments, and still be available for lessons, Charlie needed a reliable staff. Shortly after he was settled in at the club, he sent passage money for his nephew Harry Nicoll, son of his sister Jean, to come over as an assistant. Harry was the first of seven nephews Charlie helped become American professionals. He was an excellent golfer and after working a season or two at St. Andrews, returned to Montrose to win the Links Championship of 1909 before coming to the States. One by one, Harry's brothers—Bert, Willie, Charlie, Jimmy, Francis, and Arthur—arrived from Montrose to work with their uncle on their way to becoming skilled professional golfers, each one achieving notable success in the United States from New England to North Carolina and from Florida to California. Young Charlie would also soon apprentice with his father in the same thorough manner as his cousins. While at Woodland the duties of these young new assistant professionals were to care for and store the equipment of the club members, to perform clerical work in the shop, to assist in club-making and repair, and eventually to give lessons to members.

By the summer of 1909, Charlie was fully ensconced at Woodland. His family was with him, his contract was settled, his shop was established, and he was almost always fully booked for lessons. He even had his first off-season in America planned out. Harvard University had asked him to take over its intercollegiate soccer program and Charlie became the first professional head coach of the team. College soccer was played in a split season between the early winter and early spring months, which was a perfect complement to Charlie's golf schedule. He had plenty of time to devote to both of his sporting loves.

• Finding Francis •

One of the first things Charlie did on his arrival at Woodland in the early spring of 1909 was to take a survey of his new course. On a bright and sunny day in March, when the New England air still held the bitter sting of winter, he came upon a group of several young teenagers playing on the course. The boys were splaying their shots all over the fairway and mostly into the still bare bushes and stands of trees that lined the course. They turned out to be members of a nearby high school golf team who were allowed to practice at Woodland, thanks to the generosity of the members. In those days, organized golf teams in public schools were quite rare given the novelty of the game in America compared to the traditional interscholastic sports of baseball, basketball and football. Nonetheless, the enthusiastic, if not highly skilled, golf team from Brookline High School was about to meet a man who could help them tremendously as they prepared for the upcoming season. Charlie approached the youngsters and willingly gave them some valuable free advice and instruction much in the same manner that Bob Dow and Tom Morris had done for him. Soon the errant shots were a thing of the past as the grateful youngsters gained control and confidence in their game after a few lessons from Charlie.

The seemingly inconsequential event of coming across the young high school golfers proved to be a fateful moment for Charlie, one of the boys, and the game of golf itself. It was the very beginning of a relationship that suddenly changed the future of golf and consequently the history of the game.

An unassuming and lanky fifteen-year-old member of the team caught Charlie's experienced eye as having much more potential than the others. In fact, the boy had extraordinary skills and more native ability than any other amateur golfer he had ever seen—anywhere. Charlie took the youngster under his wing, voluntarily gave him individual lessons, the loan of several clubs, and soon he and the boy developed a close personal relationship that would last a lifetime. The young golfer was so eager to learn and develop his game that Charlie graciously invited him along to play Sunday afternoon rounds with him—every week—for the next several years. The boy's name was Francis DeSales Ouimet, and he was destined to become America's first golf hero.

Francis was without question the most proficient golfer on the team. He was also perhaps the most enthusiastic and dedicated young golfer in the entire United States at that time. The shy soft-spoken teenager came to Woodland and his new coach with a compelling desire to excel at the game. He came from a humble background and had learned the rudiments of the game on his own by imitating the golfers he caddied for at The Country Club located near his Brookline home.

In order to develop his skills to the championship caliber he dreamt about, Francis needed professional guidance and the opportunity to play as often as he could but that was extremely difficult for a boy of his limited means. He could not possibly afford to join a private club or even play very often at a public course. There was no doubt that he could never have been able to pay for lessons until fate brought him together with Charlie Burgess who gladly instructed Francis of his own accord. Now, Francis had the incredible opportunity to learn from a bona fide professional golfer and accomplished instructor who came from the birthplace of his beloved game. Francis was not only being taught the game by an expert Scottish professional but also by one who actually knew and had competed against his boyhood heroes—Vardon, Braid, Taylor, and the other celebrated players of the game. The great Tom Morris had even tutored Francis' new teacher. Eventually Charlie became a hero and father figure to the young golfer as they began Francis's journey towards golf immortality.

• Francis Ouimet •

Francis was born on May 8, 1893 and was raised in a small house on Clyde Street in Brookline, Massachusetts, directly across the street from the prestigious country club of Brookline—The Country Club. Just like his newly acquired mentor from Scotland, Francis grew up next door to a golf course and was destined to have the game become a defining element in his life. His parents, Arthur and Mary, having emigrated from Terrebonne, Quebec, raised Francis in their modest Clyde Street home along with his two brothers Wilfred and Raymond and his sister Louise. The section of Brookline surrounding the Ouimet house and the adjacent country club was very rural at the time. Behind the Ouimet dwelling, separated by a small wooded and swampy area, was a farmer's field used for grazing cows. It was on this field and in his backyard that Francis took his first swing at a gutta percha ball with a club he borrowed from his older brother Wilfred.

Wilfred was the first of the Ouimet boys to be involved with golf as a caddie at The Country Club. Young Francis' first encounter with the game came as he cut across a corner of the links on his way to elementary school, collecting the lost balls of the club members. A natural curiosity and interest in the game developed.

Wil, being older, would venture into Boston from time to time. He discovered that the Wright and Ditson sporting goods store had a golf department, run by none other than the Burgess family friend Alex Findlay. Findlay would allow Wilfred to trade the used golf balls he and Francis found for brand new golf clubs—at the exchange rate of three dozen balls for each club. Wilfred presented Francis with his first club, a mashie, when he was just nine-years-old.

Wil and Francis spent hours and hours, in every weather condition and at all times of the year, whacking away at their horde of salvaged golf balls on the primitive three-hole course they devised in their yard and in the field behind their house. Francis also began caddying at The Country Club and by the time he was ready to graduate from the eighth grade at the Heath Elementary School, his dream was to become a good enough golfer to win the National Amateur Championship of the United States. The first step in the direction of this lofty goal was evidenced by his desire to compete in the Massachusetts Interscholastic Golf Championship, open to all registered high school students. Francis was ready to enter high school and had developed, through his own tenacity and natural skills, into a pretty fair young golfer. His early years as a caddie provided him with enough money for greens fees and trolley fares to Boston's first public golf course in Franklin Park, where he would practice as often as he could. Francis would trudge off from home at daybreak and play as many as 54 holes before the sun went down, the darkness forcing an end to his practice.

His first chance to compete against other schoolboys came shortly after he graduated from the eighth grade, in the summer of 1908, at the Greater Boston high school championships held at the Wollaston Golf Club in Quincy. Francis convinced the secretary of the tournament that, although he had not yet *actually* attended Brookline High School, he intended to go in the fall and in fact had already registered there. After some deliberation on the part of the officials, Francis's reasoning and his entry were accepted. In his first-ever competition, Francis actually qualified for the championship rounds with a medal score of 85, but was ousted by the eventual champion Carl Anderson—a very impressive showing for Francis nonetheless.

Francis continued to caddie that summer and would make mental notes of the good shots the golfers made. After his rounds, he would emulate and practice the shots in his back yard until it was dark or until his mother called him in to do his household chores. When he finally actually entered Brookline High School that autumn, he sought out and became friendly with the other boys who had an interest in golf. His good performance at the schoolboy tournament made him a welcome addition to the team that would compete against other high schools the following spring.

When the next golf season rolled around, Francis was a full-fledged Brookline High School freshman and the golf team was registered to compete in the embryonic Greater Boston Interscholastic League. The league was made up of just five schools including Brookline. Milton, Roxbury Latin, Newton, and the thirty-mile distant Worcester High School were the other 1909 member schools.

It was at this point that young Francis and the Brookline High squad met Charlie Burgess at Woodland. Ouimet later recalled that soon after that meeting that he and the team "began to greatly reduce their scores and improved dramatically" thanks to the lessons the good-natured professional voluntarily offered to them. Francis soon admired and recognized Charlie "as a keen student of the game" and was eager to learn all that he could from the knowledgeable Scotsman.

As the spring progressed, Francis won every team match he played in except one. He also defeated another outstanding and previously unbeaten scholastic golfer named William Flynn from Milton High School. Francis impressed a great many local golf enthusiasts that spring, particularly his new instructor. By July, it was time once again for the schoolboy championships that were held this time at the Commonwealth Golf Club in Newton where Mike Brady, a new friend of Charlie Burgess, was the professional. Brady was an American-born golfer and one of the very few homebred professionals of the time. Transplanted Scots like Charlie warmly welcomed the relatively few American pros into the working-class ranks of professional golf, and a natural alliance between them soon began.

Going into the tournament Francis had improved his local reputation enough to have a writer from the *Boston Globe* newspaper describe him as "probably being one of the best all around youngsters" in the field. The Brookline team won the team championship and Francis easily qualified in the opening round of the individual championship with a score of 83. He won his afternoon match defeating a Newton High

School boy named Lawrence Manley by the impressive margin of seven holes. He worked his way to the semi-final, and then in the finals, Francis won the scheduled 36-hole match, thanks to his accurate putting and deadly short play around the greens. He defeated the powerful long ball hitter Ronald Waitt of Milton High School by ten holes with nine to play (10 and 9). It was Ouimet's first-ever golf championship and according to Francis, "a happier boy never lived." Although thrilled by his victory, he displayed the modesty about his achievement even then that would be characteristic throughout his life.

Francis turned sixteen in May of 1909 and had to give up his summer caddie job at The Country Club because of the rigid USGA rule that would have classified him "a golf professional" and would have disqualified him from pursuing his childhood dream of entering the National Amateur Championship. The strict interpretation of the USGA constitution disqualified anyone from amateur events if, after reaching sixteen years of age, they "carried clubs for hire." Simply being a teenage caddie was sufficient, according to the rigorous rules of the USGA, to make him a person who could hold "an advantage over the amateur by reason of having devoted himself to the game as his profession." Today it is hard to imagine a sixteen-year-old caddie being considered a *professional* golfer but that was the tenor of the times and so Francis, if he was to remain an amateur, was forced to abandon the summer job that he loved.

• Lessons from Charlie •

Francis spent the summer of 1909 employed at Wilson-Larrabee, a Boston wholesale dry goods store, instead of caddying. His link to Charlie now became critically important to his continued development in golf. Cooped up inside a retail store earning $4.00 a week, instead of being out on the golf course all summer, gave Francis little opportunity to continue his practice of observing and emulating the play of the skilled golfers he once caddied for. His weekly instructional outings at Woodland with Charlie became priceless opportunities for the young golfer and future national champion to improve his game. Because golf is such a complex endeavor, even a gifted natural talent like Francis must have gotten confused about exactly which part of his game he should concentrate on if he was ever to defeat other golfers who were equally talented. It was in the refinement of the young golfer's game that Charlie played a critical role.

Charlie's instruction of Francis likely began with an emphasis on accuracy and distance with the driver, as one can surmise from this passage from a book Francis wrote in 1921 entitled *Golf Tips for Young People*, years after he himself became a champion and authority on the game.

Ouimet wrote, "Last fall I had a talk with Charlie Burgess . . . as to which is the most valuable stroke in golf. Burgess . . . gives this position to the long wood shot. And he sums it up most effectively, so that anyone may understand."

> [Burgess]: "Let us take two players who are equal with the mashie and putter; one will win one day, the other the next. There is nothing outstanding in the game played by either which warrants the belief that one of these fellows is a better player than the other. Let us take, for example, a hole of 458 yards, and assume that one of these players is long and accurate with his wood and the other is only straight down the line. The long player will usually get on such a green in two shots. The accurate one takes three. Now, unless this third shot is dead to the pin, which it will not be in the long run, the golfer who consistently gets there in two is going to win such holes. It is these long holes which tell the tale in long driving versus average driving. When all else is equal, the long driver will win such matches. He is just bound to."

Ouimet continued to improve his skills during his weekly lessons with Burgess. The other lessons he received from his coach most likely followed these tenets of Charlie's teaching, later published in a 1934 issue of the Boston *Christian Science Monitor*: " . . . You are launched in the right direction if you begin by being taught rhythm, relaxation, grip, stance, and a schooling in mental confidence correctly. Then have patience and diligently practice what you have been taught . . . the secret of lessons in golf is to practice after each lesson and take more only when you have mastered those already taken."

Charlie's advice on the mental aspect of the game also became a subtle yet important part of his student's game—"At least fifty per cent is mental, mental distortion has ruined many hopeful golfers. A perfectly simple mashie shot to the green is often upset because a trap or bunker is in sight. That shot is really no different because of the hazard, but some golfers become fearful. When that needed confidence is shaken mentally, what happens? He tightens, contracts, and something goes wrong. The hazard shot becomes a needless reality, for without the tightening or contraction, the shot would have been an easy affair. Again if a golfer is afraid he will not drive far enough and presses for distance, opening the door for trouble again."

Charlie also emphasized a proper swing—to Francis and all of his students—as a crucial element in the game of golf: "If all golfers worked for form, rhythm, and timing, they would find distance and accuracy without physical or muscular application. It's not the strength of a man that sweeps the ball afar, but the perfection of the swing. An important factor in rhythm and timing is relaxation. Without that a contraction occurs deviating the club from the . . . swing . . . You notice I speak of sweeping the ball rather than hitting, for the hit, to my mind, means application of sheer power and will not do. It must revert to the true arc of the pendulum swing every time. Acceleration or speed will sweep the ball away with rhythm more smoothly than the rigidness that goes with a hit. Correct golf swinging is as graceful as any action in sport. Not only is it smooth and rhythmic, but exact. To gain the proper shot consistently, every swing must be exact. That is why we teach the driver as the first club. It requires exactitude over the greatest span of swing. From then on we teach the short-hitting clubs, not because they are easiest necessarily but because parts of the drive enter into every club used thereafter."

Burgess's instructions in regard to addressing the ball, the swing, and the follow through still are fundamentally applicable to the game today despite incredible advances in club design that have altered some of the particulars a bit. "Take a square stance to the ball. Imagine a rectangular line from the ball to its objective . . . with the square stance your hand, brought from your sides, will meet exactly in the center. Then must come a relaxed position. To obtain this be sure the arms are not stiff or taut and break the knees forward enough to avoid their locking back. There is a happy medium of speed in the backswing. Many point out that it should be done slow, but that is largely exaggerated because so many golfers are tempted to hurry. The left hand plays the important part in pushing the club back and pushing it forward, while the right merely guides. If the right begins to overpower, perfection disappears. I also find that not enough importance is attached to the completion of the swing. The proper finish means complete control of the club and should find the weight on the left leg and the body balanced. The right elbow is straight out, parallel with the line of flight, and the club shaft almost rests on the shoulders back of the head. Too many good golfers overlook this factor and apparently swing properly but contract near the finish and end up in grotesque postures."

Rhythm, relaxation, a proper stance, sweep the ball, follow through, keep a good mental attitude, and practice one element at a time until you have mastered it. Chay's method made it sound easy, and for Francis and hundreds of other students every year it produced great results.

• Back to School •

In September 1909, Francis returned to Brookline High School for his sophomore year. Francis was now an outstanding schoolboy golfer but was at best only a mediocre student. His report card from his first year was mostly filled with "C's," but as a sophomore, Francis's grades really began to tumble badly as his mind, no doubt, filled with visions of golf links rather than math equations or history lessons. In order to continue to compete as a school golf team member, Francis had to remain academically eligible, which he did—just barely.

During that fall, into the winter, and throughout the next spring, Francis and his mentor continued their weekly Sunday afternoon rounds and lessons. Francis, unable to meet the financial obligations of country club membership and private lessons at Woodland, or anywhere else for that matter, was always Charlie's personal guest. Charlie willingly gave up his own precious free time every Sunday to work with Francis. Occasionally he would arrange for one or two of his professional friends in the area like Alex Ross or Mike Brady to join him and his young protégé. Ouimet's improvement under Burgess's watchful eye was dramatic during that year. His lessons began to pay off. Francis's scores, which had been averaging around 85, began to drop into the high 70's. Practicing Charlie's philosophy, Francis's distance and accuracy off the tee box was improving dramatically. Within the year, Ouimet would be able to score consistently in the low 70's, an average that would enable him to compete and win against almost anyone. Ouimet later recalled that those weekly lessons, which continued for several more years, represented priceless "red letter days" of his life.

In the spring of 1910, Francis was elected as president of the Greater Boston Interscholastic Golf League when the representatives of the member schools met in the offices of the *Boston Globe* newspaper company to arrange and publish the year's schedule of matches. The regular season played out with the Brookline team faring very well and ended on May 18, ten days after Francis's seventeenth birthday. Next came the team and individual school championships, which were held at Woodland. Francis got off to a great start in the individual championship play winning the qualifying round medal with a score of 77. In the second round, although he shot another great 77, he lost to his Brookline High teammate Francis Mahan. Mahan shot an incredible 73, nearly a course amateur record. As humble as he was in his previous victories, Francis was gracious in this defeat as he congratulated the winner. Charlie looked at his student with pride and admiration because of the young lad's sportsmanship. Francis was of course disappointed, but he was still determined in his quest for more victories and eventually a chance at a national championship.

June 29, 1910 was Ouimet's last day as a schoolboy golfer as he quit high school after his second year to take a permanent job in Boston as a sales clerk with none other than the Wright and Ditson sporting goods company. Francis needed money in order to pay back his mother who had just lent him the $25 he needed to obtain an official "junior" membership to Woodland. Although Francis had played at Woodland for the past two years as a guest of Charlie, he needed to be an actual member of a USGA affiliated club in order to compete in officially sponsored events like the National Amateur. The Woodland members, impressed by Ouimet's play, voted to establish the special reduced rate just for him.

Arthur Ouimet was not pleased at his son's decision to leave school and to pursue the game of golf. A hard-working man, Mr. Ouimet felt that his son would be out of place among the gentrified golfing set that he observed first-hand as a gardener for the wealthy residents of Brookline. He felt the surest road to success in America was through hard work and a good education. Rather than antagonize his father further, Francis went to his mother to obtain the support and the loan of the money he needed to join Woodland and to enter the Amateur.

The 1910 United States Amateur was being held, conveniently for Ouimet, at The Country Club, right across the street from his home. What a dream come true it would be for Francis to compete in and win that particular tournament. Francis now had a handicap of only six strokes and with many of the other entrants having even higher handicaps, Francis was encouraged at his chances. Francis shot very respectable preliminary rounds of 83 and 86 for a 169 total that was just one stroke shy of qualifying for the final rounds. It was an outstanding effort by the teenager in his first encounter with golfers of national standing. A disappointed but determined Francis continued his personal tutelage under Charlie Burgess, as he entered various club competitions and local tournaments whenever possible.

• Up in Flames •

Things were good for Charlie and his family in their new home in a new land. Since his arrival, everything he could possible have imagined was going his way until the devastating event of October 27, 1910.

Charlie, young Charlie, and nephew Harry Nicoll locked up the Woodland pro shop as usual around six o'clock that night and walked home across the golf course to the little Knickerbocker where Hattie had a hot supper waiting for them. Sometime between seven and eight o'clock, Woodland's greenskeeper John Johnson saw flames breaking out around the doors and windows of the new clubhouse annex where the club office, locker rooms, and Charlie's pro shop were located. What started the fire remains a mystery. Whatever the cause, the fire soon turned into a conflagration. Johnson telephoned the police and summoned Charlie to the scene as he courageously tried to stem the flames with a garden hose. Two alarms were sounded and firefighters from the nearby villages of Auburndale and West Newton arrived with horse-drawn apparatus. By the time the firefighters got there, the entire one-story annex was engulfed in flames and was threatening to destroy the Monroe mansion itself.

The report of the fire in the newspapers the next day summed up the distressing loss and ruination Charlie suffered that night:

> "Although the firemen fought valiantly, the flames completely destroyed the annex and then spread to the main building damaging it severely. The 250 lockers in which the members had their clothing, clubs and other property stored, were completely destroyed with all their contents. Charles Burgess, the club professional, had a workshop and storeroom in the annex near the main office and all of the property, tools and clubs were destroyed. He had many bags of valuable clubs, belonging to members stored there, awaiting his opportunity to work on them. These were lost. His own clubs, ready for sale, those he was working upon and others were also destroyed."

Charlie, with his family by his side, could only stand by helplessly as the shop and all that he had worked for went up in flames. He stoically began to rebuild his business right away. He spent the winter ordering new equipment, clubs and parts from his suppliers on credit and set up a makeshift shop in the corner of the mansion's basement in order to continue his service to the members. In March, nephew Harry sent a postcard to a friend in Scotland mentioning the good news that, "Burgess is very busy just now. He is getting a lot of clubs sold after the fire. Most of the members here are getting new kits. —It is a grand course here!"

The Woodland members had immediately set about building a replacement structure for Charlie's shop, expanding it to include a new dormitory for his helpers and other club staff. Hard work and gritty determination were the only ways to overcome adversity like that in those days. Within a year, Charlie was back to business as usual.

In the spring of 1911, the Woodland Golf Club had a 36-hole medal play tournament open to all amateur golfers. Even though Francis was now a junior member of the club and could play there whenever he wished, he continued his regular Sunday afternoon instructional rounds with his coach in preparation for the many competitions he would play in. Up to this time, the best score he had at Woodland was an impressive 74. On the occasion of the spring Match Play Tournament he shot a 70 in the first round and a 71 in the second. The 70 established a new amateur course record at Woodland, but it was not the best score ever shot at the club. Francis was a great young golfer, but he still was shy of Burgess' course record of 67. The old pro still had a thing or two to show his phenomenal young protégé. The two of them continued their close relationship as Ouimet once again entered, and unfortunately failed to qualify for, the National Amateur Championships of 1911 and 1912. But it would not be long before Francis would capture the imagination of the entire country, as he became the featured player in one of golf's most dramatic events—the match that changed golf forever.

• A Championship at Harvard •

As Charlie was helping young Francis develop his championship skills on the golf links, he had also begun his tenure as the first professional coach of soccer at Harvard University in the late fall of 1909. At the time of his arrival at Harvard, the association football team—as soccer was called then—was a minor program, loosely organized, poorly supported, and coached by student managers. However, it did have a long history as an activity on the campus and actually predated American gridiron football by almost a century.

In 1903, a graduate student at Harvard organized an undergraduate group of students who wished to play intramural soccer. Several matches were held each year until the level of interest gradually grew to the point where games against other institutions were arranged. Charlie was determined to organize and develop Harvard's soccer team into a respectable program that could compete at the highest level, challenging for the recently established intercollegiate soccer championship under his leadership. His first goal was to introduce some tactics and strategies to the play of the largely unschooled players. Because the game was played in the winter and spring, many well-known Harvard gridiron football players, including All-Americans Hamilton Fish and Lothrop Withington joined the soccer team after their other season ended. The many big men he had from the football team helped him to present a team with a strong defense that could prove the edge in a close match.

Charlie also began to expand the schedule, greatly increasing the competitions against area club teams that were made up of some very experienced players, largely recent European immigrants working in the mills and factories around Cambridge. Charlie had his teams playing up to 20 games within a few years. Harvard had its first winning season in 1910-11. A strong defense kept Harvard competitive but the lack of offense kept the team from becoming a champion. The defenders were able to keep most of the games close, but there was little offense to keep the pressure off the defense and on the opponents. His 1911–12 Harvard team won nine games while losing six and tying two, and the collegiate record of four wins and two losses was the best Harvard ever had. However, the 1912 championship went to arch rival Yale who went unbeaten in the five-game league season.

Under Charlie's leadership, soccer's popularity, although nowhere near that of American football, was growing rapidly among the students and fans of Harvard. In the years prior to his arrival, the squad was small and the players largely unskilled. By 1912, 50 to 60 candidates were reporting for tryouts and several teams were available to practice against the varsity. The development of the younger players under this system would be a key to Harvard's impending success.

After the first few seasons of traveling the six and a half miles to Harvard by electric trolley, Charlie was able to travel from Woodland to Harvard's athletic fields in his newly acquired Model-T Ford. The automobile affectionately known as the Tin Lizzy was revolutionizing American society. Its arrival marked the beginning of a new form of personal transportation that took America's cities, towns, and villages out of the isolation of the horse and buggy era and into a new age of unprecedented mobility. The Burgesses were one of many American families who would acquire the popular and affordable Model-T as their first automobile during the teens and twenties.

Young Charlie the Second, now a fifteen-year-old Newton High School student was developing into a pretty fair golfer as he entered his early teen years and he often accompanied his father to Harvard to help out with the soccer team. Just four years younger than Ouimet, young Charlie Burgess was big for his age, tall but not as hefty as his father. He had a natural golf swing and was very skillful at an early age. He also had an inclination for the business end of golf that was demonstrated as he began to help out in his father's golf shop after school and during the summers. Young Charlie was a very handsome young man with an aristocratic bearing that went well beyond his years. He had the ruddy complexion of an outdoorsman and dark brown, almost-black hair that set off the striking blue eyes he inherited from his father.

In the spring of 1913, Charlie assembled his Harvard soccer squad to prepare for the intercollegiate portion of the traditional split season. During the previous winter, the team played an expanded schedule of 12 non-league games against workingmen's and semi-professional club teams from all over the region. He reasoned that the more competition the boys had against the older veteran-stocked teams, the better they would do against their college rivals. The sport was a very popular pastime outside of the college ranks owing to the thousands and thousands of European immigrants flowing into the area as labor for the many textile mills and factories of New England. Factory teams would easily draw 1,500 to 2,000 fans on a Saturday afternoon in state and regional athletic club tournaments.

Charlie also established a team training table for the first time, in his words, "being deemed advisable for keeping the players in strict training and of helping the men to know one another thoroughly." Practice began with a few days devoted to shooting and dribbling the ball and with several regular games against the second team. Practice was difficult due to the poor condition of the field caused by a late snowfall and lots of rain that spring. It was an unseasonably cold and raw start to the season and very few workouts took place in favorable conditions. With only a small amount of time for the boys to work on their game, it was hard for Charlie to get a line on his squad, but it was evident to him that this team promised to be the best team that ever represented the Harvard Crimson. Contrary to past years, the team was very fast, particularly the forward line, which had been a weak spot of his previous teams.

Harvard left Boston's South Station late on the evening of March 24, for an overnight journey to Ithaca, New York, for their first game of the college season against Cornell. The Saturday game featured, as expected, a very speedy and aggressive Harvard forward line. True to form, their tenacious offense proved the best defense as Harvard shut out Cornell 4–0. The forwards, although fast, were not particularly good goal shooters but their harassing and aggressive play and the volume of their shots on net overcame their weakness at getting off clean shots.

Haverford was the next opponent and Harvard beat them 4–2 in Cambridge on April 4. The lack of accuracy in passing and the poor shooting from the Crimson forward line had been remedied by frequent practice sessions held despite the continued rainy, cold stretch of weather. The defense began to show the trademark proficiency of a Burgess-coached team.

Harvard traveled to New Haven on April 12 to take on traditional foe Yale and the Cambridge team was victorious once again. Speedy right halfback Eugene McCall and his equally swift lineman, Daniel Needham, continued their aggressive play and frustrated their opposite numbers by keeping the ball in the Yale zone for much of the contest.

A strong University of Pennsylvania team visited Harvard on Monday, April 28 but Burgess' squad dispatched them in a hard-fought contest 2–1. Only Columbia stood in the way of Harvard capturing its first Intercollegiate Soccer Championship. Several key players had been out with injuries during the Pennsylvania game and would not be available for Harvard's last game on May 3. Columbia was also a very strong team, which had managed to tie Penn in their meeting earlier in the season. Harvard went into this last game assured of at least a tie for the championship even if Columbia won because Columbia had lost to Haverford earlier in the season, while Harvard had defeated Haverford by two goals.

As Charlie was preparing for the final soccer game of the season, several of his fellow golf professionals were making preparations to travel to England to participate in the British Open scheduled for June in Hoylake, England. Scottish transplant Alex Campbell, pro at The Country Club, planned to go directly to his old home in Troon before heading down to the Open. Three young American homebred professionals, Tom McNamara and Mike Brady from the Boston area, and John J. McDermott from Atlantic City, were making their first trip abroad and were sailing on the steamship *Olympic* for Southampton at the end of the month. The Americans were very well known to knowledgeable British golf enthusiasts because of their history-making performances in recent U.S. Opens. McDermott, only nineteen years old in 1911, was the first American-born professional to win his country's Open while Brady finished tied for second place, for a one-two American finish ending eighteen years of British domination in the event. McDermott won again in 1912 with McNamara as that year's runner-up. McNamara also had a second place finish in 1909.

Burgess, while still able to hold his own in tournaments with his fellow pros, had largely forgone competitive golf since his arrival in America because of his commitments at Woodland and Harvard, and the time he devoted to tutoring young Francis. Although his best wishes went with Campbell and his young American friends, Charlie's immediate focus was on his soccer team, undefeated through collegiate and overall play that spring. Several injured players had returned to the line-up for the final game and the team was at full strength for their final battle of the season.

Hundreds of fans gathered outside of Harvard Stadium on a long overdue warm and sunny afternoon for Harvard's last match. Columbia jumped out to an early lead with a surprising score on a kick from scrimmage at the very start of play. Then Harvard tied with a lucky accident. Columbia was awarded a penalty corner kick by the referee, and as a Columbia defender tried to clear the ball out of his zone, the relentlessly aggressive Harvard front line caused him to miss-kick the ball right into his own goal. Harvard then pulled ahead near the end of the first period with a well-executed centering pass from the left outside forward to the right forward, who scored.

Incredibly, Columbia's right forward, who scored the first goal from scrimmage to open the game, did it again at the start of the second half. The game was even at two all. Harvard responded with a goal midway through the half only to have Columbia tie it up again with a brilliant rush down the length of the field. In the exciting last few minutes of the game, Harvard's right inside forward drew the goalkeeper out of position by faking a kick and then passing the ball to his outside forward who booted the ball through the net from the other side for the winning goal. Harvard was the undisputed Intercollegiate Soccer Champion of 1913, the first ever such honor for the University.

Charlie's career in America was on parallel tracks at this time between teaching golf and coaching soccer. The common denominator was that in each setting, he was teaching a game he loved and had mastered to appreciative and talented students. He was building champions.

6 1913

> "In my years of golf study I have found that a full swing of the clubhead, beginning at the address, travels some forty-five feet from the beginning to end. It travels fifteen feet on the backswing, fifteen feet down to the impact, and fifteen feet on the follow through. Taking this surprising distance along with the fact that the sweeping of the ball comes only eighteen inches before and eighteen inches after the impact illustrates the importance of perfection."
>
> —Charlie Burgess

• Ouimet's Prelude to Prominence •

By the spring of 1913, Francis Ouimet had grown up to be a tall, lean, self-effacing young man—and a very talented golfer. On May 8,

Francis celebrated his twentieth birthday and still remained naturally reserved—almost shy—but he possessed an infectious smile that escaped his usually serious demeanor whenever he made a "good one" on the golf course. In the five years that he had been a student of Burgess, he had made incredible progress in lowering his scores and in his ability to compete with other equally gifted golfers. Francis had not won any notable events since his 1909 schoolboy championship but shortly after his mentor's Harvard soccer team won its championship, Francis broke through the field at the Massachusetts State Amateur Tournament and won the first of what would be his six state championships. Ouimet's broad smile was evidence of quite a few "good ones" he had made at the championship match held at the Wollaston Golf Club, the same course where he won his schoolboy title.

The 1913 U.S. Amateur was held in September at Garden City, Long Island, New York. Jerome Travers was the defending champion. In the opening qualifying round, Francis played extremely well and finished just behind Chicago's great amateur, Chick Evans, who won the medal for low score. In the match rounds, Francis won his first pairing and then was scheduled to go up against Travers. Ouimet played well but fell victim to the more experienced Travers, who then went on to beat John Anderson in the finals. Travers had repeated the feat of back-to-back championships with this win. In 1907 and 1908 he had also won the National twice in a row. In light of the experienced and talented competition, Francis had once again made a very respectable and impressive showing. He returned to Woodland much more seasoned and confident thanks to the friendship that he developed with Travers as a result of their meeting on the links. Although a National title was what Francis dreamed about, his Woodland coach was pleased with him and the progress he had made. Ouimet and Burgess had enjoyed a banner year so far and it was still far from over.

Even though Francis had been defeated in his quest for the National Amateur title, the young Woodland golfer had his reputation increased a hundred-fold as the result of his exhibition there. USGA President Robert Watson was so impressed by Ouimet's play that he entered him into the upcoming United States Open Championship, which would be held at the very club where Francis fell in love with the game, The Country Club in Brookline, Massachusetts. The Open was scheduled for late September for the first time in its 18-year history in order to accommodate the touring schedule of famous English professionals Harry Vardon and Ted Ray, widely acknowledged as the two greatest golfers in the world at the time. The unprecedented delay of the Open, normally held in June, proved to be a fortuitous twist of fate that allowed Francis to fulfill his destiny. Had it been played before the Amateur as it usually was, Francis would not have been discovered by Mr. Watson and it was unlikely that he would have been entered into the Open without Watson's invitation.

• A Star-Studded Field Gathers in 1913 •

Vardon and Ray were on a barnstorming tour of the United States in promotion of golf similar to the one that Vardon made in 1900 to promote his ill-timed Vardon Flyer gutta percha golf ball. In 1913, the only mass communication outlets were newspapers and magazines. Without television or radio, the public of 1913 had to rely on the printed word to read about and imagine the skills of the great sporting heroes of the day. Barnstorming exhibitions were the only other way to bring the game to the public. In America, there was a steadily growing interest and curiosity about golf, and Vardon and Ray were treated like royalty by the golfing establishment as they toured the nation. The USGA was pleased to readjust its tournament schedule in order to include the two famous stars as the headliners of the championship. The 1913 match also promised to present the strongest players ever in U.S. Open history as many other famous European stars signed on. Wilfred Reid of Barnstead Downs, England joined Louis Tellier, described as "the French Champion from LaBoulie," as entrants. Chris Calloway, an Englishman known as the teacher to European royalty at Cannes, also represented France. Several dozen other noted Scottish and English professionals joined America's best golfers to make up the largest field ever in the national championship.

The Open began with qualifying rounds on September 16, less than two weeks after the National Amateur, which meant that Francis had little time to prepare for the auspicious event. Of great concern to him was the feeling that he could not ask his supervisor at Wright and Ditson, Mr. John Morrill, for any additional time off to play in the Open. Francis had already used up all of his vacation time at the sporting goods store in order to attend the National Amateur down in Long Island. As he reluctantly approached his boss, he was surprised by Morrill's reaction. Morrill had seen Francis's name listed in the newspaper as one of the entrants. Francis, embarrassed, told Morrill that he had really had no intention of playing and that he was surprised that the USGA had entered his name into the competition. He explained that he had hoped only to be able to go out to Brookline and see Vardon and Ray perform and that he would be very grateful to him if he could go. Morrill responded with a smile and told Francis that if he was entered, he better plan on playing. Francis was happy to comply with his boss's accommodating directive.

The barnstorming European professionals and other entrants soon began to gather in the Boston area to practice for the Open. The officials of The Country Club sponsored a number of additional exhibition four-ball and other practice matches for them in the days before the Open. In deference to their unique status as the world's most famous golfers, Vardon and Ray were allowed to use the private clubhouse and locker room facilities, usually off limits to the average professional, at most all of the country clubs they visited across the nation during their tour. At the time, this was an unprecedented and major deviation from the protocol observed at almost every American golf club, where class structure and clearly defined conventions segregated the working-class professionals from the wealthy members. But the unrivaled celebrity of the British golfers created an awkward situation where an exception to the rules had to be made for them, at least to some degree, at most events. At Brookline, while not welcomed into the stately private clubhouse and member lockers of The Country Club, they were afforded more modest, but adequate, changing facilities in an nearby locker room building. Unfortunately, the same degree of civility was not extended to the rest of the professionals as they arrived in Brookline for the tournament. As had often been the case at other private clubs, to change and relax between rounds, the rank and file professionals had to make use of more spartan accommodations, in this case, the abandoned and run-down stables that once housed the club's polo ponies.

Fifty years later, transplanted English professional Jim Barnes (1916 and 1919 PGA Champion) still bristled at that insult, according to former Professional Golfers' Association of America tournament bureau chief and author Fred Corcoran in his book *Unplayable Lies.* In 1963, the U.S. Open was held once again at the Brookline course and the surviving participants of the 1913 contest were invited to return to the club for a reunion dinner. Barnes questioned that if he wasn't considered good enough to enter the clubhouse originally, why was he being invited in now? He curtly refused the invitation with the comment, "I had to dress out in the stables and eat with the horseflies then . . . Thank you, but I don't care to return."

Another not-so-subtle indication of the USGA's attitude toward the professional golfer in 1913 was the manner in which the organization referred to them in the tournament entry list and in all of its official publications. In order to distinguish between the amateur and professional entrants the USGA bestowed the distinction of listing the amateurs with the title *Mister* before their names while the pros did not receive any such honorific and were simple listed by their first and last names. Thus Ouimet, barely out of his teens, was listed in the line up as *Mr.* Francis Ouimet while his mentor and even the great Vardon and Ray did not command the title of a gentleman from the USGA. The practice continued for years, even well after the establishment of the Professional Golfers' Association of America, until it was replaced in 1931 by the simple and much less discriminatory use of an asterisk (*) before an amateur's name in Open play competition.

Charlie's entrance into the tournament marked his second appearance in the U.S. Open. He had played in 1910 at the Philadelphia Cricket Club and out of a field of 73, finished forty-seventh with rounds of 81-83-88-81 for a 72-hole total of 333. Despite his unremarkable finish, his first hand experience there was extremely beneficial to Francis as Charlie could give him a personal understanding and insight about many of the competitors Francis would encounter in the 1913 version of the tournament. Charlie knew that his young golfer had acquired all of the physical skills he needed to win a national title and so he concentrated on helping Francis with his mental game. Charlie's first-hand knowledge of Vardon's play, as well as his familiarity with the other top British and American entrants, helped Francis tremendously. The training and tutoring of his experienced Scottish teacher gave Francis a significant edge as he prepared for the challenges that lay ahead.

As Francis went off to practice, Charlie arranged for some of his fellow professionals to join him for a low-key, relaxing warm-up before the Open. Several of America's top homebred pros and a couple of fellow British transplants were welcomed to Woodland for a novel "six-some" match. Joining him in the unusual round of composite golf were: Mike "King" Brady, professional of the Wollaston Golf Club and runner up in the 1911 Open, Tommy Kerrigan, the sensational young professional from the Dedham Country Club, Willie Maguire of Houston, Tom McNamara of Boston, runner-up in the Opens of 1909 and 1912, and the candid Jim Barnes then of Tacoma, Washington.

Louis Tellier, the visiting French professional, was hosted by the neighboring Brae Burn Country Club and also participated in a series of matches with Boston area professionals including Charlie and his friends. The dapper little Frenchman enjoyed his visit so much that in 1914 he returned to America, eventually took a position at the Brae Burn club, and became an active participant in the professional golfers union movement that Charlie Burgess would establish during the twenties.

The Sunday before the Open, Francis played 36 holes with some amateur friends at the nearby Wellesley Country Club. He shot a pair of 88s on the short and rather easy nine-hole course. His score of 88 was an unimaginable 22 strokes higher than the record score of 66 that Francis had posted there just a short time before! His friends were upset and concerned that the poor rounds might adversely affect Francis in the Open, but Francis calmly told them not to worry and that the outing "had probably got all the bad golf out of his system."

Never before had any single American sporting event caused so much anticipation as did the 1913 Open with its star-studded cast of entrants. Young Ouimet did not receive much of that attention except from a few local observers who had been following his progress. Charlie Burgess was among the few who, based upon his familiarity with Francis and his knowledge of the rest of the field, would not be surprised to see the young man hold his own amongst the likes of the famous European and American professionals. The anticipation of the event was fueled by the fact that, with 164 entries, it was hailed as the largest and most remarkable field ever assembled in the history of American golf.

Besides the celebrity professionals, 22 well-known and very skillful amateurs were entered. There was a great interest to see which of the amateurs would lead his class because no amateur had ever before won the Open. Jerome Travers was a four-time National Amateur titleholder. John G. Anderson of Brea Burn was the most recent National Amateur runner-up and W.C. Fownes Jr. was also a former National Champion. Charles "Chick" Evans Jr. from Chicago was the current National Amateur Medalist and Fred Herreshoff was the National runner-up in 1911. These competitors were among the best known of the non-professionals. Francis had a mention or two by the local press, mostly because of his recent State Championship and because of his fine showing at Garden City, Long Island, in the National Amateur just a few weeks before. But to the rest of the nation and to the golfing world in general, he was just an anonymous young ex-caddie, barely out of his teens, entered into the Open for the first time—not a contender. Because of the unusually large number of entrants, the format of the tournament called for two days of qualifying play with half of the field competing one day, the other half the next. The 32 best scores each day advanced to 72 holes of stroke play over two days for the title.

• The 1913 U.S. Open: The Match That Changed Golf Forever •

The First Day—Tuesday, September 16

The opening round of the 1913 U.S. Open enjoyed brilliant sunshine and the course was in excellent condition for the contestants and the 5,000 spectators who lined the fairways and circled the greens. Among those in the gallery was former President William Howard Taft who enjoyed the play from the vantagepoint of the verandah of the clubhouse overlooking the eighteenth green. He watched with interest and applauded the shots of the various finishing pairs as they rounded the dogleg and climbed the slight rise to the final hole. His presence at the event underscored the degree of interest in the year's Open with the famous British golfers onboard. Taft remarked that he had come "just to see how the big professionals played the game."

Each contestant played two 18-hole qualifying rounds, one in the morning and one in the afternoon. The first day's challengers included Tellier, Vardon, Barnes (who was paired off with Ouimet), McNamara, USGA President Watson, Alex Ross, Charlie Burgess (who was paired with Chris Calloway), Alex Campbell from The Country Club, and Harry Vardon's brother Tom. As the golfers approached the first tee, they were all dressed in what was considered appropriate attire. Many wore long woolen pants or knickers, vests, and jackets. All wore ties and most had on hats or caps of various fashions. When Charlie Burgess teed off at 10:30 A.M. for his first round, his son Charlie, sixteen years old and a pretty fine golfer himself, joined his father as his caddie for the day.

Young Francis teed off shortly before his coach, so Charlie had the opportunity to give him a final word of encouragement and then watch with pride as Francis hit his first drive. To most of the spectators, the shy and lanky amateur looked more like one of the caddies than the serious challenger Charlie knew he was. The only person who looked more incongruous than Francis on the course that day, was his own tiny caddie, Eddie Lowery. Dressed in the requisite shirt, tie, and jacket, he also wore a cotton sailor's cap pulled firmly on his head, its brim turned down, nearly covering his eyes from view. Little Eddie was just ten years old and not much bigger than Francis's canvas golf bag. One of Woodland's youngest caddies, he had often tagged after Francis when he played there. Eddie's older brother was to have been Francis's caddie that day but was reluctant to miss school in order to be at the Open. On the other hand, Eddie was apparently not worried about his deliberate truancy. He convinced Francis to allow him to carry his clubs after assuring Francis that he would not get in trouble for skipping school for this very special event. Francis gave in to Eddie's entreaties, and the youthful golfer and his diminutive caddie marched off the first tee unaware that they were marching toward a special place in golf history.

Francis played very good golf in the morning from the start. After nine holes he shot a very solid 40 and was among the leaders. His second nine in the morning round were even better with a score of 34 and at the end of the first 18 holes he was actually leading the entire field with a 74. By the end of the day Francis qualified for the final rounds by scoring an amazing total of 152, just *one* stroke behind the famous Vardon! Behind Francis came MacDonald Smith, Alec Ross, Tom MacNamara, and Jim Barnes. Louis Tellier was eighth and Alex Campbell was ninth with a 161.

Charlie shot an 87 during the morning round and only improved his afternoon score by a stroke to finish the day at 173, a mere three strokes short of qualifying for the final rounds. Rather than being disappointed, he gladly spent the rest of the tournament by Francis's side, coaching him on as he had done so often before and watching him as he played brilliant golf. As Francis accepted the cheers and adulation of the gallery, the reporters from around the country and around the world flashed the news of the young amateur's near upset of Vardon during the first qualifying round. When the photograph of his reserved young pupil appeared on the front pages of newspapers everywhere, Charlie realized that the life of his special student and talented young friend would be changed forever no matter what the outcome of the rest of the tournament.

The Second Day—Wednesday, September 17

Many observers felt that there was more strength in the field in the second qualifying day, not withstanding Vardon and Ouimet's great rounds the day before. Besides Ted Ray, Wednesday's players included Travers, Reid, McDermott, Brady, Willie and Alex Smith, perennial contender Gil Nicholls, formerly of Woodland, John Shippen, the first African-American golfer to play in the U.S. Open, and an obscure but quite brash and self-assured young pro from Rochester, New York named Walter Hagen. The future five-time PGA Champion and Open winner was so little known at the time that newspapers constantly misspelled his name "Hagin" and even referred to him as "Willie Hagin" once. It would not be long before the name Hagen, correctly spelled, would be among the most famous names in golf.

The reigning British Open Champion Edward Ray was the other half of what was considered the main attraction of the American Championship. He was a great bear of a man with a huge walrus mustache and was a powerful and hammering hitter who drove the ball farther than any other golfer of the day. His style was very unlike Vardon who was known more for his finesse and accuracy, especially around the green.

Johnny McDermott, the young professional from Atlantic City, New Jersey, was regarded as the American professional to watch, for he was the defending champion and the first American to ever win his country's Open, in 1911. His record as the youngest U.S. Open champion ever to win that tournament still stands today. McDermott nearly won the Open as an eighteen-year-old in 1910 when, after finishing regulation play in a three-way tie, he lost the play-off by only five strokes. McDermott was just nineteen when he defeated George Simpson of Chicago and Mike Brady in another three-way play-off for the 1911 Championship. Amazingly, he also won the 1912 Championship to secure his place in history. McDermott was without doubt the most accomplished American born pro at the time of the 1913 contest. It is amazing that his monumental achievement received so little acknowledgment from the media and the golfing establishment of the day. For whatever reason, McDermott's exploits in 1911 and 1912 failed to ignite the kind of explosion of enthusiasm the game experienced after this 1913 Open.. It was a not so subtle reminder of the low regard that existed for the American professional golfer at the time.

McDermott was very confident of his chances in the 1913 contest. He had just returned from a tour of Great Britain and had faced both Vardon and Ray on several occasions. In the British Open, McDermott was the most successful American entrant *ever* in the history of that event, finishing in fifth place, just three strokes behind the runner-up Ray and two strokes behind Vardon. When the British pros arrived in the United States to prepare for the Open, McDermott doggedly pursued them on their exhibition tour, finally beating them both at the Shawnee Open in Pennsylvania just four weeks before the contest in Brookline.

As play began on the second day of qualification, a light rain shower fell on the course, but it only helped improve the play on the greens as it quickly abated. Ray went out as expected and carded both of his rounds at 74 for a total of 148, the best score of all qualifiers. To some observers it seemed that Ray was holding back just a bit on his drives for fear of getting caught up in the trees or other hazards on the relatively narrow Brookline holes. Wilfred Reid had no need to hold back his shots and the somewhat overlooked, slightly-built Englishman from Walton Heath finished a close second to Ray, qualifying with a 151. Reporters noted that Reid "proved himself a wizard with the putter . . . in a majority of the greens he putted but once to get down."

The next qualifier was the transplanted Scottish professional R. G. MacDonald formerly of Dornoch. MacDonald, Brady, and Alex Smith all qualified easily but the former Open Champion, young John McDermott, had a harder time getting his ticket for the final rounds. At the fourteenth hole in his morning round he suffered a loss of one, possibly two strokes in the most unique manner ever recorded in a championship tournament. He hooked his long tee shot into some thick rough grass and it was found resting precariously right on top of another ball, one that had been lost by some other golfer long before the Open. The question was what should be done? Could McDermott get relief? Mr. Robert Watson, President of the USGA, who failed to qualify the day before and was therefore available to make a ruling in this case, declared that the ball should be played as it was. McDermott could not move his ball without incurring a penalty stroke. His only avenue was to smash both balls and hope for the best. He did, his ball caroming wildly off at an angle into more rough, and the hole wound up costing him a six.

The lone African-American John Shippen was thirty-five and playing in his fifth U.S. Open. He posted a 154 and was in the running only seven strokes off the pace that Vardon had set the day before and nine strokes behind Ray's opening round totals. He started the morning with a relatively average round of 81 but came back in the afternoon with a most impressive 73. Shippen's 73 was one of the best rounds shot by any of the contenders during the whole of the competition.

Shippen was the first African-American to ever play in a professional tournament when he entered and came near to winning the 1896 U.S. Open at Shinnecock Hills. He learned to play the game under the guidance of Scottish professional Willie Dunn when Dunn and fellow Scotsman Willie Davis were employed to develop the course on Long Island. Shippen was the son of a Presbyterian Minister of Jamaican descent who was posted at the Shinnecock Indian Reservation. Young John and the local Indian youths learned the game by caddying, and interest in playing naturally followed. Dunn took Shippen under his wing much in the same manner that Burgess mentored Ouimet, and young John made his historic debut in the U.S. Open despite blatant racially motivated efforts to block his entry. Most of the other entrants threatened to boycott the tournament if Shippen and Shinnecock Indian Oscar Bunn were allowed to play. USGA president Theodore Havemeyer courageously stepped into the controversy and declared in no uncertain terms that the Open would be played even if Shippen and Bunn were the only two participants! The protesting golfers reluctantly conceded to Havemeyer's firm position and the 1896 U.S. Open was played as scheduled. Remarkably, despite the hostile golfers and the stress he must have felt, the then eighteen-year-old caddie finished the first round of the tournament in a four-way tie for first place with a 78. During the final round he kept up his great pace until he hit an errant shot onto a roadway on the thirteenth hole. He could not get the ball back in play without taking several shots and wound up with a 10 for the hole, which put him out of the running. Young Shippen finished the 1896 United States Open tied for fifth place among a field of over two dozen entrants.

A surprise qualifier in the 1913 Open was the little-known Walter Hagen who finished in fifth place with a 157. The top amateur qualifiers that round were John Anderson, a local player from Brae Burn and Heinrich Smith of Worcester, having scores of 160 and 161 respectively. The better-known amateur champion Jerome Travers qualified with a 165 and former Woodland pro Gil Nicholls also qualified with a 166.

As these events were being reported, an incidental story about a new innovation in sports shared the page with the golf news. September normally meant football rather than golf news, so it was not surprising to read about the preparations being made by famous local and national college football teams. But the most interesting football story involved two small high school teams from East Orange, New Jersey, because of an innovation they began. For the first time ever, they had taken the lead in "putting numbers on the backs of the men playing so that the spectators . . . may be able to follow the men in scrimmages a good deal better." Today it seems remarkable that football teams did not use the simple system of identifying players by numbers until that 1913 scrimmage in New Jersey.

The Third Day—Thursday, September 18

Charlie Burgess had spent Wednesday observing many of his friends in the second round of qualifying play. It was also an occasion to greet many of his old acquaintances and especially to exchange a word or two with his old friend Harry Vardon. Imagine the conversation they must have had about the play of Charlie's star pupil!

Francis meanwhile tried to keep out of the spotlight and had taken his day off to gather up his thoughts and composure away from the excitement of The Country Club. That did not mean he had not followed the events. Indeed when he arrived at The Country Club for the Thursday round of the championship, he was acutely aware of his situation. Francis and the other surviving contestants began to arrive at the clubhouse around 8:00 AM for the morning rounds, but there were no spectators out on the course at that hour because of some very poor weather conditions. An early intermittent rain had caused the ground to be damp and muddy and the early morning was rather cool. By 9:30 A.M. the conditions improved significantly, and the spectators who had gathered in the clubhouse began trouping out over the course, so that by noontime, a gallery of 2,000 or more fans was following the play in pretty fair weather.

Sixty-nine players were sent out in pairs every five minutes from 8:15 to 11:00 AM for the morning round of 18 holes. Reid was in the first pair to tee off, Hagen went off at 8:25 and Vardon teed off at 9:00 when conditions first began to improve. Francis drew a 10:30 tee-off time and Tellier and Ray followed near the end of the morning. Francis got off to a rocky start. In his first two holes he shot a pair of sixes and had to work hard on the back nine to finish with a 77 for the morning. Meanwhile, Ray also had a slip-up or two and shot 79 in the morning. Francis recovered well with a 74 in the afternoon for a day's total of 151. Ray knew he needed a great afternoon game and he got it. He shot a pair of 35s for a course record 70 and posted a 149 total for the day. Vardon lived up to expectations and Reid surprised as they wound up tied for the lead at 147 after the first day of the championship round.

The breakdown of the leaders found Reid and Vardon in first place, and Ted Ray tied with English-born professional Herbert Strong from the Inwood Country Club of New York for second place. MacDonald Smith and Jim Barnes were next, tied at 150 then came Ouimet, Alex Ross, George Sargent, and Hagen with 151s. Tellier had a 152 as did Charlie Thom from Montrose, McDermott had a 153, John Shippen was at 154, Travers fell off with two 78s for his 156, Mike Brady had a 157, and Tom McNamara was near the back of the pack with a 159. Twelve players were eliminated with scores of 166 or higher. Young local American hopeful Tommy Kerrigan of Dedham was among them.

It looked like the Britons were in very good positions for one of them to win the tournament. With top American-born professionals Brady and MacNamara so far behind, there seemed to be little hope of an American victory in 1913, only McDermott appeared to have an outside chance at that juncture.

America's premier amateur, Travers, was in no better position than his professional counterparts. As a result it looked like Francis was among the few American-born players—amateur or professional—who could win. It was an improbable situation, depending upon an untried amateur to overtake the seasoned professionals, Ray and Vardon, in a 72-hole final for the championship title. Moreover the amateur was not even a national figure such as Jerome Travers. He was just a relatively unknown amateur from Boston whom most of the nation had never heard of. Yet it remained that the modest young ex-caddie and schoolboy student of Charlie Burgess was America's best hope in this tournament, with growing international implications and prestige. At the end of that long Thursday afternoon, Francis walked home to spend a quiet night with his family in Brookline, while his famous British opponents were driven a few miles further into Boston's Back Bay and their quarters at the Copley Square Hotel.

Thursday Evening—September 18

After Vardon, Reid, and Ray had a late dinner, they retired to the hotel bar for a nightcap and joined a few other golfers and reporters who were replaying the day's events. From golf, the talk proceeded to politics and at that point Vardon wisely excused himself from the party in order to rest for the final day of the match. Reid and Ray continued to drink and debate. Soon the men began to have a heated exchange about everything from golf to the English tax system. Conversation rapidly degenerated to name-calling and various insulting remarks, with both men soon boiling with anger. Ray could not stand the sharp-tongued, pointed verbal thrusts of the irritating Reid for long, and suddenly the big man stood erect, leaned over, and then delivered two powerful blows to Reid's nose. Reportedly, "The blood trickled down Reid's face but the slight and somewhat frail Reid manfully struggled to his feet to offer battle to his more powerful opponent." In an instant, the headwaiter jumped in between the two and the combatants were separated—for the time anyway—and everyone went to bed. Ray refused to talk to the several reporters on hand and seemed unaffected by the incident as he retired for the night. Reid, however, was an emotional wreck, humiliated by the events at the Copley. He slept fitfully and when he finally began to doze off in the wee hours of the morning, he was awakened again by the sound of a hard steady rain falling over Boston.

The Fourth Day—Friday, September 19

All of the contestants woke up to find a day far from ideal for golf. The rain that started at two in the morning showed no signs of letting up. Unlike the conditions of the previous day, this was no morning sprinkle that would clear up. It was a downpour. As Charlie watched the contestants tee off, he was reminded of the day in 1904 when he observed Harry Vardon work his magic in the driving rains against Jack White in Edzell, Scotland. All of the British visitors were well equipped to play in the heavy rain that fell that day, most of them employing the old trick of punching a series of holes through the leather grips of their clubs, right into the hickory shafts, for better purchase in the wet conditions.

Despite the rain, a good number of spectators were on hand to see the first pair of golfers tee off. Ray, who showed no signs of any problems from the night before, and Mike Brady, the local professional from Wollaston, were off just before nine o'clock. Although the American was eight strokes behind his playing partner and ten strokes off the lead, the crowd was still hoping for an American victory over the heavily favored British pros. At this point the best hope for the USA aside from young Francis was probably in long-time transplant Barnes and the homebred McDermott who were three and six strokes off the pace.

The two leaders, Vardon and Reid, started off early as well and Vardon seemed to be having a hard time keeping his shots on line. He had a tendency to put a little cut on the ball to send it toward the right in its flight, and in the morning round, it seemed perilously close to getting him in trouble. In spite of his slight slice, which cost him a pair of sixes, and the pouring rain, Vardon did quite well in the morning, carding a 78.

Reid's performance, however, was a disaster. He showed up for the match in a mild state of panic, plainly obvious to any observer. The altercation with Ray the night before left him without rest and in a highly nervous state. It was not just the physical punishment he endured that bothered him. It was more the humiliation and embarrassment the degrading event caused to him, especially as a representative of his country in a foreign land. His morning total was 85 and that put him out of the running. He fared no better in the afternoon and fell off the pace of the eventual winners by a whopping 14 strokes. It was a colossal fall.

John Shippen was unable to come close to his previous best round of 73 and he, too, quickly fell off the pace with two 87s on the rainy final day of regulation play. Shippen finished 24 strokes behind the leaders in what would be his final Open appearance. Charlie Thom, the Scottish Pro representing Shinnecock Hills where Shippen learned the game, did a bit better but also took a big fall from his previous day's total of 152. Thom shot an 84 and an 85, 17 strokes off his previous pace to finish in twenty-sixth place with a 321 total. The pouring rain was taking its toll on many of the top players. English-born pro Herbert Strong, one of the surprise leaders going into the day's play, shot an 82 in his morning round and finished the day in eighth place. The defending champion McDermott gained a stroke on Vardon in the morning but lost one to Ray as he brought in a 77. Louis Tellier, the Frenchman, was in contention until he slipped and fell making a shot at the twelfth hole of his afternoon round and fell out of the running. Scottish-born professional

MacDonald Smith played great golf, but he too had an afternoon round that put him three behind the eventual top score.

American Hagen and long-time transplanted Englishman Barnes fared well in the morning rounds so that by the afternoon there was still hope of an "American" upset. But the most unlikely hero, Ouimet, emerged at the start of the afternoon round and began to capture the attention of the gallery, the assembled press, and the two leaders: Vardon and Ray.

Ouimet had started his morning round about an hour and a half behind the leaders and the weather was still as bad, if not worse, than before. The constant downpours worsened the deteriorating conditions of the fairways. However, the delayed start did allow Francis to get sporadic reports on the progress of the leaders and he knew exactly what he had to do to win. The sight of the slight Ouimet and his little caddie on the rain-soaked first tee was comical notwithstanding the seriousness of their business. Francis, still dressed in his woolen jacket, tie, and knickers, was soaking wet in an instant and had only his cap to protect him from the elements. His caddie was dressed in the same manner with a towel draped around his neck as the rain cascaded down over the brim of his little sailor's cap. Eddie tried to keep Francis's clubs dry by draping an oilskin cloth over the club heads and occasionally resorted to using a great large umbrella that covered the golf bag and most of little Eddie as well.

As Francis teed off for his first 18 holes of the day, he was four strokes behind Vardon and Reid (who was still a factor at that point) and two strokes behind Ray. He had prepared himself to get into a perfect frame of mind. Perhaps remembering his mentor's words that the game is "almost fifty percent mental," Francis decided to concentrate on each shot, play it for all it was worth, and then forget it. Francis got himself into a wonderful mood and his shot-to-shot approach paid off handsomely. He played beautiful golf despite the rain-soaked conditions and was bold with his putts. Most pundits thought that the British competitors would be well suited and experienced in playing in the rain, but surmised wrongly that Ouimet would be bothered by it. Francis was somewhat of a mystery player to the international golf world, and few people knew of his readiness for the rain thanks to his unusual introduction to golf as a youngster. In his very early years, most of young Francis's golf practice occurred on the makeshift course that included his backyard and the next-door cow pasture in Brookline with his brothers. However, rainy days provided the aspiring golfers a rare opportunity to sneak onto The Country Club, the very same course where he now was challenging for the United States Championship, and play as much as they wanted to. He later would recall in his 1921 book *Golf Tips for Young People* that "on wet days—the harder it rained the better I liked it—we played to our hearts' content over the well kept course without being interfered with. One of our chief stunts on such a day was to select some secluded hole and play it over and over again with mid irons and mashies. We soon found that our play suffered little in comparison with what we could accomplish in good golf weather." As a result of his early "training" in the rain, Francis acknowledged that he had developed "a great deal of confidence in [his] game when the weather conditions are far from normal." This fourth day of play severely tested his confidence in his foul weather abilities.

Francis shot a 38 for his first nine, despite getting two sixes on the eighth and ninth holes. At the end of his first 18, Francis wound up with a 74. Reid by then had played himself out of contention, and Ouimet picked up enough strokes on both Ray and Vardon to tie the great Britishers at 225 with 18 more holes to play in the afternoon for the championship!

News of his surge raced through the gallery, and interest in the young American grew with every report that came into the press tent where newspaper reporters from all parts of America and Europe were stationed. The weather conditions did not improve for the afternoon rounds as Vardon and Ray were again off sometime before Francis. As the Englishmen kept the pace and pressure up, they were both determined to insure that a twenty-year-old American amateur and ex-caddie would not deal the prestige of British golf any further harm.

Seemingly unaffected by the huge gallery that was swelling around him, Francis set off with the same sense of purpose that served to check his nervousness so well this far. Vardon finished the first nine of the afternoon at 42 and Ray carded a 43. They rounded the turn and finished the final nine with 37 and 36 respectively, tying for the championship with 72-hole totals of 304. When they retired to the clubhouse to post their scores, their young American challenger was still out in the course. Reports at the start of his final nine gave the Englishmen the idea that Francis might finally be fading. He shot a 5-4-5 for the tenth, eleventh, and twelfth holes. But a wild cheer from the gallery at the thirteenth green brought Vardon, Ray, and the people in the warm and dry clubhouse running back out onto the pouring rain to watch the incredible finish of young Francis. Francis had just holed a 30-foot putt for a three!

Ouimet shot a good five at the fourteenth and then a beautiful four at fifteen that electrified the crowd as they began to realize what the former schoolboy golfer and caddie was doing on this fateful day in Brookline. He had sliced his drive on the fifteenth but laid his chip shot from the rough right up to the hole for an easy four. The last three holes were crucial to Ouimet. He knew that in order to tie Vardon and Ray he would have to pick up one stroke better than the remaining pars of three, four, and four somewhere in the next three holes! In order to best the British, Francis had to concentrate and play against the course. On the very next hole, the sixteenth, it looked like he might have a hard time picking up the par three he needed there as he faced a difficult and pressure-packed ten-foot putt after reaching the green in two. But he elicited an audible moan from the lips of the veteran Ray when he holed the putt for par.

Now an army of five to six thousand followers, an incredibly large gallery in those days and under the conditions, was marching along with Francis over the soggy fairways of The Country Club. Among the throng, but close by his side, Charlie Burgess stood proudly and witnessed what many have called the golf "shot heard 'round the world," and "the miracle on the seventeenth green." With two holes of 360 and 410 yards to play, Francis had to score no more than a total of seven strokes, one under par. His tee shot on seventeen, and then a full mid iron shot left the ball resting on the green, giving him a difficult putt estimated between 12 and 15 feet for the crucial birdie. An eerie silence fell over the anxious crowd. Francis approached the putt with determination and with a single-mindedness of purpose that only the very greatest athletes could ever know. As the crowd collectively held its breath, and just as Francis began his stroke, the stillness was broken by a loud and persistent blast of an automobile horn from a nearby street that was only about 20 yards from the green. It seems that some impatient driver could not contain his anger at the huge traffic jam that occurred around The Country Club as a result of Francis's spectacular finish. Francis was oblivious to the distraction and was so focused on the putt that he never heard the horn and was surprised when he was told about it later. The putt went in and a roar from the crowd went up as the ball hit the back of the cup and disappeared. The cheer was long and loud, more like a reaction at a championship football game than at a golf match. Now Francis just had to par the home hole to tie for the lead, or birdie it for the win.

On the final hole Francis drove off "with a gusto that showed his heart, nerve, and ability were all behind it," according to one reporter. It was an amazing show of determination for Francis under almost impossible circumstances. "He was putting the skill and the heart of a mere youth against the skill, and long experience of two former British champions. More than that, he played in worse conditions than either of his rivals, for he had a late start and the rain came harder and more copiously as the day advanced."

Francis got off a beautiful drive so far down the long dogleg fairway that he had a relatively easy iron shot up onto the green. He had put into practice the very first lesson that he received from Burgess. The shot was long and accurate, giving him the possibility of a birdie to win. He had a fairly long putt and boldly went for the putt to win instead of playing it safe and going for a sure par. The gamble failed as the putt missed and ran by the hole by four or five feet. Francis appeared not to be disturbed by the miss as he calmly went up to the ball and stroked it into the cup for a three-way tie for the Open Championship of America. Once again a roar that could be heard for miles erupted from the crowd. The crowd went wild with excitement and the exuberant gallery rushed on to the green, lifting Francis onto their shoulders. The unpretentious local boy and ex-caddie was suddenly thrust into the limelight as a national hero. It was the most dramatic moment ever witnessed in American golf.

As happy as any man on the course was Charlie Burgess, who knew from that day on Francis would belong to the world. It was a poignant yet prideful moment for his teacher as his gifted student graduated into a whole new universe of fame and admiration. Observing the frenzied scene *Boston Transcript* sportswriter Linde Fowler described the reaction of someone else especially dear to Ouimet: "In the middle of the happy gathering stood a middle-aged woman whose face was alight with joy and her eyes sparkling with keen delight. It was Francis's mother who had been summoned from her home nearby when news of her son's gallant effort reached her. It is useless to attempt any description of what she must have experienced when she heard the triumphant shouts . . . and saw her boy hoisted on the shoulders of his admirers."

The Last Day—Saturday, September 20: The Play-off

The weather for this fateful day in golf history was still quite bad. It had been raining well over thirty hours when Vardon, Ray, and Ouimet teed off at 10 AM. By now, thousands of words had been spelled out across the newspapers all over the world and had turned this match into something like the sporting equivalent of the American Revolution of 1776. The press coverage of the match was now unprecedented; additional correspondents had continued to descend upon Brookline as the drama unfolded to report across the nation. The numbers of reporters swelled the already-overflowing press tents and telephone and telegraph stations. National pride and the tremendous curiosity of the public brought forth even larger galleries than before to watch the three men compete, head to head this time.

Before the play-off began, Francis was approached by one of his friends, an excellent golfer, who offered to take over the caddie duties from little Eddie now that the match had reached this crucial stage. The implication of the offer was that a more knowledgeable and experienced golfer as a caddie would be more valuable to Francis at this point. Francis looked over at little Eddie, who had a patriotic red, white, and blue ribbon pinned on his chest for luck. There was a tear in Eddie's eye as the little caddie thought he was finished. Instead Francis turned to his friend and simply said, "Thanks, but Eddie will do just fine."

Many of the observers were wondering whether Ouimet, despite his tremendous showing the day before, could withstand the pressure any longer. Was it a fluke that the young Boston boy had done so well? Moreover, today it was two against one and many onlookers thought it would be a day for the famous British golfers to intensify their games, as they had done countless times before, dispatching the young upstart who had embarrassed them so far in the tournament. Smart money said the young Bostonian was sure to fold and that it was merely beginner's luck that had brought him along thus far. Francis, little Eddie, Charlie, and the others closest to Francis thought otherwise. Everyone who knew him before the Open knew that he had not changed, nor would this event, grand as it was, change Francis. If Francis could keep concentrating, playing it shot by shot, hole by hole, he could win. Johnny McDermott, the youthful former American Champion, graciously went out of his way to seek out Francis and to offer him encouragement. Words that would echo the sentiments of his coach and would be a key to Ouimet's success. McDermott simply advised Francis to "play your own game."

The excitement of the previous day continued through the first nine holes of the 18-hole play-off that ended with all three men still tied up with scores of 38! Each player had made a mistake or two and each one was able to recover by the turn. Likewise, the lead never was more than a stroke at any given time for the player who had held the temporary advantage.

At the 140-yard, tenth-hole Francis finally took the lead. Vardon and Ray missed their putts, while Francis holed his short putt for a par three. On the eleventh they all shot par for fours. At twelve, Francis hit a perfect mashie (5-iron) to the green for his approach while Vardon was off to the left and Ray was off to the right of the green. Francis had at least a 12-foot putt, and if he holed it he would have gained two strokes, but this time he played it safe, took two strokes, and got another point up on his foes as they took fives for the holes. It was Vardon 51, Ray 51, and Ouimet 49 going into the thirteenth-hole. Vardon gained a point on the other two on thirteen with his birdie three; Ouimet and Ray had fours. At fourteen, all three had either a poor drive or a missed second shot and they all took fives. Ouimet was still leading Vardon by one and Ray by two strokes going into the fifteenth, and the two Englishmen began to show signs of anxiety.

Up to this point no one had landed a single shot in a bunker but Ray's long second shot on fifteen got caught in a sandtrap to the right front of the green. The ball was set close to the front lip of the bunker and he failed to get the ball out in one shot. His second bunker shot sailed out of the trap and went well beyond the green. Ray took a six, and with Francis getting another birdie four, Ray was effectively eliminated from the contest.

Now the match was really between Francis and Harry Vardon. Both of them managed par threes on the 125-yard sixteenth and they were back to the magical 360-yard seventeenth hole where just yesterday Francis stroked the putt that put him into the play-off. Francis had the honor and drove off safely, "long and accurately," to the right and had the hole open up nicely for him.

The seventeenth hole doglegged to the left and Vardon chose to try and cut the corner to pick up a stroke on Ouimet. He cut it too close and wound up in the sandtrap that guarded the bend. Vardon had to play the bunker shot out sideways and it took him three to reach the green. Francis was on in two with a mashie shot that landed about six feet past the pin. Ray continued to play out the round although it did not matter. Ray and Vardon took fives on the hole while Francis sunk his putt, with little apparent care, for his birdie three. He now led Vardon by three and Ray by seven. The last hole was a mere formality as once again the seventeenth-hole was the turning point in Ouimet's improbable victory. Francis finished the home hole with another four, Vardon had a couple of miss shots and got a six, while Ray finished with a very nice three. The final score was Ouimet 72, Vardon 77, and Ray 78.

Once again, Ouimet was mobbed and was carried into the clubhouse on the shoulders of his admirers, part of the record gallery of over 10,000 fans. Shouts of joy and adulation were heard and the newsmen rushed to their wires to spread the news around the world. The gallery, in their excitement and moved by the occasion, generously collected a purse of about one hundred dollars for Ouimet's little rain soaked ten-year-old caddie, Eddie Lowery.

No one was more overjoyed for Francis than his old teacher. After marching along with his star pupil for the last 162 holes, he witnessed one of the greatest moments in any American sporting event. He saw his Francis play his way to become what Charlie always knew he would be: a champion equal to the greatest golfers in the world.

The aftermath of this victory by the twenty-year-old American amateur may be hard to imagine today, but it rocked the sporting world of 1913 and had overtones of national pride and class distinctions far beyond the golf course. The media attention was comparable to the frenzy seen around an event like today's football "Super Bowl" and the impact of Ouimet's victory on the national psyche was as inspiring as the "Miracle on Ice" triumph of the amateur American Olympic Hockey team over the vaunted Soviet Union in 1980.

Newspaper headlines around the world proclaimed Ouimet's startling victory:

> "British Cracks Vardon and Ray Meet Their Master in Ouimet"
>
> —*Boston Sunday Globe*, September 21, 1913

> "Francis Ouimet, A Youthful Amateur, Astounds the Golfing World by Beating Veteran Masters of the Game and Winning Open Title"
>
> —*New York Tribune*, September 21, 1913

> "Golf Prodigy—American Boy's Defeat of Vardon and Ray—Iron Nerve at 20"
>
> —*London Daily Mail*, Monday, September 22, 1913

These headlines led the stories by a host of reporters and special correspondents from London, Paris, Toronto, Montreal, and Chicago. New York City had more than a dozen reporters, one who wrote "there were men from the big press associations which flashed the news by telegraph to every city and town in the United States and all countries of the world by cable." Six writers from London newspapers filed stories for England, the contingent including Bernard Darwin, a noted journalist and grandson of the famous evolutionist Charles Darwin. (Bernard Darwin also acted as Ouimet's official score keeper during the play-off.) More than 275,000 words were sent by wire right from The Country Club by a staff of ten trained operators. Another 300,000 words were transmitted from other stations in Boston each evening of the tournament. Ouimet's name was flashed to London, and his victory known there, 30 seconds after he won the championship. These were marvelous and fascinating advances in communications for the time, just ten years after Marconi's first transoceanic wireless broadcast, and it was notable that they were made in the context of a sporting event. Ouimet's victory became a colossal worldwide news item.

Francis eschewed all the attention and admiration that was suddenly cast upon him after his victory. In order to escape the inquisitive media and well-meaning fans, he and his old schoolboy friend and golf teammate Tony Colombo went into Boston to have a quiet dinner at a Boylston Street café. After dinner they attended a performance of *The Merry Martyr* at the Colonial Theater. During the intermission the new champion was recognized by a number of people, mostly golfers who insisted on offering him their congratulations. The shy Francis was clearly abashed by all the adulation. He returned to his home immediately after the performance and tried to remain out of the spotlight for a few days while he took stock of his future. But his life would be forever changed, as his celebrity born from success soon would present opportunities that were inconceivable to him at the time. The success and celebrity of Francis would also, to a large degree, alter and affect the life of his teacher and coach, Charlie Burgess.

7 1913–1914

"You notice that I speak of sweeping the ball rather than hitting, for the hit, to my mind, means the application of sheer power and will not do. It must revert to the true arc of the pendulum swing every time. Acceleration or speed will sweep the ball away with rhythm more smoothly than the rigidness that goes with a hit. Correct golf swinging is as graceful as any action in sport. Not only is it smooth and rhythmic, but exact."

—Charlie Burgess

• A Tribute to Francis •

Ouimet's improbable victory in 1913 did more to popularize golf in the United States than any event ever before. The young man's historic accomplishment blazed a trail in the world of golf for the common man to follow. Because he was an ex-caddie and was from the working-class, his sudden fame dispelled the notion that golf was exclusively a rich man's game. In emulation of Francis, thousands upon thousands of people, young and old, began to take up the game on the many new public courses that were being built across the nation. Inspired by Ouimet, the golfers who came after him began to shift the center of golfing excellence from Great Britain to America. Golfing legend Gene Sarazen was one of those golfers.

In 1913, Sarazen was an eleven-year-old caddie at The Apawamis Club in Westchester County, New York, when he heard the inconceivable report that up in Boston a former caddie and first generation American had just beaten the great Vardon and Ray. The young man, then known as Geno Saraceni and also the son of immigrant parents, was inspired. He made up his mind right then and there that he too would become a great golfer someday. He succeeded beyond his wildest imagination and in later years always recalled how the news of Ouimet's success in Brookline inspired him and was an event that changed the course of his life.

Ouimet's sudden celebrity on the international stage changed the lives of many other people, including Charlie Burgess. As the public bestowed attention on the new young golf hero, insiders around the game recognized the important role that Burgess had played as the man behind the scenes of golf's greatest moment. Charlie did not seek to profit or gain celebrity from his association with Ouimet. Even then, as in the modern world, many coaches of champions subsidized their teaching by writing books, making business deals, or by endorsing products. Charlie would have none of that. His commitment to Francis had been born out of his unselfish desire to assist a talented young golfer without the means to afford private professional instruction. His willingness to share his wisdom stemmed from his own love of the game. He never thought of any reward greater than seeing his pupil succeed.

But celebrity did come to the dedicated Scottish professional as a result of his student's success. And the degree of his pupil's success—an international championship—brought Charlie a commensurate degree of notoriety. His standing in the professional world of golf was increased significantly as the teacher of America's first golf hero.

As autumn approached and the New England weather began to change, it signaled a slowdown on the links and the start of another season of soccer at Harvard for Charlie. The candidates for the 1913–14 team gathered with great expectations. As in the past, the team would play a non-conference schedule of matches against industrial and independent soccer teams in the fall and then enter into the regular collegiate meetings in the spring. Charlie continued to introduce innovative ideas to his soccer program. This time he had an idea designed to promote and popularize soccer among the greater student body at the university. After a good deal of negotiating, he arranged for an exhibition match at Princeton University on the same day as the annual gridiron football game between the two schools, the first such soccer exhibition of its kind. In early November, the Harvard football and soccer teams and hundreds of fans traveled by rail to New Jersey for what was called the "big athletic invasion of Princeton." The soccer match between the two clubs was their first meeting ever and served as a prelude to Princeton's addition into the intercollegiate soccer league the next spring. The exhibition match was well received by the thousands of curious and cheering fans prior to the gridiron game. The experiment was a great success, but the meeting surprisingly found the experienced Harvard squad on the wrong end of a five-to-one score. The unexpected setback was one of two losses they had that fall and the team finished up with a record of seven wins, two ties, and two losses.

While Charlie was down in Princeton, the directors of the Woodland Golf Club sponsored a grand testimonial dinner for Francis held at the Exchange Club of Boston in order to accommodate all of the people who wished to honor their new hero. Although Ouimet came from poor, working-class stock, his great achievement served to overcome the class distinction that normally would have separated him socially from the wealthy club members. Instead, they warmly welcomed him into their family as one of their own—but only as long as he remained an amateur golfer. If Francis had chosen to become a professional, a logical step toward financial security for a humble young man with his talents, then the situation would have been much different. The working-class *professional* golfer was still far from the social embrace of America's country club set.

Indeed, in 1913, professionalism in any sport was looked upon with a considerable degree of disdain by most of the world's effete ruling class as evidenced by the treatment of American athlete Jim Thorpe by the international Olympic Committee that year—an action that young Francis Ouimet certainly must have thought about with regard to his own future in golf. Thorpe, a Native American born on an Oklahoma Indian reservation, represented the United States in the 1912 Olympic games in Stockholm, Sweden, in track and field. He won the pentathlon and decathlon by huge margins and set world records in both. It was widely reported that Sweden's king called him the greatest athlete in the world as he presented Thorpe with his gold medals. But the official report of the fifth Olympiad released a year later makes absolutely no mention of the great Thorpe's name. His achievements were expunged from the record books—his medals confiscated. The amateur body controlling the games discovered that Thorpe had once taken part in some semi-professional baseball games, and even though baseball had nothing to do with track and field, declared that Thorpe had violated the venerated rules of amateurism that existed at the time. He was stripped of his records. Long considered one of the most egregious and prejudicial rulings in the history of sports, Thorpe's medals were finally returned and his name posthumously restored to its proper place in history in the early 1980's. In 1913 Francis was at a crossroads between the professional and amateur worlds of golf. But, given the tenor of the times, he had most likely made his decision as to which road to take a long time before he arrived at that juncture.

Some very important announcements were made at the dinner that night that determined the direction Francis chose to follow in golf for the rest of his life. Among the few words that the reserved young man spoke to the gathering was a pledge that he would strive to remain an amateur so that he could pursue his long-held childhood dream: a victory in the National Amateur Championship—a championship he and many others, particularly the USGA, considered even more prestigious than the Open he had just won!

But how could this young clerk, son of a poor gardener, afford to maintain his preeminent position in a wealthy man's game unless he turned professional and got paid for his performances? That obstacle was ingeniously overcome by arrangements disclosed by the club's directors. As a special mark of esteem and appreciation of the honor he brought the club, Woodland elected Francis "a senior resident member for life, exempt from the payment of dues." He would also receive a host of honorary memberships at golf clubs across the state and country, and it is safe to say that he rarely had to pay for a round of golf ever again.

In order for Francis to afford to travel and compete in international competitions and still remain an amateur, a special fund was established by the club to defray his expenses in the upcoming British Amateur and Open tournaments. Subsidizing amateur players was not new nor did it begin with Francis, although he was now the most famous amateur on the face of the earth. Just two years before, in a 1911 editorial in *The American Golfer*, the practice of paying a player's expenses was called an "open secret" in regard to skirting the strict regulations regarding the USGA rules against professionalism. Still, the United States Golf Association ratified this controversial plan for Ouimet, one that to many observers seemed to be in conflict with the intent, if not the actual rules, against professionalism. The only stipulation was that Ouimet had to file an itemized list of his expenses upon his return from Europe. The USGA's approval of the Woodland arrangement might have suggested to some observers that they were looking the other way as the organization's rigid rules against professionalism were being bent a good deal in order to accommodate America's surprising new golf hero. But the secretary of the club steadfastly insisted that the "plan follows the regulations laid down by the USGA and forestalls any criticism of Ouimet's amateur standing."

And so Francis received the first of many honors and accommodations that enabled him to live and compete at the highest levels of golf as an amateur, despite his humble background and without visible means of support except for his clerk's position. He was hailed as a working-class hero and was *also* embraced by the elite establishment. In an age when amateur golfers owned the clubs, ran the competitions, and made the rules, Francis made a wise decision. He would have a good future and achieve financial security, not from the money he could make as a professional golfer, but with the contacts and social advantages he could access in the rarefied circles of the nation's amateur golf establishment.

• Pinehurst Privileges •

Francis soon began to enjoy the fruits of his labors on the links, even if the reward was not a cash prize. Celebrity status brought with it many advantages provided by the people and organizations that could profit from association with the celebrity. Many business, travel, and social opportunities presented themselves in short order and in various fashions to Francis. One of the first such perks that Francis received was the opportunity to travel to North Carolina that winter to enjoy its temperate climate and many rounds of golf at Pinehurst, the golf and sporting resort self-described as "America's St. Andrews." Whether Francis was the guest of the Pinehurst resort or of his traveling companion, Woodland member, Paul Tewksbury, is not known. Obviously, Francis could not afford such a vacation on his salary as a store clerk. Even getting the time off from his duties at the Wright and Ditson shop would have been nearly impossible if Francis had not found fame as a golfer who happened to work for a sporting goods retailer. Any newsworthy events involving Ouimet would certainly do no harm to business.

Francis accepted his vacation outing with great appreciation and much excitement. He was reported to be "anticipating his stay at Pinehurst with the keenness of a school-boy on the way to the old swimming pool on a hot summer afternoon."

Pinehurst was the brainchild of Boston entrepreneur James Walker Tufts in 1895. Tufts made his fortune in the soda fountain business, selling the ornate wooden, marble, chrome, and mirrored ice cream counters that graced the soda shops and drug stores of America in the 1890s. Tufts originally envisioned creating a sort of retirement and vacation community for winter weary northerners far away from the harsh weather of New England. He purchased 5,000 acres of land in the pine-covered sand barrens of North Carolina just west of Fayetteville. Tufts then commissioned the famous landscape architect Fredrick Law Olmstead to help create his vision. Olmstead was well known for designing New York's Central Park and Boston's famed Emerald Necklace of parklands (including Franklin Park, where Boston's first public golf course was later established). At Pinehurst, he created a quaint town of winding streets, storybook cottages, open spaces and common land, and a beautiful New England-styled central village. Important to the theme of healthy outdoor living envisioned by Tufts was the creation of the golf courses that defined the community. In 1899, Donald Ross was commissioned to build the first Pinehurst course, and then again, in 1907, he built Pinehurst Number Two, a course that is still used in championship competition today.

When Francis visited Pinehurst, three courses were in operation, all designed by Ross. The earliest greens at Pinehurst were unique in that they were not made of grass at all but were areas of hard-packed sand, which took even the best putting golfers some time to adjust to. Francis commented to the many reporters that accompanied him on his visit that his trip to the South was prompted by a desire to once again "drive a ball off the tee" and to simply play the game again in warm weather before heading off for his scheduled European journey, something he could not do very well back on the frozen turf of New England. Francis's southern visit was purely for fun and relaxation as he prepared himself for his spring competitions overseas.

• Another Championship •

Charlie Burgess had a great deal of preparation to attend to himself that spring in Cambridge concerning his soccer team. The team he carried over from the winter was well prepared for its collegiate season where the tournament format compressed the schedule into a pressure-packed month-long period. Once again he had his players sit together at a training table as practice began in late February. Harvard's opener was at home against Cornell on April 3 and the game was played on a muddy field, much of it in a pouring rain. Despite the conditions, the reconstituted Harvard eleven led 2 to 1 at the half and scored five more unanswered goals in the second half to win 7 to 1.

While he attended to his team at Harvard, Chay's thoughts were often drawn back to Francis, who had just sailed off to England for his first experience of playing against the British on their home links. Francis was scheduled to play at Sandwich for the British Amateur and then in Prestwick, Scotland, for The Open. In the meantime, he was traveling throughout the island playing in exhibition and friendly four-ball matches. He was very well received and photographs of him were selling by the thousands as enterprising vendors followed him wherever he went.

Fame followed success for Francis and did the same for Charlie and his Harvard soccer team. They were gaining more attention from the press and a full-page photogravure feature accompanied the story of the win against Cornell in the *Boston Globe*. Whereas just a few years before only a handful of loyalists showed up for the matches, now many hundred spectators were regularly attending the games held in the shadow of the great new concrete coliseum built to accommodate the university's American-style football team.

For its next match, the team traveled to the Philadelphia Cricket Club to take on the University of Pennsylvania on Saturday, April 11. Harvard lost 2–0, and Penn put itself in good position to take the championship away from the Crimson.

The squad remained in Philadelphia following the Penn game and toured the historic city on Sunday. Monday they traveled to nearby Haverford College and played a considerably better game and Harvard took home a 2–1 victory. The team returned to Cambridge and had only three days to prepare for traditional rival Yale. Yale came into the game with wins over Columbia and Cornell, but they too had lost to Penn. Harvard took the game to Yale right from the start and, supported by a strong defense, the Bulldogs could not get near the Crimson net. The final score was Harvard 4, Yale 0.

His busy spring schedule often presented some scheduling challenges for Charlie. Traditionally on every Patriots Day, April 19 (the Massachusetts holiday commemorating the holiday commemorating the beginning of the American War for Independence), Woodland opened the golf season with an important club tournament. In 1914, the holiday fell on a Sunday and Chay had to be on duty to orchestrate the events, even though he now had two of his nephews, Harry and Bert Nicoll, available to assist him. He had to manage the golf tournament in the morning, then run out to Cambridge in the afternoon, collect his soccer team, and head for Boston's South Station to catch the train for New York for a match with Columbia University scheduled for Monday. When he finally relaxed in his Pullman car, he had the opportunity to read the newspaper accounts of Francis's exploits in Britain. Unfortunately, Francis had been playing rather poorly since the start of his visit and was voicing concern about his game. It was too bad that Charlie, who had so much experience with the game as it was played in the British Isles, could not have been with his now famous student. But his duty now was with his soccer team, and Francis had to manage on his own without his reliable coach by his side.

On the return trip from New York, Charlie had a relaxing journey because his Harvard team had shut out Columbia 1–0 and were in position to move into first place as Cornell had managed to tie Pennsylvania the day before. That tie played an important role because the championship rested on the number of wins each team posted rather than a win-loss-tie formula. So, if Harvard could win their last game, they would be insured of at least a tie for the championship and the tiebreaker would be based on the number of goals scored for and against each team.

The final game against the newest member of the league, Princeton, took place on Saturday, May 3, 1914. At the end of the afternoon, Harvard secured a win thanks to two goals by the offense and another shutout performance by Brayton Nicholls in goal. The All-American goalie now had posted three shutouts in the last three games. The shutouts were also crucial to Harvard because they factored heavily in the formula that gave Charlie and his squad another intercollegiate championship. Burgess had coached his Harvard team to unprecedented back-to-back intercollegiate titles!

One week after the Princeton game, the team gathered for its annual banquet and it was announced that the sport would shift to a single fall schedule rather than the split season of the past. The players honored Coach Burgess, presenting him with several gifts including an engraved silver and crystal cigar humidor for his ever-present cigars and a matching silver lighter case.

Charlie remained as head coach at Harvard through the 1921 season, with the exception of 1918, when the team played no outside opponents because of World War I. During his tenure Harvard won 84, lost 76, and tied 15 matches. They were intercollegiate champions twice and finished second four times. The Burgess-coached teams at Harvard produced sixteen first-team, and four second-team All-Americans during his tenure. Although soccer did not catch on as quickly in America as golf did, Charlie's contributions to Harvard and college soccer were pioneering first steps toward the extraordinary popularity the game now enjoys at all levels in the United States.

• Success and Celebrity •

Francis had spent the better part of the spring touring and playing golf throughout Great Britain. He had not done very well in the Amateur Championship at Sandwich, but he won the admiration and respect of the British people wherever he went. In late May, Ouimet crossed the English Channel to enter the French Amateur held at LaBoulie, near Versailles, the home course of French Champion Louis Tellier. Warm winds and sunny weather greeted an international field of entrants. Besides Ouimet, American Amateur Champion Jerome Travers and the English champion Charles Hope were among the favorites. Francis managed to shake the inconsistent play he had shown in England and topped the field to win his first European tournament, almost at the same moment as Burgess's college boys were awarded their soccer championship back in Cambridge. Francis returned to Great Britain for the British Open at Prestwick, Scotland, where he finished far behind his U.S. Open rival Harry Vardon, who won the event for the sixth time. Somewhat disappointed by his play but much better off for the experience, Francis prepared to come home to Woodland to defend his Massachusetts Amateur and his National Open titles. He left Great Britain just as the ominous rumbling of impending hostilities was being heard and felt on the European Continent.

The homage paid to young Francis Ouimet in Europe and America was intense. Thousands of words were written about his every move and action. He was called upon share his thoughts with newsmen who were with him in Europe and the columns for several newspapers and magazines were credited to Francis as he journeyed through his European adventure. Burgess and the Woodland Golf Club also basked in the reflected glow of Ouimet's sudden fame. Woodland was attracting many visitors and guests and its membership numbers were growing. In

The Burgess Family of Montrose, Scotland, c.1888. left to right, front: David, Sr., Willie, Harry, John, Jimmy, and Anne. rear: Jean, Charlie [Chay], Albert, Annie, and David, Jr. [Burgess collection]

The Links of Montrose prior to 1904. Golfers and caddies are in front of the old Mercantile clubhouse (left) and the Victoria Golf Club. A new Mercantile clubhouse was built to the right of the Victoria in 1904, a gift of industrialist William Jameson Paton to the working-class golfers of the town. [Photo courtesy of Angus Council Cultural Services]

• • • • • • • •

Old Tom Morris standing in front of the Royal and Ancient Golf Club in St. Andrews. Morris, along with Montrose professional Bob Dow, helped to nurture the golfing talents of young Burgess. [Burgess collection]

Chay's other sporting love was football. Here he is pictured in 1898 (last row, second from the left) with his first English Team—the Millwall Football Club. Bob Hunter, team trainer is standing in the second row with the towel over his shoulder. [Courtesy of Millwall F.C. Museum]

Scottish club makers at work—Chay learning the craft in this undated photo. The other clubmaker is not known. [Burgess collection]

Chay in his final year of professional soccer. He had turned professional in golf the year before, and would concentrate on that sport for the next 42 years. [Burgess collection]

A "great triumvirate" of 1905 professional champions in Montrose. left to right: Harry Vardon, champion of the 1905 Montrose All-Professional Tournament, Chay Burgess, 1905 Montrose Links Champion, and James Braid, the 1905 British Open Champion. [Burgess collection]

The Burgess family—Chay, Harriet, and young Charles the Second, shortly after arriving in the United States. [Burgess collection]

A golfer practices in front of the Monroe Mansion, which served as the Woodland clubhouse until the 1920s. [Burgess collection]

A young Francis Ouimet and his high school friend John Sullivan shortly after Francis began his tutelage with Chay Burgess on the Woodland links. Ouimet and Sullivan became partners in a sporting goods business in 1916 and in 1918 Francis married Sullivan's sister Stella. [Courtesy of The Country Club]

• •

HARVARD VARSITY SOCCER TEAM
INTERCOLLEGIATE CHAMPION OF 1913

Top Row, Left to Right—V. B. Chittenden, '15, Assistant Manager; A. J. Lowrey, '13; S. T. Hopkins, '14; Coach Charles Burgess, S. T. Steele, '13; H. G. Francke, '14; F. H. Storms, '14, Manager.
Middle Row—G. M. Rushmore, 13; E. R. McCall, '13; Capt E. L. Barron, '13; S. Nichols, '13; B. B. Locke, '13.
Bottom Row—F. C. Grant, '14; D. Needham, '13; T. J. Hudner, '15; T. C. Hardwick, '13; C. H. Weston, '14; G. M. Carnochan, '14.

Burgess retained his links to "football' as he coached the Harvard University soccer team to its first Intercollegiate Championship in 1913. He repeated the feat in 1914. [Boston Globe, Courtesy of the Trustees of the Boston Public Library]

Chay warming up for the 1913 U. S. Open (note the familiar cigar and the watch fob which was presented to him by his champion Harvard soccer team). [Burgess collection]

Ouimet and his little caddie Eddie Lowery marching down a rain soaked Brookline fairway towards golf immortality and a play-off against Britain's Ted Ray and Harry Vardon. [Courtesy of the Boston Globe]

Ouimet, Vardon, and Ray pose for photographs prior to their historic 1913 U.S. Open play-off. [Courtesy of The Country Club]

Ouimet lifted up onto the shoulders of the enthusiastic gallery after his heroic performance in the Open. Chay Burgess (right, hatless) celebrates with broad smile, a celebratory cigar, and a "thumb up" for his now famous pupil. [Courtesy of the Boston Globe]

• • • • • • •

Chay's celebrity as a great teacher brought many famous golf enthusiasts to his practice tee to learn the game, including Boston Red Sox rookie "Babe" Ruth (back, right). Chay's frequent golfing partners and pupils also included baseball stars Harold Janvrin (front, second from left), Herb Pennock (front right), "Smokey" Joe Wood (middle row, third from left), Harry Hooper (middle, second from right), and Tris Speaker (back, second from right). [Courtesy of Bob Wood]

A Pro-Am gathering at Woodland sometime in the Teens. seated left to right: John Brady—pro at the Commonwealth Golf Club and brother of Mike "King" Brady, Chay Burgess, Jock Blair—Nashua, N. H. pro, Francis Ouimet, Harry Nicoll—Woodland Assistant Pro, Tom Columbo—boyhood friend of Ouimet, Hal Janvrin—Boston Red Sox infielder. [Burgess collection]

• • • • • • •

HERE'S TWO GOOD ONES WITH THE WOODLANDERS

CHARLES BURGESS, SR. AND JR.

Few If Any Golf Clubs in the Country, Certainly None Hereabouts, Can Boast of a Father-and-Son Professional Combination, as Can the Woodland Golf Club. Charles Burgess, Sr., Is Starting His 11th Season at the Auburndale Course, While His Son and Namesake Is Beginning His First Season as His Dad's Assistant.

Chay and Young Charlie may have been the first Father-Son professional golfers in America in 1919. [Courtesy of the Boston Globe]

Chay, Young Charlie, and Harry Nicoll outside the old Woodland pro shop. [Burgess collection]

In 1922 Jesse Guilford became the second of Chay's students to win the National Amateur Championship. [Courtesy of the Boston Globe]

• • • • • • • • • • •

Burgess (center, wearing a light-colored coat) surrounded by his fellow professionals returning to America from a winter holiday in Great Britain. The group included Cyril Walker, Jack Way, Harry Hampton, George Morris, James MacGregor, and Laurie Ayton (light coat, next to Chay). [Burgess collection]

BEST-BALL GOLF CHAMPIONS OF NEW ENGLAND

Left to Right—Jesse P. Guilford, Amateur, and Charles M. Burgess, Professional, Both of Woodland. They Had a Lead of Four Strokes in Taking the Amateur-Pro Title at Charles River Country Club Yesterday.

Shortly after Chay led the New England pros in their secession from the newly formed PGA of America, he and National Amateur Champion Jesse Guilford teamed up to win the NEPGA's Amateur-Pro Championship. [Boston Traveler photo, Courtesy of the Trustees of the Boston Public Library]

Francis, along with Jesse Guilford, was selected to represent the United States against Great Britain in the inaugural Walker Cup Match. Francis was also named captain of the team. Ouimet presented this photo to Chay in a silver frame as a memento. [Burgess collection]

Bert Nicoll, head pro at Pinehurst, was one of Chay's seven nephews who became American golf pros during the Teens and Twenties. [Courtesy of the Tufts Archives, Pinehust, N.C.]

Willie, Bert, and Charlie Nicoll together at the Buresford Country Club in San Mateo, California. [Courtesy of the Peninsula Country Club]

Chay and his progressive New England Golfer's Organization made a conscious effort to reach out to amateur golfers, particularly women's associations, including the Women's Golf Association of Boston and the Griscom Cup teams. [Burgess collection]

New England professionals enjoying a winter visit to Pinehurst on their way to the golf resorts on the East Coast of Florida. left to right: Herbert Lagerblade, Joe Stien, and Chay Burgess. [Burgess collection]

• • • • • • • • • • •

The stately new Woodland Clubhouse, built in the 1920s. Chay's pro shop was located at the right end of the building facing the small white cottage that was his home until 1954. [Burgess collection]

President Emeritus of the New England Professional Golfers' Association, Chay organized an unprecedented fund raising effort to support America's Ryder Cup team in 1928. [Burgess collection]

• • • • • • • • • • • •

Golf's greatest stars gathered at Woodland for an exhibition match to raise the money to send America's Ryder Cup team abroad for the first time. left to right: Johnny Farrell, Bobby Jones, Walter Hagen, and Gene Sarazen. Francis Ouimet was the referee and Chay Burgess was the Grand Marshall and organizer of the event. [AP Worldwide Photos]

American and British Ryder Cup Teams together after their second meeting in 1929 in Leeds, England. The British team avenged their 1927 loss in the first Ryder Cup match held at the Worcester Country Club in Massachusetts. George Duncan, Captain of the British team sits behind the coveted trophy. [Courtesy of The Country Club]

SIDELIGHTS ON VICTORY OF BOSTON'S TWO FAVORITES AT WOODLAND

On either side are the two participants in the 72-hole play-off for the national open championship executing iron shots in the course of their 36-hole exhibition tour of the Auburndale links yesterday. At the left is Billy Burke, the champion, playing a pitch shot over the trees at the seventh hole. At the right is George Von Elm, the runner-up, using an iron for his second to the first green. In the centre (left to right) are Charles Shaw, chairman of the golf committee, who acted as referee; Charles Burgess, Woodland pro, chief marshal; Burke, Von Elm and Francis Ouimet and Jesse Guilford, Woodland's victorious pair.

Chay in his accustomed role as the Marshall of special golf events at Woodland instructs reigning U.S. Open Champion Billy Burke, Open runner-up George Von Elm, Francis Ouimet, and Jesse Guilford in the rules for their 1931 exhibition match. The match served as a warm-up for Ouimet's recapture of the National Amateur Championship. [Boston Traveler photo, courtesy of the Trustees of the Boston Public Library]

Left to right: Burgess, Burke, Von Elm, Ouimet, and Guilford.

• • • • • • • • • • •

Ouimet carrying the Havemeyer Cup after his second U.S. Amateur victory in 1931. Ouimet gave his long-time mentor much of the credit for his success in the tournament held at the Beverly Country Club in Chicago when he said, "I don't know what I would have done out there without Charlie Burgess...he was always there when I needed him." [Courtesy of The Country Club]

Ouimet in the roadster that the Woodland members presented him after his great "comeback" victory in 1931. [Courtesy of Bro McLean and the Ouimet family]

• •

Chay, now a senior professional in 1934, still demonstrates the perfect swing that made his students champions. [Burgess collection]

In "retirement" Chay instructs Boston hockey star and aspiring golf professional Johnny Fitzgerald in the fine points of the game. [Burgess collection]

World War II saw Chay's grandson, Charles the Third, in the service. Here the newly wed young soldier enjoys a send-off dinner, surrounded by the lovely women in his life, before being shipped out to the Pacific. left to right: Charlie's bride Rita (a former Massachusetts beauty pageant queen), his mother Kitty, and his sister Mary Alice. [Burgess Collection]

After the hiatus caused by World War II, golf returned full swing to America in 1946. Ted Bishop won the Massachusetts, New England, and the first U.S. Amateur held after the war—at the Baltusrol Golf Club in Springfield, New Jersey. A golfing triple crown. Ted Bishop became the third student of Chay Burgess to become a National Amateur Champion—a record unrivaled by any other teaching professional in the nation. [Courtesy of the Boston Globe]

Chay and Hat enjoy their great-grandson, Charles the Fourth, in 1948. The couple had just celebrated their fiftieth wedding anniversary and Chay was finally able to retire from golf after the war. [Burgess collection]

Chay, at eighty in 1953, still had some golf to teach to his son, grandson, and great-grandson. [Burgess collection]

the years before Charlie was the professional and before Francis came to prominence, the club was barely able to keep its head above water. Many debts and uncertainties concerning its leases plagued the club. The great advances that the club made during the ensuing Burgess-Ouimet years, through course development, increases in membership, and a rise in prominence in the state and nation, put the club on firm financial footing. Ouimet's fame and Burgess's admirable reputation were largely responsible for that good fortune.

Throughout the teens and twenties, Woodland became one of the most well-known golf clubs in the country because of Francis's association with it. Charlie Burgess in turn became one of the most well-known and influential club professionals in the country because of his success in preparing young Francis. Local, national, and international writers picked up the story. One of the most read and most popular sports publications of the period was an annual series of authoritative guides published by Spalding's Athletic Library. The 1914 *Golf Guide* edited by Grantland Rice featured a full-page photo of the new U.S. Open champion and prominently pictured his Scottish mentor as well.

Business was booming for Charlie thanks to the events of the past year, because of his hard work at developing a sound pro shop, and his obvious dedication to improving the skills of all his pupils. Nephews Harry and Bert Nicoll were still with him as assistants and young Charlie was working in the pro shop during his summer recess from Newton High School. Charlie also employed some seasoned veteran clubmakers to assist him as the demand for his quality-constructed clubs was increasing. Although many ready-made sets of clubs were now being manufactured locally, such as Alex Findlay's brand of clubs by Wright and Ditson, Charlie still hand-fashioned his own clubs in his pro shop. In order to get a custom-fitted set of golf clubs, most golfers depended on the professional to make customized clubs, balanced and fitted especially for them. Charlie imported the best materials and parts from well-known Scottish manufacturers like the Winton Brothers of Montrose and was using more and more American-manufactured components as they became increasingly available.

• Most Pros Still Languish •

Charlie was doing very well, but many of his fellow club professionals were not. The working conditions for most professionals were still extremely difficult and often demeaning at many American courses. During the teens, many private golf and country clubs continued to view their professionals as mere hired hands, on a par with the domestic help many of the wealthy members might have employed in their homes or the workers in their factories or businesses. The evolution of the golf professional whom we know today was just beginning.

Very slowly, as more average Americans became golfers at public courses or began to form more modest clubs for themselves, the golf professional's skills were appreciated more and his social status began to improve. This developing appreciation of teaching and club-based professionals by golfers from a broader spectrum of social classes began to lessen the age-old gulf between the rich country club set and the wage-earning pros. The evolution of the professional golfer from servant to sports celebrity came slowly. It began during the twenties and thirties and would be complete after World War II. But in the teens, the professional still had a long and tedious journey towards respectability ahead of him.

A syndicated newspaper sports columnist of the period wrote an interesting piece about the relationship between country club members and the club professional. Sympathetic to the working professional, the gist of the story implied that the business or professional man who could afford to play golf probably made a lot more money from his profession than the average golf professional did at his. And so the businessman could and should afford to be generous as well as respectful towards his golf pro. While "the pro plays golf for a living he generally plays the game well and always fairly" the article began, " he would no more think of cheating at golf than of breaking into a bank. He is a true golfer and a strong upholder of the honorable tenets of the game . . . pros give us much value in improving our games through both lessons and opportunities of seeing them play." The author continued, "They are human beings and are entitled to more liberal consideration than they receive from many players." The article concluded with this appeal, "In making a match with a pro give him the chance to make a few dollars. That is the only way he makes a living and the only way you can pay him for the amusement and recreation you get. His charges for club repairs are reasonable and his profit on balls and clubs very moderate. He is worthy of your more liberal consideration, is self-respecting and a willing worker at his calling."

The professional golfers who read the column must have appreciated the kind words of support from the writer as they continued to labor across America without any kind of standard contract, union, or a professional organization. It would still be a few more years before they would finally join forces to incorporate and institutionalize the respect and the rights suggested in the article. Even then, the road to respect and a satisfactory professional organization would be a rocky one.

• Walter Hagen, "the Haig" •

Play for the 1914 U.S. Open began once again back at its traditionally scheduled time in early summer. It was held at the Midlothian Country Club in Blue Island, Illinois. Vardon and Ray, the featured British performers in the 1913 play-off had no plans to attend and the odds were good that an American would win. Many thought that Francis could probably repeat his feat of the previous year. However, an ambitious young pro from Rochester, New York, Walter Hagen, later known as "the Haig," had his own plans for 1914. In 1913, the unknown young pro caught the attention of the golf world with his great play at Brookline where he tied for fourth place along with Louis Tellier, Jim Barnes, and McDonald Smith. The brash and cocky Hagen shook up the staid golf establishment with bold predictions about his own success. He promised after the 1913 Open to win the 1914 championship and he did, with a four-day total score of 290. Ouimet finished a respectable fourth with a 298, tied with Boston professional Mike Brady. Louis Tellier and young Johnny McDermott were next with scores of 299 and 300.

Charlie did not make the trip to Illinois. Like many club professionals he could only venture into national or regional competitions occasionally, and only if the competitions were nearby. The demands of club duties and the scarcity of spare time to travel, let alone play, prevented many outstanding club professionals from getting the public recognition that they deserved. Financially, most American pros were better off working at a club, assured at least of steady income from lessons and profits from their pro shops. Thus a major distinction was slowly beginning to develop between the club professionals, the backbone and largest group of American golf pros, and the select few players who could afford to travel and barnstorm the country in search of the prize money that would get them to the next event.

Only a minority of American-based golf professionals could survive on their winnings from exhibitions and the few tournaments that existed at the time. For example, the maximum professional prize, in the biggest event in the country—the 1913 U.S. Open—was the $150 that Vardon earned as the top pro in the Open. Hagen and the others who tied for fourth picked up $80 each, and the final money winner, Patrick Doyle of the Myopia Hunt Club who finished in tenth place, only received $20 for his effort. By comparison, today the U.S. Open features a total purse of over $5 million and the championship prize is more than $1 million—an incredible increase of over *six thousand* times the prize Vardon won.

If the biggest tournament in the nation paid so little, it is easy to imagine how small the purses might have been at others. The life of the early touring pro was a difficult one with small prize money and a lack of decent venues. It was often a vagabond existence where he had to endure the snobbery of the country club members who hosted the events. Young Walter Hagen was greatly instrumental in ending all that. After the humiliation of situations like being assigned to the horse barns at Brookline, Hagen embarked on a course of action to demand better treatment for himself and his fellow professionals wherever he played. Hagen forever altered the public perception and social acceptance of the professional golfer as he rose to prominence during the rest of the teens and twenties. He refused to take a backseat to anyone. Not only did the Haig become one of the world's greatest golfers but he did so by thumbing his nose at convention, and as his winnings and opportunities to play for pay increased, Hagen used his celebrity to better the lot of all the traveling pros. If Hagen was refused the use of a snobbish clubhouse, he often would hire his own luxurious tent with a bar and music, set it up near the clubhouse, and entertain his own guests in grand style wearing a tuxedo. His colorful approach to life on the road and his reproach of the snobbery in golf was impossible to ignore and it gradually changed the face of professional golf with every tournament that he won.

Charlie Burgess, while outgoing and friendly, exhibited a personality that was far more conservative than the flamboyant young Mr. Hagen. So did his famous student. Charlie warmly welcomed Francis back to Woodland after his latest golfing adventure at the Open. Ouimet traded roles with Hagen in 1914 with his fourth place finish. He played well and retained his status as one of America's best young golfers although he was not the top amateur in the contest. That honor went to Charles "Chick" Evans from Chicago who finished in second place. Francis did successfully defend his Massachusetts Amateur Crown at the nearby Brae Burn Country Club after his return home to Newton. It was the second of six Massachusetts state titles he won during his career. He then spent the rest of the summer preparing for the tournament he wanted to win most of all, the National Amateur, which was going to be held in September at the Ekwanok Golf Club in Manchester, Vermont.

• Charlie Burgess and "the Bambino" •

Boston and New England had been a hot bed of sporting activities for the past several years. Beside Ouimet's win at the Open, back-to-back Harvard soccer championships, and the first undefeated season of Harvard gridiron football in 1913, Boston sports fans had two major league baseball teams to root for, the National League Braves and the American League Red Sox. The hard-luck Boston Braves of the National Baseball League had not won a championship since 1898, but in 1914 the Braves provided Boston fans with considerable excitement. They were in last place on the Fourth of July that year when suddenly they went on an unprecedented winning streak—and kept on winning and winning and winning! They captured the pennant, then dramatically beat the Athletics of Philadelphia in four games to win the World Series.

The Red Sox had just won the World Series in 1912 and were rebuilding their team to position themselves for another run at the pennant. On July 11, 1914, they brought up a big strong young pitcher from the Providence Grays minor league club. His name was George Herman Ruth, soon to be known as "the Babe" and "the Bambino," and soon to become probably the greatest baseball player that ever lived. Shortly after he joined the Sox, he got his first lesson in golf—from Charlie Burgess.

During the teens and twenties, baseball teams went from city to city by railroad. As a result, the schedule for the season included many travel days for the visiting club. For the home team it was a day off, sometimes to practice and sometimes to enjoy a relaxing diversion from baseball. Lots of major league ball players enjoyed golf and many were quite good at it. There was a strong link between the Woodland Golf Club and the Boston Red Sox. A couple of Woodland Golf Club members, prominent Boston attorneys, often invited Red Sox players out to the Newton course. If they were already skilled at the game, they would join their hosts and the club professional for a VIP round. If they were novices, like the young Ruth, Burgess would take them aside for some instruction before they were let loose on the course. Over the season and over the years, Ruth's golf game improved rapidly under Charlie's instruction and he became a devoted adherent of the game. Ruth played often at Woodland while he was with the Red Sox, and even after he was traded to the Yankees in New York, he remained a regular visitor any time he was in town. Charlie and the Babe enjoyed a warm relationship that lasted many years, and despite Ruth's popular moniker, Charlie always referred to him by his proper Christian name whenever they spoke. Ruth was not Burgess's only baseball playing student and golfing companion. Red Sox stars Tris Speaker, Harry Hooper, Herb Pennock, "Smokey" Joe Wood, and local boy Hal Janvrin were regulars in Burgess's continually growing stable of celebrity students.

• Challenging Charlie •

The summer months were hectic as usual for Charlie and his staff at Woodland. Nephew Bert Nicoll had just left Charlie's employment to take a teaching position at the nearby, Donald Ross designed, Belmont Springs Country Club. With lessons scheduled from dawn to dusk almost every day, he depended on his nephew Harry Nicoll to run the pro shop. Harry was assisted by young Charlie who was now seventeen and already showed considerable skill as an instructor besides having a keen interest in the business side of golf. Ever since Charlie brought Harry over from Scotland, he sensed that the young professional was itching to get in a match to test his skills against him. Charlie was forty years old and still a few years away from entering the senior phase of his career. Harry, in his twenties, was on top of his game and was beginning to feel pretty sure of himself, even a bit cocky, about his game. Like his uncle, he was a former Montrose Links Champion and had trained with Scotland's best golfers at St. Andrews before coming to the States.

Finally, one day in the summer of 1914, Harry got his chance to challenge his uncle head-to-head in a twosome. Charlie recalled the contest with Harry this way:

> "Our match was all even going into the eleventh-hole that paralleled Grove Street, a fine 390-yard hole with an elevated green, and we both hit good drives right up the middle. Harry's mashie second was on the pin all the way and mine looked equally as good. When we reached the top of the hill only one ball was visible. We figured one ball had gone down into the deep pit back of the green. On the way to look for the missing ball Harry said, 'That's my ball on the green!' and it was. But my ball was in the cup, which gave me an eagle two. I held on to the one hole advantage until Harry squared the match at the long seventeenth. The eighteenth tee was at the corner of Washington Street and the road leading to the Woodland train station. The green was in front of Monroe Mansion, the clubhouse. Harry's iron to the home green was dead on the pin and brought great applause from the members gathered on the front steps when it stopped six inches from the pin. It looked pretty bad for me because the best I could hope for was to tie the hole, which would have been a moral victory for my nephew. So you can imagine the reaction of the gallery, not to mention Harry, when they saw my mid-iron shot roll by Harry's ball and plunk into the cup for a hole-in-one."

Young Harry went back to the pro shop with a renewed sense of respect and admiration for his uncle's still quite formidable talents.

8 1914–1919

> "To gain the proper shot consistently, every swing must be exact. That is why we teach the driver as the first club. It requires exactitude over the greatest span of swing. From then on we teach the short hitting clubs, not because they are easiest necessarily but because parts of the drive enter into every club used thereafter."
>
> —Charlie Burgess

• The 1914 U.S. Amateur and Jesse Guilford •

In September of 1914, Charlie joined Francis at the Ekwanok Country Club in the bucolic southern Vermont town of Manchester where the twentieth National Amateur Championship was being held. Even though he had won the U.S. Open less than a year before, the Amateur was the event that he had always dreamed about winning. Francis played extremely well in the qualifying rounds finishing with a 145, just one stroke behind the low scores of W. C. Fownes, Jr. and R. R. Gorton, who tied for the medal. Francis worked his way through the tournament match play rounds defeating W. R. Marston from Baltrusol, W. I. Howland from Chicago, and the 1909 winner Robert Gardner in his first three matches. In the semi-finals, Francis met and defeated co-medalist Fownes while defending Amateur champion Jerry Travers had defeated Walter J. Travis of Garden City, New Jersey, in the other semi-final bracket. The experienced Travers was the odds-on favorite to win his fifth national title. But on September 5, the final day of the tournament, Francis pulled off another huge upset on the national stage in fine fashion by beating Travis by six holes with five to play. Ouimet's boyhood dream was now a reality, and within the span of twelve months the twenty-one-year-old ex-caddie won both the National Open and the United States Amateur Championship title!

In the very same fashion that Francis first came to the notice of the national golfing establishment the previous year, even though he had fallen short of victory, another young golfer entered into the tournament garnered a great deal of attention through his good play and remarkably long drives. The player was nineteen-year-old Jesse P. Guilford, a local boy of sorts from Hooksett, near Manchester, New Hampshire. He was that year's great new discovery.

When Charlie and Francis met Jesse, they discovered that they had much in common. In remarkably similar circumstances to both Francis and Charlie, Jesse learned the game as a caddie and was practically born on a golf course. He also grew up with the game in his own backyard, as the Hooksett course actually used part of his father's farm for one of its fairways. The personalities of the three golfers, who would soon become a team, were also quite compatible, although they did differ markedly in the degree to which they were comfortable around others. Charlie was good-natured and outgoing, while Francis was quiet and reserved until he became familiar with someone. Jesse, however, was extremely reserved, almost painfully shy, and his temperament was often mistakenly thought of as somewhat sullen.

Jesse picked up the game as a ten-year-old and was the youngest person ever to win the New Hampshire State Amateur title at age fourteen in 1909. Jesse had won the title a total of three times before his entry into the 1914 National Amateur. Stoutly built and extremely powerful, Guilford could hit the ball a country mile. Similar in style to the famous Ted Ray, Jesse did not try to finesse the ball—he simply smashed at it with all his might and it flew. Drives of 275 or 300 yards were not uncommon for the teenager. Today it seems impossible that these distances could have been achieved with the simple wood-shafted clubs of the day, but the young farm boy often achieved them. Guilford's shots were so powerful that sportswriters dubbed him "the human siege gun" after watching his performance. Both Boston sportswriter Linde Fowler and the famed Grantland Rice have been credited with pinning the nickname on Guilford.

In a similar arrangement to the one that Woodland members had for Francis, Jesse's golf prowess earned him the financial support of appreciative members of the club he was representing. The members of the Intervale Country Club in Manchester, New Hampshire, created a trust fund that was approved by the USGA to help him with his development. Again the apparent hypocrisy about the rules on professionalism came under fire. But the practice of trust funds that allowed certain talented amateurs of meager means to travel and participate in contests all over the world continued. Jesse was sent down to Boston to get a few pointers from Scottish professional Alex Ross at Brae Burn and received rave reviews in the Boston press when he did quite well there, reaching the semi-final rounds of the club's amateur championship.

Jesse returned to his parents' home on Front Street in Hooksett and, apparently escaping the attention of the USGA and its strict rule on professionalism, spent the next year working as a golf instructor at the Intervale Country Club while still competing as an amateur. He also enjoyed one of the privileges his newly recognized abilities provided for him. As Francis had done the previous winter, Jesse accepted an invitation to Pinehurst and participated in the annual North-South Tournament. Jesse legitimized his place on the national golf scene by winning that championship and defeating Ouimet in the process. Jesse then solidified his reputation by venturing to Massachusetts to win the state's Amateur Championship, after winning the New Hampshire crown again in 1916. He then made another bid for a national championship at the 1916 U.S. Amateur held at the Merion Cricket Club in Haverford, Pennsylvania.

Guilford continued to improve his standing on the national scene by lasting until the semi-finals where he lost 4 and 3 to Robert Gardner. Gardner in turn lost to the eventual champion Chick Evans. Overall, it was a fantastic start for Jesse as he made the decision to move down to Massachusetts and join Ouimet and Burgess at Woodland.

Jesse moved to Newton when he was in his early twenties and was warmly welcomed into the Woodland Golf Club. He took up residence, boarding in a multi-family home that literally backed up onto Woodland's current eighteenth tee. He worked as a clerk and later as an accountant, but his real ambition was to become a full-time, yet amateur, golfer in the style of Ouimet, Travers, and Evans. Guilford's association with Woodland brought him together with Ouimet and under Burgess's wing. During the rest of the teens and through the twenties, Woodland became known as the "home of champions" by virtue of the accomplishments of its three gifted golfers.

• Francis Banned •

Charlie's success as Francis's coach, and now as the mentor of young Jesse Guilford as well, enhanced his reputation as one of the foremost instructors of the game. Lessons from Burgess were in great demand, and he and his nephews were busy from morning until night at the club.

Meanwhile, Francis received some good news from the Massachusetts Golf Association (MGA) and some very bad news from the United States Golf Association in the spring of 1916. The MGA posted the rankings of Massachusetts golfers each April, and Francis was the number one golfer in the state with a better than scratch ranking of "plus one." It was the second year Francis topped the list. That was the good news. The bad news was that the USGA declared him ineligible to compete as an amateur any longer! The reason given was that because he and his old high school chum John Sullivan had recently entered into a sporting goods business together he had violated a new USGA rule.

The organization ruled that his engagement in the sporting goods business came under their newly adopted and very strict ban on professionalism. At the most recent annual meeting, the leadership adopted its strongest position ever on the separation of professionals and amateurs. The measure was designed to help rid American golf of what the USGA perceived to be the creeping taint of professionalism into the amateur arena. The rule stated that professionalism resulted from "accepting or holding any positions as an agent or employee that includes as part of its duties the handling of golf supplies or engaging in any business wherein one's usefulness or profits arise because of skill or prominence in the game of golf." The executive committee explained that this ruling was designed to achieve the "greatest good for the greatest number of players, and would at the same time declare for pure amateurism in American golf."

It seems hard to comprehend that this decision was made by the same organization that still allowed clubs to raise thousands of dollars for expense accounts for star amateur players and allowed the practice of waiving membership fees and providing transportation and housing for visiting celebrity amateurs. There seemed to be a considerable amount of inconsistency and wavering on the part of the USGA concerning its interpretation and application of the rules on professionalism. Francis appealed the ruling to the USGA and was backed by the directors of the Woodland Golf Club and many other supporters from around the country. After a hearing on June 18, 1917 he received a letter from Howard Whitney, Secretary of the USGA. The letter informed him that his statements presented before the Executive Committee "proved that [he] was still engaged in the sale of golf supplies . . . and [he] presented no facts, which would alter the decision." Thus the committee voted unanimously that his business venture made him a non-amateur. As a result of the new rule, Francis could not participate in any more USGA-sanctioned tournaments as long as he owned or was employed in his sporting goods store. It was remarkable that Ouimet did not give up on the USGA and turn professional. First, he was forced to stop caddying at age sixteen in order to remain an "amateur" and now he was banned from USGA play because he opened his own sporting goods business—a business *exactly* like the one he was working in when he won the Open. Days after the denial of his appeal, Ouimet entered and won the 1917 Western Golf Association Amateur championship held in Chicago because that region had balked at adopting the strict definition of professionalism that the USGA incorporated.

Major life-altering events seemed to descend upon Francis in the summer of 1917. The rumblings of war that were heard in Europe in 1914 had escalated into the greatest armed conflict the world had ever witnessed and America was preparing for war. Within weeks of the USGA decision to uphold the sanction against him and just shortly after his Western Open victory, Ouimet's number (2165) came up in the draft. Francis was among many prominent athletes who were drafted into wartime service. Ironically, Francis's time in the Army would pave the way for his eventual reinstatement as an amateur by the USGA after the war. America's late entry into the war had come well after hostilities broke out, but the American Red Cross and thousands of American citizens were doing all they could to attend to the suffering of the people of Europe well before troops were sent overseas. Rather than worry about the USGA sanction against him or the draft, Francis teamed up with Jesse Guilford and devoted himself to playing in scores of fundraising exhibition four-ball matches benefiting the Red Cross war effort. Guilford and Ouimet both soon served in the armed forces and their talents were used to support the war effort in a most effective manner. They remained in the U.S., and while both were assigned military duties, they were also an almost unbeatable team playing exhibition four-ball golf matches up and down the East Coast throughout (and well after) the First World War raising money for the troops.

• The PGA of America •

At the same time that the USGA was trying to "rid golf of professionalism" through tightening its rules, American professionals were marshaling their energies to form an organization mindful not only of their own interests but also for the good of the game as they saw it. Early in 1916, a number of pros were invited to a luncheon in New York hosted by Mr. Rodman Wanamaker, a prominent businessman and department store owner from Philadelphia. This was the same Wanamaker who had hired pioneer golf promoter Alex Findlay to oversee his golf equipment operation. The object of the gathering was to discuss the feasibility of forming a national association of professional golfers similar to The PGA of Great Britain. The official records do not indicate that Findlay was a participant in the New York meeting, but given his well-known involvement in golf's development, it may be assumed that he had a strong influence on Mr. Wanamaker's desire to help the professionals organize. Wanamaker also offered to sponsor an annual American professional championship similar to the *News of the World* tournament held in Great Britain.

The assembled golfers at the gathering in New York felt that there were many matters connected to the game in which the professional needed protection. They voiced concern that the professional in the United States "absolutely has no voice in the selection of championship courses or in the conduct of a tournament. [The professional] may suffer from the laxity of club members who fail to meet their financial obligations and with a powerful organization in back of him, . . . would be much more able to meet such situations." Further, the professionals all agreed that "the cooperation of some amateurs is necessary to the complete success of their movement and amateurs will be invited to accept places on the controlling board." Ouimet was among several prominent amateurs (even thought he was barred as one at the time) who were present and who spoke in favor of forming the organization. But Francis declined an offer to join the professional organization, sure that he would be reinstated as an amateur again soon.

Mike Brady was part of a three-man delegation from New England sent to the meetings. He brought forth the support of Burgess and the other professionals from the Boston area who had been involved in attempting to organize their own regional association for the past two years. By February, the representatives drew up a constitution and a set of by-laws, which were approved, and the Professional Golfers' Association of America was born. Charlie and his fellow New England golfers were included in the large eastern section of the PGA and would remain there through the war years.

Charlie did his part to swell the membership roster of the young PGA of America with significant representation from his own family. Nephews Harry and Bert Nicoll had been groomed by him to become head professionals. Bert was contracted to the Belmont Springs Country Club, a club designed by Burgess's old friend Donald Ross, and Harry Nicoll would leave for the Haverhill Country Club within the next couple of years. Finding replacements was not a problem for Burgess. He only had to send the passage fare to his sister Jeannie back in Montrose, and off to America another nephew and potential PGA member would come.

The next nephew in line was Willie Nicoll, and shortly thereafter Charlie brought over his namesake Charlie Nicoll. All of his nephews met with great success as head or teaching professionals at well-known clubs across the country and all became members of the new Professional Golfers' Association. Charlie was also grooming his own son for a career in golf until the American involvement in the war in Europe put so many things on hold. It would be just a short while before young Charlie joined his father and cousins in the ranks of professional golf.

• The Great War •

The First World War, known then as the Great War, brought many sporting activities to a halt when the nation mobilized for the war effort. Ouimet and Guilford's domestic fundraising efforts did not exempt them from active duty but were additional duties the young men were asked to perform. Jesse had signed up for the Aviation Corps and his mechanical ability was rumored to be so good that he could take apart a plane and put it back together himself in short order. Francis joined the Army National Guard and was stationed at nearby Fort Devens in northern Massachusetts. Francis was near enough to home to court his business partner's sister, Stella Sullivan, and they were married when Francis accepted a commission as lieutenant in September of 1918.

Young Charlie Burgess had enlisted in the army in June of 1918. By November of that same year the Scottish-born soldier was made a naturalized U.S. citizen because of his enlistment. That month he shipped out of the States after being trained in the new and dangerous Chemical Warfare Corps. When the troop ship carrying Burgess and his company passed by Newfoundland, it was signaled by radiotelegraph to turn around and return to America as an armistice had just been signed, ending the war on November 11, 1918. Young Burgess was discharged and sent back home by Christmas.

As the three young men prepared to return to civilian life, a horror at home as bad as the trench warfare in Europe still was raging. The great influenza epidemic of 1918 has been called a nightmare of epic proportions, killing many more people than did the Great War itself. Estimates of 500,000 American deaths and over 40 million worldwide were attribute to this mystery flu pandemic. At Fort Devens, where Francis was still stationed, 8,000 soldiers were dying in the base hospital. Closer to home the former Woodland clubhouse, the Woodland Park Hotel, was taken over as an emergency hospital annexed to the nearby Newton Hospital. In September the hotel was initially set up with 50 beds, but shortly was crammed with spaces for 200 patients as the mysterious flu peaked. As mysteriously as it first appeared in the spring of 1918, the "Spanish Flu" had disappeared by the winter of the same year.

In January of 1919, the USGA reconsidered Francis's amateur standing and ruled as follows: " Whereas, Francis Ouimet, upon entering the service of the United States, severed his personal connection with the management of Ouimet & Sullivan, and thereby discontinued the practices which were decided to be in violation of the amateur rules of the USGA [he] . . . is reinstated as an amateur golfer." In fact, Francis and his new brother-in-law Jack Sullivan had sold out their sporting goods business during the spring of 1918, so that alone would have cleared the way for the United States Golf Association to reinstate Francis as an amateur. Whatever the rationale, the USGA no doubt was glad to have found a way to gather the nation's premier golfer back into their fold. In the spring of 1919, Francis was discharged from the Quartermaster Corps and had an offer from the prestigious financial firm of Burgess (no relationship to Charlie), Lang and Company to work for them as a salesman of securities. Francis accepted and started work there after a short trip south for some golf and relaxation.

• Young Charlie •

Just as Francis was returning to amateur status, young Charlie Burgess, now age twenty-one, became a full-time professional and an associate member of the Professional Golfers' Association of America when he became the assistant to his father at Woodland. Woodland had the distinction of being the only club in the entire country at the time that had a father–son combination as its professionals. One local scribe hoped that "if Charlie Junior proves to be a chip off the old block, like his popular and ever cheerful father, then a trip to Woodland by a visitor would be doubly pleasant in the future." Time would soon tell.

Young Charlie had grown up in relative affluence and was a very bright and able young man. Tall and good looking, he had a confident manner that went well beyond his years. Although he had the opportunity for as much schooling as he wished, he had little interest in his academic studies. Part of his indifference to school might have been attributed to the worldliness he acquired while being exposed to the business of the golf club and the environs of Harvard during his teenage years. He was, however, a willing worker after school and during the summers at the club. He often filled in at the desk of the pro shop when Chay and Harry were busy and made no objections to carrying clubs around the course when asked to caddie. He became rather blasé about meeting the growing number of celebrities and sporting stars on the Woodland Links. For example, a casual entry into a journal that he kept simply noted that on April 22, 1915 he "caddied for Strunk of Philadelphia." Strunk was *Amos* Strunk, the star first baseman of the Philadelphia Athletics who was later traded to the Red Sox when they won the 1918 World Series. The Athletics were in Boston that week for a series against the Red Sox, and Amos had a layover day that he used to pick up a lesson and play a round of golf with Charlie and some Woodland member friends of his. Most American teenager boys would have been very excited to meet a famous baseball player like Strunk, but it was not uncommon for Charlie to see and caddie for a host of famous sports stars and other celebrities who frequented Woodland to take lessons from his father.

The elder Burgess used the Wright and Ditson sporting goods firm as a supplier for many of his pro shop items. Young Charlie would often venture into Boston by train to pick up orders or pay bills for his father after school. By many accounts he was a very good son and a willing worker. In addition he was a skillful golfer and was developing his game to the point it became obvious that he had professional potential.

As a teenager, he and his friends, perhaps with their girlfriends along, would look forward to spending an occasional afternoon or evening at nearby Norumbega Park. The park was one of the many "trolley parks" erected at locations across the country around the turn of the century by the new street railway companies as a way to increase ridership on their electrically powered streetcars. Norumbega was opened in the summer of 1897, ideally situated on the banks of the meandering Charles River in Newton, about ten miles via streetcar from Boston. Young Charlie and his friends enjoyed the park, which featured band concerts, picnic areas, a zoo, a boathouse, penny arcade, a carousel, and other rides powered by the same electrical current that drove the streetcars. It also had the Great Steel Theater with a seating capacity of over three thousand, hosting vaudeville, comedies, musical plays, and motion pictures. Later, this theater would be converted to a dance pavilion called the Totem Pole Ballroom. Between the Great Steel Theater and the Totem Pole, the Newton amusement park would host the very best and most famous musical entertainers and big bands of the twenties, thirties, and forties. Because of the park's proximity to Woodland, many of the golf-loving band leaders, singers, and entertainers who played the park, like Bing Crosby and Al Jolson, often got in a few rounds and lessons with Charlie, Sr. when they were in town.

By the time young Charlie had reached his final year of high school in 1916, he was eager to be done with school and anxious to get out into the world. His father helped him into the ranks of professional golf at the early age of nineteen. For the next few years, Charlie continued his education on the golf course and was employed by various clubs around New England, particularly summer resorts, as a golf teacher. His brief golf career was interrupted by the war, but in 1919, when young Charlie was discharged from his service in the Chemical Warfare Corps, he was appointed by the directors of Woodland to be his father's full-time assistant.

• Opposition to Golf •

As the game of golf fast became an American obsession, igniting the passions of so many of its adherents, it also caused some controversy as well. Just before the exciting decade known as the Roaring Twenties, a most unusual and contentious trial began in the Newton, Massachusetts, Police Court. Two men stood before the judge because they had been playing golf—on a Sunday. The case centered on the so-called Sunday Blue Laws in Massachusetts, which dated back about 300 years to the Puritan ban on public diversions or sports being played on the Lord's Day.

The Massachusetts Golf Association (MGA) stepped into the case on behalf of the two defendants, Brae Burn Country Club members Edward Kimball and Howard Emerson, who were charged with "taking part in a sport and with taking part in a game on the Lord's Day." The MGA said it was their intention to carry the case right up to the United States Supreme Court, if necessary, in order to overturn the law and defend the two golfers. Sometime before, the defendants and several members of the Woodland and Wollaston Golf Clubs had volunteered to test the law. Until the last possible moment the MGA kept secret the location of the course where the act of civil disobedience was to take place in order to avoid a media frenzy as the situation had caught the attention of newsmen from all across the nation.

Two officers of the State Police, Officers Frank G. Hale and Frank Hardiman, went to the Brae Burn Country Club on a Sunday afternoon in August of 1919 and watched the defendants tee off. The police then actually followed them around the course. They testified that they saw Mr. Kimball "knocking a small white ball around with his sticks" and that they heard Mr. Emerson propose that he and Mr. Kimball play a round together. When Kimball and Emerson approached the fifth green, the police who had been stalking them intervened, taking their names and addresses. Summonses were issued to the golfers on the Tuesday after the match.

The two golfers had not been keeping score originally, but at the start of the fifth hole they began keeping score against each other and that was the key to the local judge's ruling against them. Judge Bacon of the Newton Police Court ruled that the playing of golf without a score allows the players the chance to merely play for exercise or diversion and hence was not a "sport" as defined by the statute. However, once scores were kept, the outing changed to a competition and they were found guilty of the second complaint and were fined a token amount of $5.00. Thus, the judge seemed to keep the door open for legally playing

Sunday golf as long as no scores were kept. That concept of golf as a game, not a sport, was expected to encourage Sunday golfers and put the matter to rest. But the MGA and the two golfers still appealed the case to the State Superior Court. Before the court could act, the State Legislature promptly passed a bill, the so-called Sunday Baseball Act, which allowed baseball, golf, and other sporting activities on Sundays, subject to the approval of the local authorities in each city or town.

Now the ball, so to speak, was placed in the hands of the Newton City Board of Aldermen. On April 21, 1919 in a long, heated session the matter was debated by over 200 citizens who packed the chambers. Because the wording of the bill used "baseball" and not "golf" as the main target of the legislation, it drew passionate arguments from both sides. Many social workers, probation officers, and civic groups spoke favorably about the bill because it would give some of the troubled youth of the city "proper physical exercise as they were at work during the week." It was argued that the minds of the young men of the city "are active and if not given a physical outlet they will gamble and tell bad stories."

As expected many clergymen spoke against the bill. Mr. C. Peter Clark spoke in opposition representing the First Church of Newton Center. He thought that, "The Ten Commandments had worked very well so far," and that Sunday sports should be banned. But it was Mr. Rubin Forknall, Newton Alderman and vice president of the council, who stood most steadfastly opposed to Sunday sports. He accused the "golf players" of being behind a plot to pass the law through " . . . a clever subterfuge of tying their case in with one to help disadvantaged boys play ball." In his comments he referred to the landing of the Pilgrims and the ideals brought to America by them, and how disgraceful it would be we indulged in "movies, gala days, baseball and other legalized sports, including golf, all on the Lord's Day." He then reiterated "that the propaganda sent out to us on Sunday baseball is the propaganda of the golfers. The golfers were wise and pulled the trick, but they won't always fool the people." His opposition to the measure continued as Alderman Forknall stalled passage of the ordinance by invoking a series of delaying parliamentary procedures. Finally, in mid-May, Alderman Forknall put up one last gallant stand, endeavoring to filibuster the bill, but he was outvoted by the board and the measure for Sunday sports passed by a vote of 18–2. Sunday golfers were at last freed from the specter of having their game interrupted by the local police. Thankfully, history has proven that golf on Sunday and religious observances have peacefully coexisted, in Newton and elsewhere, ever since that much-debated Board of Aldermen's vote of 1919.

9 1920–1921

"At address take a square stance to the ball. Imagine a rectangular line from the ball to its objective. From this imaginary line place the left heel one-third of the distance to the left of the ball and the right two-thirds from the ball. If the ball is played off the left heel as sometimes advocated, either your hands must advance to properly direct the ball or the sweep will drive away from the line of the objective causing a slice."

—Charlie Burgess

• The Twenties Begin •

After the controversial Sunday golf case was resolved at the turn of the new decade, the twenties brought a period of sustained economic growth and prosperity for many Americans. Circumstances were just right for building hundreds of new golf and country clubs across the nation, as interest in golf grew significantly during the 1920s. The advent of the eight-hour workday, the five-day workweek, and increases in the daily wages of American workers created conditions that let them enjoy many new leisure time activities. Members of the working class began to advance to the middle class as the middle class continued their pursuit of upward mobility. And new golf heroes like Francis Ouimet, Walter Hagen, and a youngster from Atlanta, Georgia, named Robert Jones were attracting thousands of new fans to the game. In the state of Massachusetts alone, over 50 new golf clubs were constructed from 1920 to 1929, and Charlie's adopted hometown of Newton had five active clubs during the decade, with the addition of the Charles River Country Club in 1921.

A sour note for Boston sports enthusiasts at the very start of the decade was the sale of the popular baseball star Babe Ruth to the rival New York Yankees on January 5, 1920. Red Sox owner Harry Frazee was said to have sold the great Ruth to the Yankees for the relatively meager sum of $100,000 and a loan of $300,000 secured by a mortgage on Fenway Park. Whatever Frazee's motives for selling Ruth was, the effect of the sale arguably lasted for decades. Red Sox fans have long decried the sale and the alleged "curse of the Bambino" which seemed to have been levied on the franchise for generations. Ever since Charlie's enthusiastic golf student was sold to the enemy, the mantra of "wait till next year" has been the perennial rallying cry of loyal Red Sox fans until 2004, when Boston finally won another World Championship.

To add to the woes of sports fans from Boston and the rest of the nation, Congress passed the Eighteenth Amendment, known as the Volstead Act or Prohibition, that same month. The Volstead Act banned the production, distribution, and consumption of alcohol in the United States and forced a drastic change to commonly accepted social behavior at most sporting events. Social drinking was a large part of the golf club scene and Prohibition greatly altered clubhouse life during the twenties, although it was not unusual for well-connected country club members to find a way around the law if they chose to.

For the Burgess family, the twenties proved to be a very busy time and a period of relative affluence. The pro shop was prospering, and

Charlie's lesson times were always fully booked allowing him to make a few investments in the stock market and other business ventures. Charlie, now more often called Chay by family and friends to avoid confusion with his grown-up son, was forty-five and actively involved more and more with the concerns of his fellow club professionals in regard to the new PGA of America. Young Charlie was sharpening his skills and had developed his own following because of his fine golfing and teaching abilities. Harriet kept busy with domestic duties, charitable works, and had her own small-scale cottage knitting industry that had evolved from her volunteer efforts for the Red Cross during the Great War. At the outbreak of the war in Europe, Harriet knitted woolen socks, mittens, caps, and sweaters for the boys fighting at the front. After the war was over Hattie earned a little extra income by offering her hand-made goods to the golfers who passed through her husband's shop, particularly during the chilly early spring and late fall seasons.

• Jock Blair's Misfortune •

The recent organization of U.S. golf pros by the PGA of America was a long overdue necessity. Finally gaining some protection and representation in contractual matters, the unification of the American pros focused attention on the need for some sort of insurance against a catastrophic illness or disability. The importance of having an active and sound benevolent fund for professional golfers in need was made clear by the heartrending story of Jock Blair, the fine teaching professional at the Nashua Country Club in New Hampshire. It is a poignant example of the kind of misfortune that could easily ruin the life of the early professional unless relief could be found through the philanthropy of their fellow pros.

Jock was born in St. Andrews in 1888 and immigrated to Canada in 1910, where he worked as a club pro in Ottawa and Toronto for several years. He then moved to the United States and joined the staff at the Commonwealth Country Club in Newton, Massachusetts, and became associated with the well-known American homebred professionals John and Mike "King" Brady. Jock was part of the early informal alliance of

Boston area professionals that Chay Burgess was reported to have organized a few years before the establishment of the PGA of America. Only sketchy references to this 1914 organization of Boston area professionals have survived, but it likely included American-born pros Mike and John Brady, Jock, Chay, and the other transplanted Scottish teaching pros active in the Boston area.

The Nashua Country Club in New Hampshire opened in 1916 and hired Jock as its first professional. Shortly after his arrival, Jock began to suffer from a rapid onset of crippling arthritis and other related health problems. The severity of the condition was such that after about two years he was unable to walk, let alone play golf, without extreme pain and was forced to retire from his position in 1918. By the summer of 1920 Jock, just thirty-two years old, was bedridden most of the time, without income, insurance, or any means of supporting himself, his wife, and his two small children. His condition continued to deteriorate with each passing day.

Fellow PGA professionals, in what was then the Eastern Section of the PGA, organized a benefit affair for the ailing pro. Louis Tellier, Brae Burn professional, and Mike Brady, Blair's former colleague, arranged an exhibition match at the Brae Burn Country Club between Francis Ouimet, Jesse Guilford, and themselves. The charity match between the two amateur stars and the Boston pros followed the same format that Jesse and Francis used on behalf of the American Red Cross in four-ball, best-ball exhibitions during the war years. Brady and Tellier had teamed up against Ouimet and Guilford several times before and the matches were fairly evenly split. Since all four golfers were rated as among the best in the entire nation at that type of play, the teams easily drew a large gallery at 50 cents per person. Several thousand dollars were raised through the receipts and other contributions. Blair survived only a few more months, supported by the welfare of friends, some generous club members, and his fellow pros. Jock passed away in February of 1920. Soon after Jock's death, Chay Burgess and some of his many New England associates began to draw up plans for a method of insuring that no other area professionals would ever again be unprotected from the kind of catastrophic event that befell poor Jock Blair.

Jock was replaced at Nashua by his young understudy Joe Stien. Joe was one of a new breed of American club professionals who desired to work at a club and still have the option to play enough competitive golf to make a name for themselves in that arena as well. Blessed with matinee idol good looks and an engaging personality, he became very closely associated with the great Walter Hagen and was his partner in many four-ball competitions throughout New England and all over the South as the seasons changed.

Hagen invited Stien to join a team of competitive American professionals that he assembled to tour Europe prior to the 1926 British Open. The Hagen led exhibition team was instrumental in paving the way for the Ryder Cup Challenge, the first permanent established team competition between American and British professionals.

Stien remained close to Hagen throughout the twenties as he managed one of Hagen's golf courses in Florida for several years. He eventually left golf to pursue business opportunities in other arenas during the thirties.

• A Return to Scotland •

By the 1920's, many American club professionals employed in the northern climates of New England and in the Midwest began an annual winter migration to the South. With their home courses frozen or covered with snow and ice for months at a time, more and more of them sought seasonal employment at the winter resorts in the southlands. Chay's nephew Bert Nicoll became a well-known and successful dual club pro. He spent three-quarters of the year at his home club in Belmont, Massachusetts, then wintered at Pinehurst, where he was head professional on the staff of Donald Ross who managed golf operations at the resort. Later in his career, Bert spent many of his winters as head pro at the Palm Beach Country Club in Florida.

Chay was only an occasional visitor to the South for a few weeks at a time each year. Until this time he had spent most of his winter months in his Woodland shop repairing and hand crafting golf clubs. Later in the decade, he and his son Charlie would open a very successful indoor winter golf school, but during the winter of 1920, he and his family traveled back to Montrose to see old friends and to stock up on golf supplies for his shop. It was his first visit back home in eleven years.

The family sailed on the most famous liner of the day, the *Mauretania.* This Cunard Line ship was the fastest in the world as well as being one of the most luxurious ships on the sea. Even the *Titanic* had been no match for the *Mauretania*'s record speed of 27 knots that she set in 1909. The *Mauretania,* like most of the British Empire's sea going vessels, saw military duty during the World War as a troop carrier and hospital ship. Her sister ship was the ill-fated *Lusitania,* sunk in 1915 by a German U-boat.

After they docked in Southampton, the family finished their journey with a daylong railroad trip through the English heartland, into the hilly green border country of southern Scotland, and then up the northeast coast to their beloved Montrose. The Scottish winter was seasonably cold, yet not one flake of snow fell on the village during the two months the Burgess family was there. As a result Chay, unencumbered by teaching duties, had enough time to play as many rounds of golf during his visit as he would have played back in the States during an entire season. He hit his stride on the familiar links course and shot the course in under par record rounds of 70 twice that winter. His fellow Montrosian Harry Hampton, another transplanted Scottish professional, was also visiting his old hometown. Hampton was the professional at the Beverly Golf Club in Chicago and played with Chay often that winter as he also posted a record 70 on the dry but chilly Montrose Links.

After a pleasant extended stay in Scotland, the Burgesses were ready to head back to America along with a contingent of other golf pros who had also taken advantage of the slow season to get back to their respective "old" countries. Joining them on the return voyage were Harry Hampton, Englishman Cyril Walker, and Scottish golfer Laurence "Laurie" Ayton. Also on board were professional golfers, Jack Wade, James MacGregor of the Misquamicut Golf Club in Rhode Island, and George Morris who had settled in Pennsylvania working at the New Bethlehem and Harrisburg courses. The long sea voyage gave Chay and his friends ample opportunity to meet and share information regarding the current state of affairs of professional golf throughout America and discuss the relative effectiveness of the new American PGA among other things. Seen most frequently at the dining table or on the parlors with Chay during the return voyage were Walker, Ayton, and Hampton.

Harry Hampton was a bit of a vagabond throughout his professional career and, like many other transplanted Scottish pros who contributed greatly to the development of golf in America primarily through their teaching ability, has been largely overlooked. Hampton made several strong runs at national championships while still maintaining his links to club work. Born in Carnoustie, he moved to Montrose as an adult and was the winner of the famous Montrose Links Championship, the Boothby-Campbell Shield, in 1908. In 1909, he succeeded Burgess as the winner of the Mercantile Golf Club Badge and the Coronation Tankard. When he immigrated to the United States shortly after Chay, Hampton became a perennial contender for the U.S. Open and later the PGA Championship. Initially, he worked in the Boston area taking a position at the Donald Ross designed North Andover Country Club and then moved later to the Western Massachusetts town of Lenox. He entered the Open more than a dozen times, representing clubs from Richmond, Detroit, Memphis, and Chicago. In his early years, he often finished in the top dozen or so and never worse than the top twenty-five. His PGA record was quite competitive, but he never won a national championship. From 1919 to 1926, he advanced as far as the quarter and semi-final PGA Championship rounds, losing to such stars as J. D. Edgar, Johnny Farrell, and to Jock Hutchison twice.

At the time of the crossing, Cyril Walker, the pro at the Englewood Golf Club in Detroit, still had his best golf before him. In 1922, he finished thirteenth out of 262 in the U.S. Open, and then in 1923, he finished in twenty-fourth place. At Oakland Hills, Michigan, in 1924, Walker had his best showing and won the event, beating the famed amateur Bobby Jones by three strokes. Throughout the twenties, Walker was known for his many PGA tilts with the giants of the game—Jim Barnes, Walter Hagen, and Gene Sarazen. His best PGA finish was a 5–4 loss to Hagen in the semi-final round of the 1921 PGA championship after he had beaten Sarazen in the quarterfinals.

Laurie Ayton, from St. Andrews, received much of Chay's attention during the passage and the two spent many hours together in conversation. It was Ayton's first trip to the United States after accepting a job in Illinois with the Evanston Golf Club. Burgess described Ayton as "one of the finest types in the game, clean cut in every particular, clean living and a great player, one who should hold his own in any company." Ayton's recruitment to Evanston was highly publicized and the generous treatment he was given by his new employers was noted by many of his fellow professionals and travelers as a positive sign of a slowly growing regard for the professional golfer in America. After Ayton arrived at the Evansville Golf Club, he wrote to Chay and described how the club generously arranged a grand dinner to which all the professionals in the Chicago district were invited in order for him to meet his brother professionals in "a most pleasing manner."

Ayton joined the ranks of club professionals, which included more and more homebreds, who were venturing from their clubs from time to time in order to participate in the many new tournaments that were being established. They were starting to capture the imagination of the golfing public that truly admired the skills of the pros and accorded them developing celebrity status. Ayton's first American tournament was the 1920 U.S. Open held at Inverness in Ohio, where he finished seventeenth out of a field of 265. Like Harry Hampton, he was a perennial competitor through the twenties, and his best outings came in 1925 when he finished six strokes back, in ninth place at Worcester Country Club in a field of over 400 in that Open.

• Two Kinds of American Pros •

After returning back from the pleasant trip to Scotland with his family and fellow professionals, Chay returned to Woodland to find his star pupils in fine form and ready for another competitive season. Success for Jesse Guilford and Francis Ouimet was measured now by what they accomplished off the links almost as much as by what they did on them. Jesse continued in his accounting business and was extended a life membership at Woodland by the club in deference to his great play. Francis was a full-fledged golf celebrity, frequently asked to pen an article or story for various newspapers and magazines. In a magazine called *St. Nicholas*, Francis thoughtfully mentioned his mentor's special teaching ability and interest in young people. In the story he told of a young girl just seven years old who learned the game from his old master and commented on how she quickly developed a "free, easy and graceful swing" under the watchful eye of Burgess. Francis described Chay as the ideal professional, "one who possessed great skill in the execution of the game and who could effectively teach it to others."

The American professional was beginning to enjoy a new place in the pecking order of the game, due in great part to the growth of the PGA during the twenties. The official objective of the PGA was to "promote interest in the game of golf; to protect the mutual interest of its members; to hold meetings and tournaments periodically for the encouragement of the younger members; to institute the benevolent fund for the relief of deserving members; to hold meetings at which the subjects of greenskeeping and course architecture are discussed by professionals and experts . . . to act as an agency to assist any professional golfer or club-maker to obtain employment, and to effect any other object of a like nature as may be determined from time to time by the association."

Many members of the PGA were observing that there were two distinct classes of professionals developing at the start of the twenties. Chay Burgess represented one type of professional, an all-around man and teacher who was occasionally able to get a few days or maybe a week off from his club as needed to play in one or two professional events. The other type was the pro who was allowed to spend nine or ten months away from his home club in order to tour the country in search of tournament or exhibition money. If he was successful, his club benefited from the association of its name with his and the pro gained celebrity. Some pros like Sarazen and Barnes had arrangements with their home clubs to spend months away from their shops and club responsibilities in order to travel to as many tournaments as they wished. Other professionals, like Hagen, became so successful that they did not need any affiliation with a club at all.

Soon all the professionals in America had to make the choice between a club job that called for 95 percent of their attention, or the other that required travel around the country for nine or ten months of the year.

Most of the early imported British professionals like Chay had come to America assuming a club-based teaching position because of the great need for their services by club members unschooled in golf but eager to learn the game. The earliest professionals were wedded to a home club where their income was derived mainly from lessons and the sale and maintenance of equipment. Initially, few competitive tournaments or exhibitions existed that paid enough for even the most successful pro to survive on full time. So the relative security of a club position, rather than life on the road, was the choice of the vast majority of America's first professional golfers from the late 1890's to the teens.

Even with the continuing expansion of the game and the development of the Professional Golfers' Association of America, there were still very few well-paying tournaments for the traveling pros and almost no competitive venues for the American teaching or club-based professional to play in during the early 1920's. Much of the traveling pros' income derived instead from barnstorming exhibition matches set up by all manner of promoters and producers eager to introduce the game and often to make a quick buck for themselves if possible. Walter Hagen became a master of surviving on the early PGA road show circuit and was wise enough to insist that all spectators be "tagged" with a visible pass to insure that they had paid the admission fee. According to author Herb Graffis in his comprehensive history of the PGA of America published in 1975, this now-familiar way of regulating the gallery at an event was adopted by the PGA in 1921 for admission to all of its championships. The USGA followed suit and in a cooperative initiative designed to help the professional golfer charged admission to the U.S. Open in Chicago the next year.

Since the establishment of the PGA in 1916, only three national PGA Championships had been held (there were no tournaments in 1917-18 because of the war). Regional qualification rounds were held and a few lucky club pros had the opportunity to get in some competitive golf against the likes of Walter Hagen, Jim Barnes, Jock Hutchison, Harry Hampton, Leo Diegel, Gene Sarazen, and Bill Mehlhorn. Mike Brady, Louis Tellier, and Tom Kerrigan were perennial New England area qualifiers for the first three championships which each featured a total purse of $2,580 to be shared amongst the field of 32 players. Jim Barnes, the champion in 1916 and 1919, received $500 for each of his victories. Five hundred dollars was also the top prize when Jock Hutchison won the 1920 PGA Championship. Second prize each year was $250, and anyone finishing below the top ten got very little prize money for their efforts.

Today the prizes are astronomical in comparison, even accounting for inflation; the PGA Championship has a top prize of nearly $1,000,000 and a total purse of over $5,000,000. Even the last place money winner, finishing as far back as sixty or seventieth place usually wins nearly $10,000—about four times the total 1920 purse!

Relatively small purses and few qualifying spots limited the appeal of the first few PGA Championships to a handful of American pros. In response to the limited opportunities most club pros had for tournament play in 1920, a group of New England-based professionals led by Chay Burgess began to formulate ideas for their own organization that would follow the tenets of the national PGA but would be much more responsive to their own needs. The New England pros wanted to serve their clubs and still have the opportunity keep up their skills and to play for prize money without making that 95 percent or else choice. Chay and his colleagues began to talk about taking action to address that issue and many other matters of great importance to teaching professionals all across America.

• Chay's Second National Champion •

As American professional golfers continued their slow progression towards respectability and recognition, America's amateurs still continued to capture the interest of the nation's public and soon would make an impact on the international stage. Chay's students at Woodland led the country's amateur ranks with the one-two combination of Ouimet and Guilford. Even the famous little Woodland caddie, Eddie Lowery, was now making a name for himself in the region's amateur golf ranks. In 1919 he won the Massachusetts Junior Golf title at age sixteen and repeated again in 1920. But it was still Ouimet and Guilford who dominated the regional and much of the national golf scene in the twenties. The two Woodland amateurs were an unbeatable combination when they paired up for four-ball matches, as they did often. They were also each other's friendly but serious rivals in match play.

Francis was twenty-eight, married to the former Stella Sullivan, in the banking business, and had outgrown his boyhood awkwardness to become quite friendly and worldly. Jesse, two years younger, was also married. He and his wife Louise had two little girls. An accountant, he still remained reserved and quiet around anyone but his closest friends. He was extremely shy, and because of his serious demeanor, many people presumed Jesse to be unfriendly. Perhaps it was just the contrast between him and the affable and more outgoing Ouimet that made Jesse seem that way to others.

In September of 1921, Jesse and Francis headed out west to the St. Louis Country Club in Clayton, Missouri, for the twenty-fifth National Amateur Championship of the USGA. It was the first time the tournament was held west of the Mississippi River and the field was studded with the world's greatest amateur stars. Besides the young men from Woodland, George Von Elm, Jesse Sweetser, John Anderson, Chick Evans, Robert Gardner, Bobby Jones, and Scotland's Tommy Armour all teed up against each other in 1921.

Francis got off to a fast start and led the field in the qualifying round with a 144 for the medal. He won his first match but was knocked out of the running in the second round by H. R. Johnson from St. Paul, Minnesota.

Jesse had a very tough first round draw in Von Elm of Salt Lake City to start the tournament. Guilford's long hitting prevailed and he dispatched Von Elm 5 and 4. Jesse then met Dewey Webber in the second round and beat him 3 and 2. He made it to the semi-final by taking out Ouimet's vanquisher H. R. Johnson in the third round. In the semi-finals, he faced the formidable 1920 champion Charles "Chick" Evans of Chicago and won convincingly 5 and 4. Jesse then swept past Robert A. Gardner 7 up with 6 to play in the 36-hole final, winning the National Amateur Championship of 1921.

It was a most impressive and attention-getting win for the long hitting "Siege Gun" of Woodland. He was not only the new Amateur Champion of the United States but the road to his championship was acknowledged as the most difficult series of matches ever seen in *any* previous championship. At each draw, he faced and defeated an established champion golfer. First, it was Von Elm, the Pacific Northwest and Trans-Mississippi Champion. Then, he beat Webber who was the Chicago District Champion. Next, he faced Johnson who was the Minnesota Champion, and then he defeated the defending champion, Evans, before winning the final against Bob Gardner, another former U.S. Amateur Champion.

Chay's two star students were the talk of the town and of golf enthusiasts across the country because of their efforts in St. Louis. On the Sunday before the tournament itself, Jesse and Francis teamed up in a best-ball stroke play match. They won first prize with a score of 69 in "the finest and largest field that ever competed for the National Best-Ball Championship," winning the American Golfer trophy for their effort. Then Francis won the 36-hole qualifying medal with a 144-stroke performance, shooting a new course record of 69 for the first 18, then following with a solid 75 for the second. Finally, Jesse's great win over the star-studded field was the victory that made a clean sweep of all the championships at St. Louis for Charlie Burgess's prize pupils.

When Guilford stepped forward to accept the championship trophy, the notoriously shy winner amused the gathered spectators quite unintentionally when he gave this brief response, "If I'm expected to make a speech, I'm sorry I won." Despite his frightful reluctance to stand in the spotlight, the Woodland members gave him a royal celebration banquet on his return to Newton. The most difficult task the event organizers had was to force the reluctant Guilford to utter even a few simple words of acknowledgement at the dinner.

• Professional Team Play •

The increased popularity of golf, both amateur and professional, in the 1920s brought with it the development of new opportunities for the exhibition of the sport. In early 1920, plans were being drawn to play international professional team matches between America and Great Britain. This proposal for international team play predated the establishment of international amateur team play for the Walker Cup (1922) and the professional Ryder Cup (1927) team competitions, but it was not the first formal team match between United States golfers and their European counterparts.

The forerunner to all international team competition between the USA and Europe began with the 1913 excursion of homebred pros Tom McNamara, Mike Brady, and John McDermott to Liverpool for the British Open at Hoylake. The three Americans took a side trip to Versailles to take on a French team led by Arnaud Massey and Louis Tellier. Alex Smith, the long-time transplanted Scot (he had been in Chicago since 1898), joined the American team to lend it some stability. To the surprise of many, the strong U.S. team was severely trounced in that encounter. The coming of war in Europe held off any further attempts at international team play by either professionals or amateurs until after the conclusion of combat, and the 1920 proposal was the first postwar attempt at renewing international professional team competition.

The exhibition matches were to be played prior to the 1920 U.S. Open at the Inverness Club in Toledo, Ohio. Initially, it was proposed to make up three teams, one comprising homebred Americans, one native-born Scottish team, and one English team to play each other. The plan was ripe with controversy over the makeup of the teams. Walter Hagen, John Barnes, Jock Hutchinson, and Mike Brady objected to the suggested organization of the teams and proposed that the match be played between a team representing resident American professionals, regardless of their national origins, against a team of British "invaders." The so-called invaders were expected to be Vardon, Ray, Abe Mitchell, George Duncan, and Laurie Ayton among others.

The renowned British stars Vardon and Ray were once again conducting a lucrative barnstorming tour of America similar to their 1913 visit. They were joined by the now equally famous team of Mitchell and Duncan, who had been attracted to the growing golfing opportunities in the States ever since Ouimet's populist victory in 1913. Laurie Ayton, who had just settled in Illinois after his voyage to America with Chay Burgess, joined up with his former British colleagues when they arrived.

The proposal by Hagen met the approval of many other U.S.-based professionals who felt that when someone had been in America as long as Jim Barnes, Jock Hutchison, and Gil Nicholls, they should be included on a team representing America, especially since they would be playing against a team of foreign professionals who were in the country for only a short visit or had only just taken up residency. But disagreements continued, the matter was not resolved, and the 1920 U.S. Open went ahead without the hoped-for international team play exhibitions.

England's Edward Ray won the Open with a 295 four-round total and vindicated the 1913 play-off loss to Ouimet he endured on his last visit to America. However, Ouimet was not among the 265 entrants in the 1920 contest. The top American amateur was Chicago's Chick Evans who finished with a 298 behind Harry Vardon, Jack Burke, Leo Diegel, and Jock Hutchison, all of whom tied for second place at 296.

• A Rebellion in the PGA •

At the start of the twenties, a growing dissatisfaction with the new Professional Golfers' Association of America was evident to Charlie Burgess and many of his fellow professionals throughout the country. In the first five years of the association's existence, a great effort was made to attract and organize all of the nation's professional golfers, who now numbered more than one thousand. In return for their annual dues, the club professionals who made up the bulk of the membership seemed to get little in return. Aside from the PGA championship qualification matches, the scarcity of regional professional tournaments was a concern of the grassroots members who wanted to keep up their competitive skills and have an opportunity for some prize money as well.

In addition, the recent hardship of Jock Blair dramatically pointed out the need for an effective benevolent fund that would be responsive to the needs of the members at the local level. It was clear from the discussions Chay had with the other professionals on his recent voyage that many of the concerns he had about the effectiveness of the new PGA were shared with many other club-based pros in every region of the country.

In January of 1921, Chay assembled the leading New England professionals who agreed to secede from the PGA of America and to create a formal regional organization dedicated to what they felt were their own particular needs. The group incorporated and called itself the New England Professional Golfers' Organization (NEPGO). The founding fathers were Charlie Burgess as president, John J. Keenan as vice president, C. Harry Bowler as secretary-treasurer as well as Bert Nicoll, George Dernbach, Donald Vinton, and David G. Tait, who served as directors of the nation's first independent professional golfers organization established since the founding of the PGA.

According to its charter, the corporation was formed to "promote interest in the game of golf, to hold meetings and tournaments periodically for the encouragement of the members, to institute a benevolent fund, and to affect any other object of like nature that may be determined from time to time by the organization." The goals of the organization were almost exactly like the national PGA. The key difference was that now the New England pros could establish and direct their own affairs, tournaments, and anything else that was of local concern without waiting for a far-removed national body to act.

Within weeks after the establishment of the NEPGO, dozens of area pros signed on. Soon members had an abundance of competitive tournaments, all within a reasonable distance from each professional's home club. The NEPGO quickly grew into a strong regional body. Its rapid success sent a strong and clear message to the PGA of America that, in order to survive, a reorganization of its top-down administrative structure was necessary before other regions followed the example of the independent New Englanders and joined them in their secession.

The inaugural New England Professional Golfers' Organization tournament was held in Massachusetts in April of 1921 at the Winchester Country Club and, according to published accounts, "from any and every angle the tournament . . . was a great success." Forty-four starters came from all parts of New England and "there was no end of distance hitting and first class long iron play in the course of the day." Willie Ogg of Worcester was the winner, although the little Frenchman Louis Tellier had led the field for the first nine holes with a gallery-pleasing 39.

More important than the outcome of the match or the size of the field was the spirit of the day. Boston sportswriter and avid golfer Linde Fowler called the gathering of the region's golfers the "family-izing" of the New England professionals. Secretary-Treasurer Harry Bowler reported to the members, who met after the match, that in less than three months, the organization had grown to 79 members with more applying each week during the spring. Financially, the group had collected dues and donations from sporting goods houses and private individuals and the treasury was growing substantially.

Besides running tournaments, the NEPGO acted as an employment agency placing members in advantageous positions as it constantly was on the lookout for desirable professional opportunities for its members. The NEPGO also began the establishment of a benevolent fund that spring. The group made its objectives clear by demonstrating that it was a real working body, one that would keep in close contact with the affairs of the entire district and had no desire to be antagonistic to the Professional Golfers' Association of America.

The NEPGO leadership envisioned that all professionals, greenskeepers, and other golf industry professionals throughout the country would follow the example of the New England golfers. They also were open to be affiliated with one central body like the PGA of America, but they desired to work along the lines of the USGA where each region made local decisions and only matters of general national impact would be the province of the parent body.

The credibility of the newly established organization was evident from its inception. Longtime New England resident and nationally esteemed golf professional Donald Ross made an important gesture of support and encouragement to the organization when he donated a handsome perpetual trophy in his name to be awarded to the annual NEPGO champion. Ross evidently believed that Charlie's group was going to be around for a long time.

Chay and his group also made a deliberate effort to reach out and work cooperatively with the United States Golf Association and the regional amateur golf associations in all of the New England States. In order for the New England pros to be successful, they needed the support and collaboration of the many USGA member clubs that allowed them to use their facilities. A much stronger professional association emerged as a result of establishing a reciprocal organization that reached out and sponsored many exceptional golfing opportunities for the region's amateurs in addition to strictly professional events.

In May, the organization sponsored its first Amateur-Professional Best Ball Tournament, which was held at Woodland. Bert Nicoll and H. H. Marden from the Belmont Springs Club won the event with a 36-hole total of 136. Seventy-eight players entered, and it was a veritable who's who of the region's golfers. Former Ouimet caddie Eddie Lowery and his professional partner Ed McPhail were just a half-dozen strokes off the pace. Young Charlie Burgess paired up with Wilfred Ouimet and won a prize for the best afternoon card, which was a 68. It was another successful outing for the young organization.

Next up was a mixed foursome match featuring the pros of New England paired with the ladies of the Women's Golf Association of Boston and their guests. It was a precedent-setting, historic occurrence since it was the first such pairing played in the country as a regularly scheduled event sponsored by a professional organization, and it was the forerunner of many other interesting co-ed matches held nationwide. Louis Tellier and Miss Elizabeth Gordon of Rhode Island tied for low gross with an 81, and Harry Bowler was paired with an up-and-coming young golfer named Glenna Collette.

After her debut in the NEPGO event, she became one of women's golf's greatest stars. Between 1922 and 1935, Glenna won 18 major U.S. championships including six Eastern Amateur Championships, six North-South Championships and six U.S. Women's Amateur Championships.

• New England Professionals Prosper •

By June, the NEPGO had 105 members, more than ten percent of all the pros in America, and it was still growing. In the first New England Professional Golfers' Organization tournament held at the Brae Burn Country Club, Louis Tellier shot a record-tying 72, a warm-up for his anticipated run at the Massachusetts Open and at a national championship. Another professional tournament was held in June at Woodland, then an amateur-professional match at Winchester, followed by another open mixed foursome at the Oakley Country Club. NEPGO sanctioned play continued with a four-ball tournament in July at Belmont, which Bert Nicoll won with an individual round of 69, a record score for the course.

The New England pros continued to reach out in association with amateur organizations when it ran a mixed foursome competition with the women members of the Boston Griscom Cup team at Woodland. The Griscom Cup was established in 1889 as one of America's first inter-city golf competitions for women, and teams from Philadelphia, New York, and Boston have competed for the trophy since 1902. It was the first formal co-ed affair with professional golfers for the ladies. The NEPGO held two more amateur-professional tournaments in Hartford, Connecticut, and Nashua, New Hampshire, in summer of 1921. The organization, led by president Chay Burgess, was a sudden and continuing success. The plethora of golf tournaments available to the professionals of the region continued into September when the Massachusetts Golf Association sponsored the State Open. Louis Tellier and John Cowan tied for the crown after 72 holes of play. In a dramatic 18-hole playoff Tellier beat Cowan by one stroke on the last hole 80-81.

Another interesting amateur-professional match was held at Woodland during the late summer of 1921. The now-celebrated team of Ouimet and new National Amateur Champion Guilford was scheduled to play an exhibition against famous British pros George Duncan and Abe Mitchell. Duncan and Mitchell were once again back in the United States on a golf exhibition tour. The famous British stars were beginning to spend more time in America than in their own country, which was either a powerful indicator of how much the game had grown in the United States or how much it had recently declined in Great Britain.

Woodland officials expected a record number of spectators to be on hand for the famous amateur's play against the British stars, mainly because of Mitchell's reputation as a long ball hitter. Many golf enthusiasts were anxious to see a showdown between Mitchell and the "siege gun" shots of Jesse Guilford. The exhibition had the distinction of being the first golf match ever to be insured in the United States. Woodland member and insurance man Fred Driscoll wrote up a policy to cover the club against financial loss in the event of a cancellation caused by rain. The arrangement with the Hartford Insurance Company indemnified the club against the loss of the guarantee required by the professionals should rain drive away the spectators and the club's revenue from their admissions. It turned out that the weather was fine, the crowds were large, and the match was a battle royal right to the end of the scheduled 36 holes. Jesse was able to match Mitchell's prowess off the tee, but surprisingly it was Mitchell's deadly putting that gave the British team the edge as they won by two strokes on the very last hole.

The final and biggest event in the inaugural year of the NEPGO was held on October 17, 1921 at the Myopia Hunt Club in South Hamilton, Massachusetts. Louis Tellier, Gil Nicholls, and John Cowan were the odds on favorites to win the first New England Professional Championship and take home the coveted Donald Ross Trophy. Sixty-four of the best regional and national professionals teed off for the 36-hole match. Scottish veteran Gil Nicholls beat Tellier by one stroke and Cowan by four. The contest went right down to the last few holes when at the thirty-third hole, Teller, the transplanted Frenchman, pushed his third shot into a trap. He then three-putted for a disastrous seven. Nicholls took the hole in five for a two-stroke lead. Tellier picked up a stroke on the next to last hole, but only managed to halve the last hole with a five, and Nicholls took the title and the very first Donald Ross Cup as the NEPGO Champion. Unfortunately the annual end of the season tournament for the Boston Newspapermen's Golf Association was scheduled on the same day as the first NEPGO Championship, which made press coverage a bit difficult for golf-loving reporters. However, many of the scribes finished their 18-hole meeting just in time to meet their deadlines as they joined their non-playing colleagues covering the pros at Myopia. Eddie Lowery, now working as a young newspaper reporter for the *Boston Traveler*, took the best gross score prize at the event for the newsmen with a 73.

In a separate division of the NEPGO Championship, young Charlie Burgess won fourth place with a cash reward of $10 in the 36-hole medal play for assistant professionals, greenskeepers, and other golf club staffers. It was his best professional finish so far and he seemed to be very focused on becoming as successful as his father was in professional golf. Perhaps his recent introduction to Kitty McCarthy had something to do with it. Young Charlie met Catherine "Kitty" McCarthy one evening at a dance at the popular local riverside ballroom called Nutting's on the Charles, in nearby Waltham, Massachusetts. Charlie fell head over heels for the charming, attractive Irish-American girl with hazel eyes and a smile that melted his heart. Soon he and Kitty became steady dance partners and became a successful team mastering the waltz, foxtrot, and rumba in numerous competitions. They began a courtship that was in full gear during the summer of 1921. Anytime he was free from his duties on the golf course, he was with Kitty on dates into Boston or on beach outings to Cape Cod and Boston's North Shore.

The New England Professional Golfers' Organization won wide acclaim for the splendid achievements made in the short time of its initial year. It held fifteen tournaments, distributed $2,626 in prize money, had over 115 members join within eight months, started a benevolent fund, and began an employment service for its members. Charlie Burgess, as President and Harry Bowler of Winchester, as secretary-treasurer, made incredible progress in improving the lot of the professional golfer in America, particularly that of the club or teaching professionals. They also made tremendous strides in gaining the respect of the nation's golf establishment through their efforts to include the region's amateur golfers in their activities. Charlie was credited by Boston sportswriters with designing and leading an assembly of golf professionals who were "probably better organized . . . than any other group of golf instructors in the country." Thanks to the excellent management and enthusiasm of the officers and the active participation of the rank and file members, the NEPGO became a yardstick for the rest of the nation's professional golfers to measure up against.

The group had its sixteenth and final tournament of the season at Wollaston in November, but it was held in the aftermath of a terrible tragedy that rocked the golfing world all the way from Newton, Massachusetts, to LaBollie, France, and beyond.

• The Tragedy of Tellier •

As we have seen, the life of the early professional golfer was far from an easy one. Constant pressure to perform up to public expectation or personal standards often took a mental and physical toll on even the most stalwart pros. Financial worries, difficult working conditions, and subtle but clear social segregation all combined in varying degrees to stress many early American professional golfers.

On November 3, Louis Tellier, Brae Burn Country Club professional and former French Champion, took his own life by hanging himself from a beam in one of the course rain shelter houses located just a short distance away from his home.

Tellier was one of the most renowned European-born golfers of the era, often representing France in international competition with fellow countryman Arnaud Massey. (Massey was the first non-British winner of the British Open in 1907, Champion of the first French Open in 1906, winner of the first Belgian Open in 1910, and the initial Spanish Open Champion in 1912.)

Tellier traveled in the foremost golfing circles and was married to the sister of English professional Wilfred Reid. After joining Reid, Vardon, and Ray and on their celebrated 1913 American tour, Tellier and his wife returned to the States in 1914 to take several golfing positions that were offered to him, including a short stay at The Country Club before assuming his final job at Brae Burn. He became Chay Burgess's neighbor, living at 1900 Washington Street, across the street and a few yards from the Woodland Golf Club entrance drive. Tellier just had a short walk from his backyard to the grounds of the Brea Burn course and clubhouse.

Chay and other close friends believed that chronic depression and a state of mental unbalance had plagued Louis for some time. The recent traumatic death of a friend and several recent physical illnesses of Tellier were said to have been contributing factors to his state of mind. He was also reported to be deeply disappointed in his recent loss to Gil Nicholls in the NEPGO Championship. Tellier had shot a tremendous 72 for the first half of the match but scored an 85 on the last 18 holes, giving the tournament to Nicholls, who shot consistent 78s for a one-stroke margin of victory. That final stroke was not given up until the match went right down to the last heartbreaking hole for Tellier. It was a tremendous disappointment for the dapper little Frenchman, and sadly it may have been enough, given his depression, to drive him to such a desperate measure as suicide.

Tellier, seemingly in the heyday of his golfing career, was just thirty-five and had been in the running for the National Open title three times. Once, in 1915, he led the field only to fall victim to some bad luck, when he lost his footing on a crucial shot, and finished tied for third. Tellier's passing marked a sad and poignant end to the otherwise successful New England golf season that year.

10 1921–1929

"With the square stance your hands, brought from your sides, will meet exactly in the center. Then must come a relaxed position. To obtain this be sure the arms are not stiff or taut and break the knees forward enough to avoid their locking back. I do not agree with the theory so strictly preached that the left arm must be straight at the top of the backswing. You cannot do it and maintain relaxation."

—Charlie Burgess

• An Anniversary Back in Scotland •

On December 13, 1921 the Burgess family once again set sail for Scotland, this time to celebrate Chay and Harriet's silver wedding anniversary with family and friends in Montrose. The plans were for Chay and Hattie to spend the entire winter back in the old country, while young Charlie was to come back directly after the celebration in order to ready things for the spring season at Woodland. Harry Nicoll, now the head professional at the Donald Ross-designed Oak Hill Golf Club in Fitchburg, Massachusetts, and his brother Willie, the latest nephew Chay had sponsored as an American golf pro, joined his aunt, uncle, and cousin on the voyage. Several other prominent golf professionals who frequently traveled back to Great Britain in the winter months were also on board.

For this trip the family sailed on the largest Cunard vessel in service, the *Aquitania*. She had a gross tonnage of 45,647 and her length (901 feet) and width (97 feet) were even greater than the *Titanic*'s had been (882 and 92 feet respectively). Like her sister ships, she had served in the war and was refitted in 1919 with her original lavish furnishings, objets d'art, and with new oil-fired engines. She was one of the best-decorated Atlantic liners afloat, with a first-class dining room done in Louis XVI style among her many amenities.

At 10:00 A.M. on the morning that the ship sailed from New York, Kitty sent a bon voyage wire to her young fiancée from the Postal Telegraph Office in Boston where she worked. It was the first of many wires and letters between Charlie and Kitty during the voyage. The correspondence gives some insight to the nature of transatlantic travel, society, and the interest in golf at the time. The first person to write back to Kitty from the ship was Harriet, who had taken an instant liking to her and warmly welcomed her into the family.

December 13, 1921—4 p.m.

Dear Kitty

Here we are speeding along to Bonnie Scotland. We sailed just at mid-day, started in with a good lunch. Chay and I have been walking along the decks, the water is just lovely up to the present. We have met with three golfers, Willie Park and Tom McNamara and an Englishman Jack Way who came over in the same boat with us years ago. [Way was pro at the Canterbury Golf Club in Cleveland, Ohio] . . . A few days have elapsed since I started this. Charlie and I have just come from church. You may know by this scribble the boat is pitching a wee bit so I won't say anymore just now.

Best Love,
Harriet

Young Charlie also began a series of letters to Kitty, one each day throughout the journey, some are excerpted here:

Dear Kitty,

I received your telegram and was very happy indeed to get it . . . I bought this writing paper to attempt to put a few remarks on paper. I say "attempt" for this big ark is rolling to beat the band and a lot of faces have been missing from the table the last two meals. Willie Nicoll has been in his bunk since seven o'clock. Well dear I'll stop now as I see a steward approaching with tea and cakes-jolly-eh, what? The deck-hands are predicting rough weather to-morrow. I hope to be among those present—so far so good.

. . . We have just passed the banks of Newfoundland on our northern course and have now swung straight east for Europe. There was a movie show in the dining room last night and after that at 10 o'clock I went to bed. You must pardon my penmanship as the old hooker is doing her best to roll over . . .

Well we are fully halfway over now and making good time. The sea has gone down quite a little and a lot of the people who were seasick are appearing on deck again.

After lunch Tom MacNamara who was a "Pro" and who now is in the wholesale golf supply business in New York came through and I took him down to the folks' stateroom where they were ensconced in bed with magazines and fruit galore and we talked all afternoon. Tonight there is a concert and as it is for charity and as father and mother are going and want me to go with them, I suppose I'll go. . . .

We are two-thirds of the way across now having run 547 miles in the last 24 hours. We may land in Southampton Monday but I am inclined to think it will be Tuesday morning . . . Yesterday was "sports day" on board—the children's sports were in the morning so they could attend a Santa Claus and Christmas tree affair in the afternoon. Every kiddy on board went thru to First class where an immense Xmas tree was laden with a present for each one. They each had a Xmas stocking filled with fruit and candy and then each one got a game or a toy with their name on it besides. There was a Santa Claus and six reindeer and then about a dozen clowns, etc.

. . . Last night we had a dance with the ship's brass band for music. . . . I paraded mother out at the first note of every dance but one, which she danced with another pro on board. She did wonderfully well. It made no difference to her, one step, fox trot or waltz she was there! I know she was tickled silly at getting away with it. Will write to you tomorrow our last full day on board.

. . . this is our last full day on board, for at noon we'll be in France at Cherbourg and at Southampton, England by night. We won't land however till tomorrow, Tuesday forenoon. Yesterday we went along to church service and after that came back and took some pictures.

Your Charlie

Young Charlie continued his correspondence with Kitty as often as he could when the party finally arrived in Montrose. He had plenty of time to write, as the winter of 1921–22 was one of the worst ever in the northeast of Scotland. Blizzards raged, fueled by the fierce winds and bone-chilling moisture from the North Sea. Storms lasted for days at a time and snow covered the ground most of the time the Burgesses were there. The men were hard pressed to get in even a single round of golf. Despite the poor weather the family enjoyed their holiday to their homeland, which was highlighted by Chay and Harriet's silver wedding anniversary party. The celebration was held in the elegant Victorian era Guild Hall on High Street in the center of town. The supper and dance was a grand event featuring an assembly of many friends and relatives most of whom were at the wedding 25 years before. Chay and Hat extended their visit to Scotland until the end of March, while young Charlie was off the very next day after the anniversary party, anxious to return to America and his fiancée.

• The Golf Center Shifts to America •

Young Charlie brought some insightful and interesting news back to the States with him regarding golf's relative fortunes in Great Britain and America. The remarks he made prompted the *Boston Traveler* to run a banner headline across the Friday edition of the sports section, which read: "BURGESS DECLARES GOLF CENTER SHIFTING TO UNITED STATES." The paper's newest young reporter and golf enthusiast Eddie Lowery wrote the story. It was his first major byline. Lowery, the one-time caddie for Francis Ouimet, did very well as a golfer in his own right. As a teenager, he had served as the summertime caddie master at Woodland on Chay's staff for a while and won two Massachusetts State Amateur titles before assuming his position on the *Traveler* staff. He would team up with Chay Burgess to tie for lowest net in the final NEPGO Am-Pro of the 1922 season and then go on to win the 1927 Massachusetts Amateur before leaving to settle in California where he made his fortune as an automobile dealer. In the West, he teamed with Byron Nelson to win the Bing Crosby Pro-Am in 1955. He became a mentor to young golfers himself and among his protégés were 1964 U.S. Open Champion Ken Venturi, 1956 U.S. Amateur Champion E. Harvie Ward, and tour pro Bob E. Smith.

Lowery's report on young Charlie's trip to Scotland clearly documented the rise of American golf and the diminishing British dominance in the sport. Between his own observations and in conversing with other professionals, young Charlie came to the conclusion that the world's golf center, which had been the British Isles for centuries, was now clearly in the process of shifting to the United States and would do so within two years. He also reported that golfing conditions were never so bad in the history of the game in England as they were at the time. The aftermath of the World War and the flu pandemic were still acutely felt in Britain. Thousands of young men and women who represented a generation of new golfers had been lost. Money and resources used to combat war and disease left Great Britain in extremely difficult financial times.

He spoke of the experiences of George Duncan, the well-known British professional who along with Abe Mitchell had just toured the United States. Included in that tour was the widely publicized match with Ouimet and Guilford. "Duncan was the most popular golf instructor in the British Isles at the time yet he averaged less than two lessons a day since returning from his last American tour. Under normal conditions Duncan would have averaged between 10 and 12 lessons each day." Charlie continued, "If Duncan, who is the most popular pro on the other side of the Atlantic is not making enough out of the golf game to live on, what can all of the other professionals be doing? There is only one outlet to the present golfing situation on the other side and that is the United States. It is safe to predict that every one of the leading British professionals, and many others, too, will leave for the United States just as soon as they can get signed up with some good club . . . "

When Duncan and Mitchell finished their tour of the United States the year before, they emphatically declared that they would not be back again in any time soon. However, when they discovered the downturn in the British golf scene, they quickly decided to sign up with the next touring group of British stars heading for America in 1922. The group included Chay's old friends Jimmy Braid, John Henry Taylor, Harry Vardon, and Alex Herd. As far as purchasing golf clubs in the old country was concerned, young Burgess stated, "It was almost impossible to buy in any quantity Winton or Stewart clubs." The reason? Both of the factories were contracted by American concerns for their entire output and the contracts were for the foreseeable future, at least for months ahead.

Charlie had decided to return on the *Aquitania* hoping its large size would provide a greater amount of comfort to him in the rough winter seas than would one of the smaller vessels he had been thinking about using. It was a wise decision and it would be hard to imagine the kind of voyage a smaller ship would have made on the rough crossing he experienced. The seas were so rough that at one point, the captain ordered all power stopped and the giant ship "hove to" for the comfort of the passengers. Even with the ship's "sea anchors" out in place, the great vessel was fiercely tossed about and the waves smashed in 17 portholes and flooded parts of the lower deck. The damage continued and in the midst of the rush of seawater on board, a fire broke out as well to add to the seriousness of the situation. Thankfully no one was injured and the damage to the ship was discovered to be relatively minor.

Young Charlie succeeded in returning safely to the United States and brought with him a special new club called the "rustless iron," which was all the rage in England. The club was described as an ordinary steel club with a secret "special composition" that kept it from rusting. The Winton firm of Montrose, which produced the club, was sure of its success and planned to open up American agencies in New York, Boston, Philadelphia, and throughout the West to promote their advanced product.

Further evidence of Charlie's prophecy of eventual U.S. golf supremacy was borne out by the increasing dominance of American golfers during the decade of the twenties. American-born golfers demonstrated their ability to master the game even on British links. From 1922 to 1930, Walter Hagen and amateur Bobby Jones won The Open seven times between them. When Jones won his first British Open in 1926, it was also a 1–2–3–4 finish for the USA. At home after Jesse Guilford's 1921 U.S. Amateur victory, Jones won America's National Amateur Championship four times (1924–25–27–28) during the decade, accentuating the continuing ascension of American-born golfers in the world of golf. Homebred American pros Hagen and Sarazen became internationally renowned stars as evidenced by their six American PGA championships during the twenties. Between 1922 and 1930 the U.S. Open was won by Americans, Sarazen (1922) and Jones (1923, 1926. 1929. 1930), five times.

It was clear that American golf had entered a new era, an era ushered in, to a great extent, thanks to the enlightened guidance of the early transplanted Scottish teaching professionals who had taught America the game at the thousands of clubs that had been created throughout the nation during the past three decades.

• The PGA Reforms •

Chay and Hat returned to America in April on board the *Mauretania*. They made the crossing without incident and brought back with them another nephew, Frank Nicoll, to work as a clubmaker in Chay's shop.

The still independent New England Professional Golfers' Organization met in May and elected Chay Burgess as their leader once again. They announced another full tournament schedule of 14 events, from May until November. Of the 14, ten were at Massachusetts clubs, with one each in Maine, New Hampshire, Connecticut, and Rhode Island, the idea being to give the members in those states at least one opportunity to play in a PGO event without the need of a long journey. As golf reporter Larry Paton of the *Boston Transcript* put it, "The tournaments give the boys a chance to see one another often and to get practice which they otherwise would not get, what with their nose at the instruction grindstone six days a week." Paton was a better than average golfer himself and was often among the top finishers in the Pro-Ams and golf writer outings.

At the annual meeting of the New England professionals, a very important step was taken towards reconciliation with the Professional Golfers' Association of America. The initial and almost instant success of the New England golfers in running their own affairs and meeting the needs of members was well noted in golfing circles around the country and particularly by the PGA leadership.

As a direct result of the 1921 insurrection of Chay's New England golfers, a thorough reorganization of the PGA of America began at once and was completed by 1923. The constitution of the national body was completely revised to allow each regional section to be entirely self-governing. Instead of large unwieldy sections, often thousands of miles in area administered by the national office in New York, the PGA adopted a structure of smaller associations run by locally elected officers who had the needs of the district fully in mind. Each section also elected a member to sit on a national executive committee to deal with matters of nationwide importance.

Having successfully made their point, the New Englanders voted to become affiliated once again with the Professional Golfers' Association of America, as a sectional body, without in any way losing their identity as a strictly New England organization for New England golf professionals. The NEPGO Executive Committee also decided to appoint four delegates to the PGA annual meeting, one serving as a member of the PGA executive committee. After the New Englanders rejoined the national group, the PGA referred to them as the New England Professional Golfers' Association (NEPGA), with Chay Burgess remaining as the group's president. However, the members of the New England press corps still often referred to the New England pros as the New England Professional Golfers' Organization, or NEPGO, for many years after, and the legally incorporated NEPGO did not formally dissolve until 1942.

The 1922 summer schedule of NEPGO (now NEPGA) events continued with the great success that had been enjoyed the previous year. In May, Chay was enjoying a fine round of golf in an amateur-pro event at the Commonwealth Golf Club in Newton. He and his partner were among the leaders going into the final few holes when he was struck on the shoulder by an errant drive of the amateur player in the group behind him. The affable Burgess, who still retained his delightful Scottish brogue, jokingly shouted back to the apologetic player that, "the shot does na count unless you hit me in the head!" Apparently none the worse for wear, Chay and his partner went on to finish in a tie for third place with a net score of 140 for the 36 holes.

In June, the 72-hole NEPGA Championship for the Donald Ross Cup was held at Woodland. Both Chay and young Charlie were entered, although Charlie would play only 36 holes, as he was still a Class C or assistant professional. The one-time Woodland pro Gil Nicholls won the four-round event once again with a score of 299. Nicholls led the field by nine strokes in his impressive win. Chay, now forty-eight years old, finished in the middle of the pack, shooting 82 for each round. Young Charlie was nowhere to be seen when play ended. Perhaps personal matters preoccupied him, as he was to wed his sweetheart Kitty McCarthy the very next week. After a brief honeymoon, young Charlie was back on the job witnessing first-hand his confident prediction that the golf center of the world was shifting to America.

Young Charlie's recent observations on American golf seemed well substantiated considering the many promising new faces among the nation's professionals like Leo Diegel, Johnny Golden, Bill Mehlhorn,

Johnny Farrell, and Gene Sarazen. These newcomers joined experienced national professional performers Walter Hagen, Jim Barnes, Mike Brady, Tommy Kerrigan, Jock Hutchison, Gil Nicholls, and many other successful homebred or long-settled transplants. Great new American amateurs Jess Sweetser, Fred Wright, and George Von Elm joined experienced amateur golfers Chick Evans, Bob Gardner, Francis Ouimet, and Jesse Guilford to clearly tip the scales of golf supremacy from Britain to the United States in the twenties. Finally, perhaps the most influential golfer of the time to join the list, amateur or pro, was Atlanta's Bobby Jones, who only played competitively from 1923 to 1930, yet in that time won thirteen major tournaments including his "Grand Slam" of the British Amateur, the British Open, the U.S. Open, and the U.S. Amateur all in one year. It was the golden age of golf in America.

• Jesse, Francis, and the Walker Cup •

Chay's prize pupils Ouimet and Guilford were central figures in regard to the who's who of American golfing stars responsible for the 1920's balance of power shift to the United States.

Francis's latest win was a victory in the Houston Invitational in the summer of 1922. Since his National Amateur title in 1914, he had won the Massachusetts Amateur three more times, the Western Open in 1917, and the North South Amateur at Pinehurst in 1920. He was runner-up to Chick Evans in the 1920 National Amateur, and in 1921 was the medalist in the opening round of the National Amateur. During the war years Francis and Jesse had combined to play in countless exhibition and charity four-ball matches against the world's best golfers.

Jesse, for his own part, was the latest National Amateur Champion and would join Francis on the first Walker Cup team to challenge the British for the championship of amateur golf between them. George H. Walker, former president of the USGA in 1920 (and grandfather and great-grandfather of American Presidents George H. W. Bush and George W. Bush), put up a trophy for the international team play between American and British amateurs. Both Ouimet and Guilford had been chosen to participate in an informal version of the competition in

1921 that was held at Hoylake, England, just prior to the British Amateur of that year.

The first formal Walker Cup matches began in 1922. Ouimet, Guilford, Bobby Jones, Chick Evans, Robert Gardner, Max Marston, William Fownes Jr., and Jess Sweetser represented the U.S. against the British team of Cyril Tolley, Roger Wethered, John Craven, Colin Aylmer, W. B. Torrance, W. W. MacKenzie, C. V. L. Hooman, and Bernard Darwin.

Darwin, the British journalist who covered the 1913 Open win of Ouimet, was sent to report on the Walker Cup matches but had to step in to play against the Americans at Southampton, New York, when the British team captain fell ill. The United States team took that initial Walker Cup match and won again in 1923 at St. Andrews, in 1924 at Garden City, again at St. Andrews in 1926, and also in 1928 at Chicago. Jesse was on the team in 1922, 1924, and 1926, while Francis was a player and captain of the squad eight times from 1922 to 1934 and non-playing captain of the Walker Cup Team four times from 1936 to 1949.

• Golf Grows in the Twenties •

During the twenties, the remarkable building boom of new golf courses and country clubs in every state of the nation was another measure of the continually growing interest the citizens of United States had for the game. The 50 new golf clubs established in Massachusetts alone, from 1920 to 1929, were indicative of the continuous expansion of the game in America during the decade.

In 1923, the Woodland Golf Club had Donald Ross remodel the course and a new clubhouse was built to replace the old Monroe Mansion, which the membership had long outgrown. The handsome new Georgian-styled brick building was tastefully built to provide all of the comforts and conveniences a modern golf club should have, including a thoroughly modern and well-designed shop and sales area for its professional. Much of the business of the New England Professional Golfers' Association was done in Burgess's new shop and, in its third year, the organization was firmly established as the voice of the region's professionals. Chay stepped aside as the NEPGA president, but young Charlie was elected secretary-treasurer of the group for 1923 and kept the family close to the organization. The season passed with another full slate of NEPGA-sponsored events and the usual golfing activities of the New England summer.

In August, John Cowan of the Oakley Country Club in Watertown, Massachusetts, won the monthly New England PGA tournament after a playoff with Herbert Lagerblade of Bristol, Connecticut. Chay experienced one of his most memorable moments of the season on the seventeenth green during the first round of that outing. Seconds after word of the arrival of his first grandchild was shouted by one of his friends in the gallery, he missed an easy two-foot birdie putt. Shortly after that, his excitement under control, he celebrated the birth of little Charles Burgess III in more characteristic fashion by shooting his final round in 36, inclusive of a six, which observers noted wasn't bad for an old grandfather!

Cowan won the contest but runner-up Lagerblade attracted a lot of attention by using his controversial steel-shafted golf clubs. This was a period when manufacturers and golf innovators were trying out many new materials and types of equipment. The USGA had banned the use of the steel clubs in their events but the NEPGA, once again showing leadership and concern for its members, had allowed them in their event. It would not take long for the USGA rules to adapt to the new clubs that were being so heavily advertised and promoted by manufacturers, who naturally stood to gain from the change over from hickory shafts to steel. Of course, the club pro would also have an interest in the new clubs, both on the course and in his shop.

The Horton Manufacturing Company from Bristol, Connecticut, which was Lagerblade's hometown, created the Bristol steel golf shaft, patented as far back as 1910. The advertisements they ran in the monthly magazine published by the PGA for its members extolled the virtues of the steel shaft and suggested that the change to steel would be inevitable. An early golf magazine advertisement read: "The Bristol steel golf shaft is going big. Golfers are buying it because they like it. They are telling their friends of it. Nothing can stop this word of mouth advertising. . . . You will find the Bristol steel golf shaft does not become shop worn. Neither will it rust, crack or warp." The eventual introduction and acceptance of steel-shafted clubs was just one of the many advances in the golf industry that flourished in the twenties. Experimental clubs and balls of all types were common. Improvements in greenskeeping techniques through the use of chemical fertilizers and insecticides for the first time literally changed the look and play on America's courses during the 1920s. Common fungi and other diseases that plagued many courses such as "dollar spots" on the greens, were now controllable, thanks to the innovations of the era.

Another interesting indicator of the great popularity of golf during the twenties was the proliferation of indoor winter golf schools. The indoor facilities were created so that the northern golfer, unable or unwilling to travel south, could try to maintain or improve his game when the courses were covered with snow and ice. Actually, even snow-covered links did not stop the hardiest golfers. Charlie had a bucket of red paint handy during the winter months to color the golf balls that were used when a light coat of snow covered the fairways. But most of the golf "played" in New England during the winter was done indoors at cleverly created sites. Chay and young Charlie initially strung up three netted shooting areas within the spacious basement of the new Woodland clubhouse, and many other teaching professionals set up indoor golf shops throughout the Boston area. Fred Low, pro at the Unicorn Club, had two roomy nets at the Boston Athletic Association building, and Matt Campbell of Essex set up shop in the sporting goods department of the Jordan Marsh Company in downtown Boston. Chay and Charlie later established an elaborate indoor golf facility in Boston, at the site of an underused automobile parking garage in Park Square near the luxurious Statler Hotel. The golf school featured "holes" that were canvas targets painted to resemble greens in the distance, real sand traps, putting greens with artificial turf, and even a brook with running water and real goldfish to add to the faux outdoor atmosphere. Their winter golf school attracted many Boston businessmen who would often take an hour off from work to get in a few swings and a lesson from Chay or Charlie.

• Guilford and Burgess Win New England Crown •

Chay may have tried one or two of Herb Lagerblade's innovative new steel-shafted clubs around this time, but he was still playing with his own "Cha" Burgess Special handcrafted hickories when he teamed up with Jesse Guilford for the biggest attraction of the 1924 season, the New England Amateur-Pro Championship. The tournament was held at the new Charles River Country Club in Newton in late September. Due to a scheduling quirk the championship was held the day *after* daylight savings time had ended and many of the two-man teams were still out on the course as darkness fell. Conditions were made even tougher because there was a brisk breeze all afternoon and the holes were reported to be cut in "rather ticklish positions, not exactly conducive to low scoring," especially in the glare of an early setting autumn sun and then in the dusky conditions that followed.

Guilford had just returned to Boston after a rather poor showing in the 1924 National Amateur held at the Merion Cricket Club. He had faced off against his friend Ouimet in the middle round of the tournament and unfortunately both of Chay's students were not playing as well as expected. It seemed to a casual observer that neither one of the great stars wanted to beat the other in that match-up as, they were both pulling shots and missing putts they normally would have made easily. Francis finally won the match 4 and 3, with both he and Jesse shooting in the low 80's. Francis went on to the next round, but lost the semi-final to Bobby Jones. Jones, the "Atlanta Peach," then finished off George Von Elm, 9 and 8 in the final.

Partnered again with his old friend and instructor in this New England match, Jesse shook off his recent drab national play and shot two very sharp rounds of 74. The former national champion's play alone could likely have carried the team to victory but old Chay Burgess, or "good old Charlie" as he was also often called now, was on top of his game as well. At nearly fifty-one, the senior professional was shooting some of the best golf he had in a while, as he recently recorded successive rounds of 75, 74, and 73 at Woodland as a tune-up for the championship.

Chay started the first round of the Amateur-Professional Championship with a birdie three, and when Jesse exploded for a seven on the final hole of the same round, Chay got another birdie to save the hole. He continued to pick up whenever Jesse faltered and his excellent golf accounted for saving the team three strokes in the last round. Burgess and Guilford posted combined scores of 68 and 72 for a 36-hole total of

140 and captured the "Down East" Championship by four strokes over the home club pair of John Keenan and amateur Edmund Childs. Chay and Jesse's names went on the impressive championship trophy right next to the names of their good friends Harry Bowler and Francis Ouimet, the unsuccessful defending champions. The NEPGA Pro-Am was one of the last events of the season, and it was a very meaningful win for the old pro to share with his good friend and pupil.

Young Charlie, now a new father himself, remained an assistant to his father for most of the 1920s, except for brief summer stays at the Hatherly Country Club in North Scituate, Massachusetts. Hatherly was located about 50 miles away from the Newton Lower Falls apartment where Charlie, Kitty, and baby Charlie resided. It was a long commute by the steam train lines, first to Boston and then south to North Scituate, but once Charlie arrived at the picturesque Hatherly course, one can easily imagine why he suffered such a long ride to get there. The first several holes of Hatherly were set against a backdrop of salt marshes, salt-water inlets, and the Atlantic Ocean. The sea breezes blowing over the links were reminiscent of his boyhood home in Montrose. The Hatherly Club was probably the closest thing to a real links course in the Boston area, and young Charlie was able to enjoy a couple of seasons at this summer-only club. Hatherly was only open from Memorial Day to Labor Day, so Charlie still could retain his links to Woodland and Newton as he obtained his senior rating there in 1925.

At home, the youngest Burgess family member was getting his share of attention from Chay and Hat. When Baby Charlie was learning to talk, he got a bit confused when addressing Chay and Hat. The adults attempted to teach baby Charlie to call Chay "Granddad," and to call Hattie "Nana." But little Charlie got them mixed up and wound up calling Chay "Nana" and Hat "Grammy." The names stuck. So Chay Burgess, renowned professional golfer, internationally known football player, and champion coach was now also a Nana!

Times were very good and the fortunes of the Burgess clan were continually rising in the 1920's. Both Chay and his son were doing quite well. A large and prosperous membership at Woodland assured them of plenty of lessons and customers in the pro shop. Chay had a healthy bank account and was able to invest a bit in stocks, bonds and other investments. Lavish presents at Christmas time, like an incredibly detailed rocking horse imported from France, were given to baby Charlie. Even a purebred Scottish Terrier pup named Thomas David of Perth, or Tommy Ta-Ta, as baby Charlie called him, graced the Burgess household in this period of comfortable living. A baby sister joined little Charlie in 1925. All her family would know Mary Alice Burgess simply as "Sister," as she and her brother grew up in the exciting and now quite prosperous golfing world of their father and grandfather.

• The PGA, the USGA, and the Open •

The successes that Chay enjoyed in the twenties, including the success of his New England Professional Golfers' Organization, were well documented and he was grateful for his good fortune. But the fortunes of other professional golfers and the PGA of America were still very much dependent upon the administration of the United States Golf Association. As the final arbitrators of golf matters in America, they retained the last word on the professionally dominated but amateur-administered U.S. Open.

Changes to American golf in matters advantageous to the interests of the professional golfer often came very slowly and usually very reluctantly. As recently as February of 1923, the PGA of America had made an important appeal to the USGA regarding the format for the qualifying rounds of the National Open. The pros desired to have sectional qualifications, one in the East and one in the West, to lessen the congested play that had been plaguing recent Opens and to make it easier for PGA members to try and qualify at a course that was closer to their homes. The USGA dug in its heels over the issue and refused to give in to the PGA's rather modest request citing that it was foreseen as being too difficult to secure three different courses for national open play each year, one for the Open itself, the other two for the sectional qualifications. They also somewhat paternalistically asserted that they thought the PGA considered the Open as a sort of "old home week" for their professionals as they got together from all over the nation. They thought that they were doing the PGA a good service by allowing the pros to count on gathering together in one spot every year. The USGA could not understand why the pros would object to a single-site format that also served as a convenient reunion opportunity for its far-flung members.

The 1923 U.S. Open and qualification rounds went on as scheduled at the originally planned single site, the Inwood Country Club in Inwood, New York. Out of the 360 entries, 77 qualified, 69 of that number pros, but *Mr.* Robert T. Jones, the almost invincible amateur from Atlanta, won the event after a play-off with professional Robert A. Cruickshank from the Shackamaxon Country Club of Westfield, New Jersey.

In 1924, the PGA's reasoning regarding regional qualifications ultimately prevailed and the USGA arranged for two qualifying rounds for the Open. One in the East at the Worcester Country Club in Massachusetts and the other in the West at Oak Park Country Club in Illinois. The finals were held in Michigan at the Oakland Hills Course, and the 1924 Open Champion was Chay's associate, transplanted English professional Cyril Walker. Finally, by 1926, 13 cities from coast-to-coast hosted regional U.S. Open qualifying rounds, allowing increased access to the tournament for many more of the nation's hardworking club and teaching pros.

• America's Forgotten Champion •

One of the saddest stories in the struggles of the early professional golfer in America is that of Johnny McDermott, a young professional from Atlantic City, New Jersey. Today he is remembered, if at all, as the answer to the golf trivia question: Who was the youngest American to win the United States Open? McDermott established his all but forgotten record in 1911 when he was just nineteen years old, winning the national championship after a three-way play-off, against Mike Brady and George Simpson. McDermott was also the *first American-born* golfer to win his country's Open. Just the year before McDermott *nearly* won his first U.S. Open at age eighteen, when he lost to Scotsman Alex Smith in another three-way play-off that also included Alex's brother MacDonald Smith. Incredibly McDermott repeated as national champion in 1912 as a twenty-year-old. But his remarkable accomplishments of 1910, 1911, and 1912 have been overshadowed and practically ignored compared to the attention-getting triumph of Francis Ouimet in 1913.

Why? Why were the tremendous achievements of young McDermott, a younger Open champion than Ouimet *and* the first American-born U.S. Open Champion, relegated to relative obscurity by the chroniclers of the times and later by golf historians? The simple answer lies in the fact that he was a professional. Despite his youth, McDermott's status as a professional detracted from his achievement in the eyes of the amateur-controlled American golfing establishment and national press. Ouimet, on the other hand, was the first *amateur* and the first *American* amateur ever to win the nation's Open. In doing so, he had also defeated the world's greatest professionals—including the defending champion McDermott and an assembly of many great British and European champions featuring the legendary Vardon and Ray. The world embraced Ouimet's win as a victory for the common man, an amateur who played the game for sport and not for gain. McDermott's tremendous accomplishments were quickly forgotten after Ouimet's heroics in 1913.

Sometime after relinquishing his U.S. Open crown to Ouimet (reports differ, either in 1914 or 1915), McDermott suffered a physical and mental breakdown and was institutionalized in a sanitarium for about nine years before he attempted a comeback in 1924. McDermott was hospitalized in Norristown, Pennsylvania, where his condition and state of mind was reported as "grave . . . and at times of utter blackness."

In 1922, a glimmer of hope for a recovery began as McDermott expressed a desire to once again play golf. A temporary six-hole course was created on the spacious grounds of the sanitarium exclusively for his rehabilitation. America's new golfing hero Walter Hagen was a frequent visitor to the stricken golfer and made a visit in 1924. Hagen hopefully predicted that "McDermott would again be a factor in American championship golf should the restoration to health be completed."

On December 13, 1924 McDermott left the grounds of the hospital for the first time in about ten years to play in an exhibition best-ball match at the Whitemarsh Valley Country Club in Philadelphia. He declined a suggestion to play under the more lenient winter rules that permitted teeing up the ball for fairway shots and insisted that he play each shot as it lay. He shot 38 for the first nine holes, an amazing performance given his long confinement, and he and his amateur partner defeated two leading area professionals in the match. After his one-day outing, he went back to the hospital, remained confined, and did not take any further advantage of his private course as his friends hoped he would. Worse, he never ventured outside of the grounds to play golf again and his hospitalization continued without much hope of improvement.

Throughout McDermott's long confinement, his fellow professionals remained faithful and attentive to his needs. During August of 1928, they arranged a series of benefit matches for McDermott. Various PGA sections were urged to organize fund-raising exhibitions and the Metropolitan, Long Island, and New Jersey bodies took the lead. Hagen and Gene Sarazen made substantial personal donations to the McDermott fund, as did golf-loving entertainer Al Jolson. The money was used to help pay for his continuing care.

Sadly, the hoped-for recovery of the two-time National Open Champion never occurred and McDermott remained institutionalized for the rest of his life. He died in 1971, a few days before his eightieth birthday.

• Saving the Ryder Cup •

1927 marked the frequently attempted and often-delayed beginning of official international professional team play with the establishment of the Ryder Cup competition. Previous attempts at establishing permanent professional team play between American and British golfers, such as the 1920 proposal, were unsuccessful until English businessman and golf enthusiast Samuel Ryder offered his support. Ryder proffered a trophy and his financial support as incentive for establishing continuous competition between the nations of Great Britain and the United States.

Prior to the British Open in 1926, Mr. Ryder had observed the informal match between Walter Hagen's team of visiting Americans and their English counterparts and thought that the competition should be formalized to become a recurring event. Hagen's American team included Joe Stien, the young New Hampshire pro, Joe Kirkwood, Al Waltrous, long-time transplanted Scotsman McDonald Smith, and British-born but also long-time resident-American professional Jim Barnes.

The establishment of the Ryder Cup competition was also significant as one of several recent watershed events in the relations between the USGA and the PGA of America. The USGA, the official organ of the United States in international golfing affairs, could have had total control over the pre-Ryder Cup event but instead asked Hagen to captain, select, and completely organize the 1926 exhibition team. This gesture by the USGA, not long after the decision to hold and expand regional qualifications for the Open, signaled another subtle but important change of attitude toward the professional game. The USGA made still another significant overture to the professionals proposing that the PGA manage all future international professional team play themselves.

The first official Ryder Cup match was held at Worcester, Massachusetts, in 1927 and the professional golfers of New England were called upon by the PGA to assist with the many details inherent in running this important new international golfing event held in their district.

An important stipulation for the formal 1927 competition was that all members of the United States team had to be American-born and all members of the British team must have been born and currently residing in Great Britain. Unfortunately, the rule left long-time American-based but British-born pros like Barnes, Smith, and many others out in the cold, unable to play for either team. There seemed to be no practical alternative plan that could have satisfied everyone.

Walter Hagen was chosen captain of the U.S. team and was joined by Leo Diegel, Johnny Farrell, Johnny Golden, Bill Mehlhorn, Gene Sarazen, Joe Turnesa, and Al Waltrous. Mike Brady and Al Espinosa were named alternatives. Ted Ray led the invading British team, which included Aubrey Boomer, Archie Compston, George Duncan, George Gadd, Arthur Havers, Herbert Jolly, Fred Robson, and Charles A. Whitcombe. The U.S. team was triumphant, beating the British by a substantial margin 6½ to 1½ in the eight-a-side single match contests and 3 to 1 in foursomes.

The return match of the biannual series was to be held in Leeds, England, in 1929. The PGA of America was now solely responsible for raising the funds needed to send the team overseas. The leftover monies from the gate receipts of the 1927 Worcester match was a relatively meager $1,833.72, not nearly enough to send a ten-man team plus officials overseas for the first return match. It was estimated that the PGA needed nearly $14,000 to send the Ryder Cup team to England. Although the PGA of America was still a relatively young organization, it had grown to include 24 regional sections from across the nation. The largest was the Metropolitan, which included New York with 258 members. Next was Illinois with 187 members, then New England with 158. Total memberships in the PGA of America were nearly 2,000 but unfortunately, less than two-thirds of the members were up-to-date with their dues. The PGA was in dire financial straits. Headquarters put out a desperate plea to its member sections for help. Without a huge and rapid response, the Ryder Cup Challenge series would end almost as soon as it began.

The overwhelming majority of professional golfers in the PGA of America were club-based or teaching professionals. The more high-profile touring pros that made up the Ryder Cup team were few in numbers compared to the rank-and-file club pros. Still, Chay Burgess and his once rebellious teaching pros came forward with a brilliant proposal to save the Ryder Cup, knowing that the continuation of the matches was important for all of golf and for all professionals no matter how they earned their living.

The New England PGA agreed to arrange a unique and unprecedented fund-raising Ryder Cup exhibition match at Chay's home club, Woodland. Young Charlie Burgess was serving as secretary-treasurer of the NEPGA and as such was primarily responsible for the section's fund-raising effort on behalf of the traveling Ryder Cup Team. Who better to organize the event than his father, good old Charlie Burgess, the experienced tournament organizer and founder of the New England Professional Golfers' Organization?

Chay began to call upon his many friends and acquaintances to pull the match together. He assembled a star-studded field of America's greatest and most famous players: Walter Hagen, Gene Sarazen, Johnny Farrell and the incomparable Bobby Jones. He paired up Hagen with Sarazen and matched them against reigning U.S. Open Champion Farrell and Jones, the king of amateur golfers, for a 36-hole best-ball, stroke play match. The participation of Bob Jones in this event to support professional golf was an important and most gracious gesture, symbolic of his personal respect for professional golf and the men who played it. The support of the world's most famous amateur golfer sent a strong message to the rest of the golfing establishment. The time had come to abandon the long-held view that the professional game was a tainted version of a gentleman's game and Jones was willing to donate his time and talents to support the PGA in its time of need.

Hagen, Sarazen, and Farrell were all members of the victorious U.S. Ryder Cup Team of 1927. Hagen was a three-time British Open Champion, including the 1928 contest at Sandwich. He also was a past U.S. Open winner and four-time PGA Champion at this stage of his career. Sarazen had won the PGA twice and had won the U.S. Open in 1922. He would win another U.S. Open, another PGA Championship, and the British Open before his career was over. Johnny Farrell was the new kid on the block having just won the U.S. Open at Olympia Fields. Bobby Jones, the world's most famous amateur, had won the U.S. Open twice and would win it twice more. He had won the U.S. Amateur three times so far and would capture his fourth title in just a few days at nearby Brae Burn Country Club. He would win the National Amateur one last time in 1930 as he would also win the British Amateur, the U.S. Open, and the British Open that same year—his history-making "Grand Slam." Jones was a perennial Walker Cup Team member and probably would have won the PGA Championship as well if he had ever turned professional! It was an incredibly impressive foursome; at the time of the match, the assembled group of players already held 23 major titles between them.

Over 5,000 ardent golf fans flocked to Woodland on a warm and sunny September morning to witness the exciting first round. Chay's renowned celebrity pupil Francis Ouimet volunteered to act as the match's official referee. Francis was still a top-ranked competitor himself, and the addition of his name to the event enhanced its appeal even more. Chay was the Grand Marshal and ruled the exhibition with a firm hand, ensuring that play would not be impeded by the thousands and thousands of eager fans who turned out to see the popular golf stars perform. He often had to halt the gallery's excited rushes with a loud military whistle his nephew Willie Nicoll had used during his tour of duty with the Fifth Black Watch Division in the Highlanders Camp at Verdun fourteen years earlier in the Great War.

Hagen and Sarazen took the lead after the first 18 holes by five strokes. Jones was powering the ball off the tee, his shots a good 10 to 15 yards out in front of Sarazen, his nearest rival for hitting honors. Johnny Farrell was not up to his usual brand of golf. The reigning U.S. Open Champion often hit erratically off the tee and pushed his drives time and again, making the bulk of the work fall on his amateur teammate Jones.

Hagen, or "Sir Walter" as the press often called him, had a great individual round of 67, and his partner's score was a 68 for a dazzling best-ball score 64. Bobby Jones shot a 70 and Farrell scrambled back mightily to get his 73 for the first 18 holes, giving the team a best-ball score of 69. Several poor putts by Jones added to the Jones–Farrell team's problems. His favorite putter, affectionately called "Calamity Jane" by Jones, let him down on a couple of five footers that would have won the holes and brought the team to within three.

Jones and Farrell staged a strong comeback surge in the afternoon round, climbing back from the five-stroke deficit to just one-stroke with one hole to play. The gallery had swollen to over 10,000 by the time the match had wound down to that final hole. At least 5,000 of the spectators crowded around the clubhouse to watch as Bobby Jones, the Atlanta Peach, set up the last shot, an eight-foot putt that could win the hole and finish the exciting match in a tie. Jones drew out his famous putter and took a bead on the line of the putt across a mildly sloping green. He carefully judged the break and slowly drew back on the putt that meant defeat should he miss. His ball started on a perfect arc for the cup but held up a second too long and missed the break by just a fraction of an inch to roll by the upper lip of the cup.

Officially the match went to the Hagen–Sarazen team by one over Jones and Farrell. But the real winner that day was the game of golf and the PGA Ryder Cup team, which benefited from the exciting exhibition sponsored by the New England Professional Golfers' Association. Secretary-Treasurer Charlie Burgess II reported that the match netted over $10,000. The unique fund-raising effort encouraged other PGA sections and individuals to contribute to the Ryder Cup fund as well. The New England PGA became by far the largest single contributor to the fund, and Chay Burgess became the man who saved the Ryder Cup because of his extraordinary ability to organize and produce the important event. The match at Woodland insured that the Ryder Cup challenge would continue and become the revered international event that it is today.

• A Tribute from Francis •

A very special recognition of Chay's special contributions to golf came at the close of the 1920's. In April of 1929, the members of Woodland proposed a celebration of his 20 years of service to the club. Over that 20-year span, the evolution of the professional golfer and respect for his profession in America had come very slowly, even as the game grew very rapidly. A generation had passed since Chay's arrival from Scotland, and in that time most American country clubs and the USGA had finally come to recognize the important contributions of the professional golfer—club and touring pro alike.

Americans were playing golf in record numbers as golf firmly took hold in the national landscape by the end of the twenties. Thanks in large part to the PGA professionals, now numbering in the thousands, America had learned the game and fell in love with it as well. Boston sportswriter Linde Fowler noted that Chay's length of service with one club was an extraordinary accomplishment during the period of golf's rapid growth in America. At the time, his 20 years at one club exceeded the tenure of any other professional in the region if not the country. This longevity was taken as a sign of great respect and a compliment to the man himself because golf club life was something very changeable. The Woodland club had undergone many changes as many old members and club officers left and others took their place. Yet Chay remained with Woodland despite many flattering offers from other clubs. He had renewed his contract after his first year at Woodland with a just a handshake and a gentleman's agreement because he said he would remain and had faith in the club's treatment of him. For his part he never saw the need to alter that agreement for he held that his word was as good as his bond.

As a teacher, Chay estimated that he had easily given over 12,000 lessons since he arrived from Scotland. On a good day in the summer he often was out on his practice tee from seven o'clock in the morning until seven at night. Instead of finding his long hours of teaching irksome and wearing, Chay said that he found them, "interesting because [his] own interest in the game never waned." He went on to say that his interest in the progress of his pupils "over-balanced the physical strain and the monotony of doing the same thing over and over."

Chay had the good fortunate to have been publicly recognized and appreciated for his personal contributions to golf while still active in his profession. And on the occasion of his twentieth year at his club the membership tendered him an evening that he never forgot. Besides the usual platitudes and gifts, he was presented with two thousand dollars in gold coins, a tremendous sum of money at the time. Twenty $100 gold pieces, one for each year of his service, were presented to him on a lovely silver platter that was also part of the tribute. Even more important to Chay than the money and gifts were the words his dear old friend and pupil Francis Ouimet prepared in homage to him that night.

During the middle of March, just a few weeks prior to Chay's testimonial, Francis had been suddenly stricken with a major abdominal ailment. He had to remain hospitalized while others took over his expected role as master of ceremonies at Chay's celebration. The words that Francis would have given in his speech, words that would have been delivered that evening and then left only to the listener's memory were, in a serendipitous twist of fate, preserved forever in a letter that he sent to be read at the gathering.

The handwritten letter read:

> "It is with deep regret I am unable to be among those of you who have gathered tonight to honor 'good old Charlie.' I use the word 'old' merely as a term of affection because after all Charlie is still only a youth and one who will never grow old.
>
> It was my good fortune to meet Charlie soon after he became associated with the Woodland Golf Club in 1909. We had a golf team at Brookline High School and Woodland

generously allowed us to play many of our matches over their course. Thus it was we came to know him because each time we appeared on the scene Charlie was there with his cheery hellos and general good nature.

Whatever progress I have made in golf I owe directly to Charlie Burgess. In 1910 and 1911 I played with him often—took lessons—and had the satisfaction of seeing my scores drop from around 85 to the low seventies. I would give anything if I could play those Sunday afternoon matches over once more because they represent red-letter days in my life. He always had the faculty of putting me in the proper frame of mind when entering an important match and I repeat he taught me whatever I know about the game.

I think it is wonderful that our club has been so fortunate as to have had Charlie's services for twenty years and he is just as important—in my opinion to the future welfare of Woodland—as anything we can possibly have.

It is useless for me to continue on because I fully realize it is impossible in mere words to do justice to Charlie's twenty years of honest and faithful service. His first thought has always been directed to the members of the Woodland Golf Club. If you were taking a golf lesson from him and your time was up—he gladly gave you an extra fifteen minutes and many times more. I only bring this point up to show his unselfish disposition. I would like him to know that I sincerely wish him continued years of good health and prosperity because they don't make them any better than 'good old Charlie.' Regards to all."

Sincerely, Francis Ouimet

The moving tribute from Francis and the Woodland members was a wonderful way for Chay to start the new golf season. The year was also off to a great start for Chay as his New England Professional Golfers' Association began its ninth year and young Charlie was again elected as Secretary-Treasurer of the NEPGA. The organization once again came up with a strong slate of regional tournaments and the membership continued to grow.

• The End of the Decade •

During the summer of 1929 Chay had the pleasure of seeing another one of his rather special amateur pupils achieve remarkable success on the links. Young Pearly Crosby had been working with Chay for the past couple of seasons after initially learning the game from nearby Sandy Burr Golf Club professional Ralph Thomas. Crosby had a severely crippled left hand as a result of a childhood accident. Unable to close his hand around the club shaft, he had to rely on a built-up grip to compensate. Adapting a club grip was not a difficult task for a skilled club maker like Chay, and he started working with Crosby between 1925 and 1928. In 1928 Crosby went to the finals of the New England Amateur Championship and lost 75–73 to twenty-two-year-old Bill Blaney of Brae Burn. Crosby broke amateur records at a number of area clubs, including one at the South Shore Country Club in 1928. The previous record he broke at South Shore was a 71, which Francis Ouimet had set there just the week before! In 1929 he held the amateur record on a newly reconfigured Woodland course. Crosby competed and excelled with no consideration given to his handicap except the built-up grip on his clubs. Pearly shot a 70 at Woodland, which also tied him with the professional record holder—his instructor Chay Burgess.

Jesse Guilford, meanwhile, had slipped just a bit in his game, but only just a bit. When the Massachusetts Golf Association handicap list was published in 1929, Jesse had dropped in the rankings to a one-stroke handicap. One handicap or not, Guilford managed to win his second Massachusetts Open that year. Francis Ouimet remained the state's only scratch golfer.

Another bit of good news for Burgess was that Francis had recovered enough from his intestinal condition to resume his golf and prepare for the National Amateur at Pebble Beach, California. Francis went out to the September event and made a valiant effort to try and recapture the crown he had won in 1914. Francis began as one of 140 starters and defeated the sensational new West Coast star Lawson Little by two holes with one to play (2 and 1) in the third round. Interestingly, Ouimet's encounter with Little marked still another link to Charlie Burgess. Little was a pupil of Chay's nephew Willie Nicoll, who had become the professional at the Buresford Country Club in San Mateo, California, in 1923, and the seaside course at Buresford was the only West Coast course designed by Chay's good friend Donald Ross. Francis made it as far as the semifinal round of the National at Pebble Beach where he lost 6 and 5 to Harrison Johnson, the eventual tournament winner.

The failure of Francis, now in his early thirties, to win another National Amateur was causing many observers to speculate that he was all through with championship caliber play. They said that his star was in decline because so many younger more promising players were moving up the ranks and that it would be unlikely for Ouimet to ever win another major tournament again. It was a prophecy that Chay took great exception to and was one that his most famous student would soon dispel.

As the decade drew to a close, Chay was most thankful and pleased with his success and good fortune. He reflected on the amazing growth and prosperity both he and the game of golf enjoyed in America since his arrival in 1909. But the unprecedented disaster that befell the nation on October 24, 1929, when the stock market crashed, soon turned the American dream Chay had been enjoying into a nightmare. Chay and his family did not experience any sudden dramatic personal or financial consequences, but the dark days of the Great Depression soon slowly began to erode the good life they had come to know through golf, and the survival of the game itself was in danger.

11 1930–1934

> "There is a happy medium of speed in the backswing. Many point out that it should be done slow, but that is largely exaggerated because so many golfers are tempted to hurry. The left hand plays the important part in pushing the club back and pushing it forward, while the right merely guides. If the right begins to overpower, perfection disappears."
>
> —Charlie Burgess

• Ouimet and Guilford Challenge Von Elm and Burke •

The $2,000 in gold coins Chay received in April could not have been presented to him at a better time. A modest stock and bond portfolio he had acquired over the years quickly fell victim to the October 1929 crash. A small savings account, the devalued stocks, the family sedan, and the inventory of Chay's golf shop comprised the Burgess family estate at the beginning of the thirties. The relatively affluent existence they enjoyed throughout the twenties did not suddenly come crashing down, but the effects of the Depression inevitably hit home as the economy ground slowly to a near halt.

As the fortunes of wealthy golf club members declined, every club and teaching professional in America began to suffer. The very existence of a private country club in the 1920's and 1930's revolved around the affluent members of society. As the net wealth of the upper classes lessened, sometimes slowly, sometimes overnight, membership in a golf club was one of the luxuries given up early. With fewer members, the professional at the private clubs had a much smaller customer base and business slowly began to dry up.

Woodland managed to keep the specter of closure away from the Auburndale links despite the constant fear that it would go under, as many other clubs did, thanks to the many good years the club enjoyed before the Depression. The club had enough golf enthusiasts still able to get out for a round to forget about things for a while, as sports and entertainment were a needed form of relief during the troubled decade. Despite the Depression, Chay was once again able to be a part of another great exhibition match for the public's enjoyment at the beginning of the decade.

Just after the 1931 U.S. Open and weeks before the National Amateur, Chay and his friends from Woodland staged another golf extravaganza reminiscent of the successful Ryder Cup exhibition match of 1928. Thousands of golf enthusiasts lined the Woodland course in late August as the current U.S. Open Champion Billy Burke and George Von Elm, the runner-up to Burke in an unbelievably dramatic 72-hole play-off, came to Woodland as part of a barnstorming exhibition tour. They were challenged to a 36-hole best-ball team match by Woodland's amateur stars Guilford and Ouimet.

The 1931 U.S. Open at the Inverness Club in Toledo, Ohio, was one of the most sensational and exciting golf tournaments ever played. In order to participate in the Open, the PGA championship, and almost all of the major tournaments worldwide, regional qualification matches were now commonly required. In over a dozen qualifying rounds held all across the nation, over 1,140 players vied for just 151 qualifying spots. Of that number, only 63 made it on to the 72-hole championship rounds. Out of the final 63, Burke and Von Elm survived, tied at 292 for the championship at the end of regulation play, each averaging 73 shots per round. An all-star line-up of professionals finished close behind. Leo Diegel, Wiffy Cox, Bill Mehlhorn, Gene Sarazen, Mortie Dutra, Walter Hagen, Al Espinosa, Johnny Farrell, and MacDonald Smith all were within seven strokes of the leaders.

A 36-hole play-off was held. In the first round Burke took the lead 73–75 only to have Von Elm shoot a 74 to Burke's afternoon round of 76. The play-off match ended all tied up again at 149!

The next day, the two men were off once more in *another* grueling head to head 36-hole play-off. In the morning round, Burke shot his worst round of the tournament, a 77. Von Elm did better with a 76 but did not seize the opportunity presented to him as the 76 for Von Elm was also his worst outing so far. In the final 18-hole round, Von Elm shot a strong 73, but Burke managed an extraordinary 71, erasing his deficit, and he won the unprecedented 72-hole play-off by *one stroke* and the Open victory was his!

Burke and Von Elm were savvy enough to realize that a nationwide tour would be a profitable venture. Von Elm particularly was known as a "businessman golfer," one of the early sportsmen also who were entrepreneurs. Von Elm came from the amateur ranks before turning professional just prior to the Open. As an amateur, he won the National Amateur Championship in 1926, beating Bobby Jones, and was runner-up to Jones in 1927. Von Elm passed up an interesting and unspecified but reportedly lucrative offer to cover the upcoming 1931 National Amateur Championship for a national radio news syndicate because the amount offered was much less than what he and Burke were each able to get for their exhibition matches. The money they earned was a guaranteed appearance fee and a percentage of the gallery gate, often substantial. Whether or not they won was less important than their participation, as long as they could pull in the spectators. However, they could not afford to lose too often and played hard to enhance their reputations and future drawing power at the gate.

The two Woodland amateur stars were not in the match against Burke and Von Elm for the money, although they were also players that people always enjoyed seeing in competition. As far as the upcoming National Amateur was concerned, Jesse had all but decided to pass it up while Francis was very intent on going to the Beverly Country Club in Chicago to recapture the crown that had eluded him for the past 17 years.

Chay took up position on the first tee in his now-accustomed role as chief marshal and started the best-ball, match-play competition. The traveling professionals got off to a great start shooting a combined 66 for the first 18 holes and had a three-hole advantage at the end of the first round. Individually, Burke had a 72 and Von Elm shot a course record-tying score of 70. Guilford and Ouimet were quickly down in the first round as Jesse was often wild off the tee. Guilford's individual total for the morning round was 77 while Francis was superb, matching Von Elm's record tying performance. The combined best-ball score of the local pair was a 69.

In the afternoon round, the Woodland team began a rally in an attempt to defend their impressive 10-year record of never losing a best-ball match on their home course (since their two-stroke loss to Duncan and Mitchell in 1921). The home team rallied, won the first four holes in succession, and changed their three-hole deficit into a one-hole lead. Burke and Von Elm hung on after that and managed to tie things up at the twenty-fifth hole. Jesse and Francis were determined not to be outdone and clinched the victory at the thirty-fourth hole, 3–2.

Ouimet played brilliant golf, burning up the course with an afternoon round of 69. Even with Jesse's score of 75, the team scored a combined 64 thanks to Francis' great play and the timely great hole from Jesse when it counted. After the match, Burke said,

> "I have heard a lot about Ouimet but I never had seen him play before. After watching him today I cannot imagine any amateur in the field at Chicago beating him. He is so far ahead of the amateurs I have seen play this year that there is no comparison."

Von Elm's reaction was similar,

> "I have always realized Francis was good, but I never realized he was so good until today."

The comments of Burke and Von Elm were most interesting because of the perpetual rumors floating around that after 17 years without a major victory, Francis was considered to be washed-up as a national champion and had little chance to win in Chicago.

Before leaving the Woodland Clubhouse on his way to the next stop on his tour, Von Elm had a few pointed remarks on the USGA's stand on its poorly enforced and often violated expense rule for amateurs. The former amateur star, well qualified to offer his opinion on the matter, commented frankly that:

> "There are very few real amateurs according to the strict interpretation of the rule, very few people who will play in Chicago next week will pay their own expenses to the Windy City. I know for a fact that there are several who will play who cannot stand the expense but they will be there just the same."

Von Elm's remarks echoed the thoughts of many others in regard to the idea of the questionable "special accounts" for needy amateurs. The same type of expense fund that Francis Ouimet and Jesse Guilford were provided with many years before was still allowed by the USGA, in what seemed like a resourceful but somewhat disingenuous design to prevent other promising young amateurs from defecting to the professional side because of financial concerns.

It was a much different situation for Francis in 1931 than it had been in 1913. He had done very well in the banking and trade business and was financially secure enough now to maintain his amateur standing through his own livelihood. This time it would be Francis's old friend Chay who would be the beneficiary of the Woodland members' generosity through a special fund.

Besides being his coach, teacher, and friend, Francis had often referred to Chay as his good luck charm whenever he was beside him in an important match and sincerely wanted him to be with him at the National Amateur in Chicago. As a gesture of the high esteem that the Woodland members held for "Old Charlie," they underwrote his expenses for the trip with Francis. Charlie, the younger, was left in charge of affairs at the clubhouse and Chay depended on his son to take care of business at home. Young Charlie, still as handsome and personable as ever at thirty-four, was able to enjoy the exciting developments of 1931 around the club with Kitty and their children, now ages eight and six, by his side.

• Ouimet's Great Comeback •

Chay left for Chicago by rail on the famous and luxurious train known as the Twentieth Century Limited, catching his sleeper car in Boston before being pulled through to New York for the final run to Chicago. The train rivaled the ocean liners of the day for the comfort and opulence surrounding the passengers on board. The dining car was adorned with heavy oak carvings and thick, sound-absorbing velvet curtains that could create private dining areas. In addition to the formal dining car, there was always a delicious buffet available, a library car, a smoking car, barbershop, observation lounge, staterooms, and game lounges.

The deluxe train ride to Chicago was complemented by the accommodations the Ouimet party found in the Windy City. Chay, Francis, sportswriters Linde Fowler and Bill Cunningham, and the rest of the Boston contingent were quartered at the lovely Del Prado Hotel on the south side of the city. Long a favorite with the golfing crowd because of its proximity to the better Chicago links, the Del Prado billed itself as "distinctly a golfer's hotel," as it also adjoined the Jackson Park Golf Course where it extended its guests free privileges. The hotel was located about a 15-minute automobile ride away from the Beverly Country Club, and one of Chicago's fine woman golf stars, Mrs. Lee Mida, winner of the 1930 Woman's Western Open, graciously acted as chauffeur for the Ouimet group during their stay.

During the practice rounds on Saturday and Sunday, a fierce gale blew up so hard that many of the players picked up and quit or gave up trying to keep a score. One golfer described as a "modest young man from San Francisco" had an outstanding day, despite the gale force winds, and the press quickly picked up his name as a dark horse contender. The player was Lawson Little, who shot a 73, two over par. He had a 38 going out and a 35 on the home nine, which was quite an accomplishment in the difficult conditions. The trick to playing the winds was one that Burgess and other Scottish pros had had to master or else they would have perished on the seacoast links courses of their native land. Because Little was the pupil of Chay's West Coast nephew, Willie Nicoll, it was no surprise to Chay that young man must have learned to "cheat the wind" at his oceanside course in California just as it was done back on the links of Montrose.

As play began for the qualifying rounds, Bobby Jones was present this time only as a newspaper observer and a radio commentator because he had recently decided to retire from competitive golf at the early age of twenty-eight. His surprise retirement and Von Elm's recent switch to the professional side of things left the field wide open for a new National Amateur Champion to emerge. And there were plenty of new, young, and promising contenders for the crown. One hundred and fifty-one hopefuls assembled at the Beverly to participate in the National Amateur after surviving their grueling regional qualification matches.

At the end of the first day's qualifying round, a local Chicago boy, Jack Westland, fired a 72 to lead the field. Behind him was Gus Moreland, a twenty-year-old from Dallas, with a 73. Francis, now thirty-eight, showing great iron play and playing the wind to perfection, was in a five-way tie for the next position at 74. In the afternoon a strong and steady rain fell, reminiscent of the conditions during Francis's famous Open victory of 1913. He shot a 78 for a qualifying total of 152 just four strokes off the pace set by the medalist Johnny Lehman, another local Chicago golfer.

The first round of tournament play began with 32 survivors paired off in match play brackets. Francis was up against John Shields of the Rainier Golf and Country Club in Seattle, Washington, who had qualified with a 151.

Francis almost put himself out of the running in the first round, not by his play, but because of a simple accident with a match. Francis, like many of the adults of the era, indulged in the habit of smoking cigarettes. Francis would often light up a cigarette while playing a round of golf, perhaps to relax him. On this occasion the wooden match sputtered, backfired, and flared up when Francis struck it, and he burned himself badly on his index finger. Now an injury to a finger of a golfer in a big tournament might not seem like a serious problem, but as one newsman put it, "it is like a bad charley horse in football or a sprained thumb in a boxing match." It could have caused havoc with Francis's grip. In fact, the burn did fester and swell even with ointment and covered with adhesive. Fortunately, Francis seemed to be able to adapt to his temporary disability well enough to continue his play. Bill Cunningham of the *Boston Post* suggested that from then on whenever Francis desired a smoke while playing in a big contest, someone else should light his cigarette, unless Francis was presented with a windproof lighter. Cunningham suggested that cigar-smoking Chay Burgess keep a close eye on Francis and do the honor of lighting up for his pupil because "the match was never born that could burn old Charlie's callused dukes!"

Even with a burnt and swollen finger, Francis advanced through the first 18-hole match play round 4–3 and through the next round in horrible rainy weather 5–4 against Frank Connolly of Lake Shore, Michigan. The rain had begun the night before and came down so hard and long it flooded the greens, filled up the holes with water, and made the fairways look like swamps. An idea of the intensity and volume of the rain can be understood from the fact that when Mrs. Mida picked up Francis, Chay, and Linde Fowler to drive them to the course, she had to detour around several underpasses because dozens of automobiles were disabled and submerged in them.

Chay woke up very early that morning, and before he and Francis had breakfast, Chay took a moment to sit and write a note to young Charlie:

September 2, 1931
Hotel Del Prado

Dear Charlie,

Had a fine trip out. I am having a good time here. Harry Hampton is Pro at this club and was asking for everybody. The course is about eight miles from Chicago. Francis and I drive out in the morning and night. Might you will have seen, he is playing fine. I have just been in to wake him up as he starts at 9:30 and it is now eight o'clock. How is everything? Hope you are selling a package of tees now and then. Well Charlie, I think we will leave here Saturday night, but will let you know before we do so. I sent a card to little Charlie yesterday. I hope he and Mary are well. Tell them I will see them next week. I hope Francis wins out as I know it will help me. Will give you all the news when I come back. I am hurrying for breakfast. Be good.

Your loving pal
Chay

The torrential rain continued the next day and in the rain-swept third round of the event, Francis faced twenty-one-year-old Paul Jackson of Kansas City. Much had been made about Francis's supposed decline because of his advancing age, but age proved not to be a factor when Francis cleanly dispatched his younger challenger 7–6. Nineteen-year-old sharpshooter Billy Howell from Richmond, Virginia, was Ouimet's opponent in the next day's semi-final as the weather finally let up. Perhaps Francis felt a little bit like Vardon or Ray must have felt when he faced them as a youngster in 1913, now playing the role of the older and more experienced champion. But Francis was not about to let Howell enjoy the thrill of a similar victory if he could help it.

As the match progressed, the Boston entourage followed Francis closely around the course. Chay as always was never far from his side and was a steady, reassuring presence for Francis, keeping him calm and providing him with timely advice when necessary. For example, at the thirteenth hole Francis pulled his tee shot into the rough to the left of the fairway. Francis looked at the resting place of the ball from the tee, then looked over to the right side of the fairway, where there was a fence and out of bounds markers running down the hole. Out of bounds in the tournament meant a loss of stroke and distance. Francis turned to Charlie as he done countless times before, and as if he was reading his mind, Chay said to Francis, "That's right, err on the safe side, better thirty yards too much to the left than one yard too much to the right on this hole." To which Linde Fowler joked to anyone in hearing distance about the rather obvious advice, "Canny boys, these old-time Scotch professionals!"

Having endured first the incredible winds, then a burnt finger, the driving rain, and a series of opponents all under twenty-five years old and reportedly on top of their games, the thirty-eight-year-old Ouimet dispatched young Howell two holes up with one to play to reach the finals.

Ouimet had labored throughout the entire tournament thus far handicapped by something he never anticipated—the gallery, which followed him around out of curiosity, but always cheered for his opponent. Francis's play was terrific, holing putts of 20, 30, and even 50 feet, but he never received more than a polite smattering of applause. If one of his younger opponents sunk a five-footer or reached the green from the trap, it would draw echoing roars from the audiences. Later, Francis would comment on the how much the encouragement of Chay and his small circle of friends meant to him during the matches, but in typical fashion he never mentioned the fans that cheered against him. Francis also kept a close touch with home, sending as many as three to four telegrams each day to his wife Stella and his little girls Janice (who preferred to be called Jane) age seven, and Barbara age ten. Family and close friends were whom Francis relied on when the going got tough in Chicago.

In the final round, Francis met Jack Westland, the impressive young Chicagoian, and some interesting things began to develop. The gallery for the final day's match started out rather small for such an important event. As the morning round headed towards the finish, more and more people came out to see if the "old" veteran could handle still another young challenger. The crowd swelled to three thousand, then four, five, and six thousand or more as they followed Ouimet and Westland around the final 18 holes. Even though Westland was a local boy, much of the gallery now began pulling for Ouimet, who had suddenly become the sentimental favorite. Could the former champ pull it together one more time to take home the trophy that had eluded him for so many years?

Throughout the morning round Westland seemed off his game, playing his irons poorly and putting erratically, while Ouimet was in fine form playing great golf, perhaps his best ever. Messenger boys on bicycles relayed the hole-by-hole account of Ouimet's surprisingly strong play back to the press tent. At the end of 18, it was Francis Ouimet five up. Westland came back on the first hole of the afternoon round to cut the lead to four. Ouimet bounced back and won the next two holes to climb to six up. Westland halved the next hole to end Francis's run, but then lost the twenty-third hole by a stroke, falling behind by seven. Westland had a two-hole run and got the match back to five, but could do no better.

The 390-yard, thirty-first hole was the clincher. Ouimet drove 10 yards beyond Westland out to the 260-yard marker. Each man chipped up onto the green within a foot of each other on their second shots, both 20 feet above the hole. Ouimet putted first and the ball stopped six inches short of the hole but directly in the path of Westland's ball. In those days each player had to putt around or over his opponent's ball, there was no rule then about marking the ball to allow your opponent a clear putt. Instead the "Stymie" rule held that you could position your ball in the path of your opponent, and if he hit your ball while attempting his putt, he would be penalized. Thus Francis effectively stymied Westland's ball by blocking his line of putt, and the hole and match belonged to Ouimet six holes up and five to play.

Francis had regained the National Amateur Championship after a 17-year drought by the same 6–5 margin he defeated Jerome Travers by in 1914. Observer and special news commentator Bobby Jones expressed himself as "tickled to death" that Francis won. Ouimet's triumph at Beverly was one of the most remarkable comeback stories in the history of golf. Ouimet was considered by most observers as a seasoned but somewhat washed-up old veteran when the tournament began, the type of player that goes just so far and then is usually eliminated by a younger opponent along about the third round. Francis fooled the gallery and a lot of the experts because so very few knew he had been at the top of his game for the first time in years. Chay naturally was delighted and was able to share his happiness with Francis and also with Hat, young Charlie, and Kitty as he and Francis made long-distance telephone calls back to Massachusetts that afternoon. The champion and his friends, wasting little time in celebration, headed out to catch the train for home that same evening.

• A Hero's Return •

An incredible welcome greeted Francis at the train station in Newtonville late Sunday evening when the Twentieth Century Limited pulled in at 10:24 P.M. Over 5,000 friends and admirers crowded the platform and jammed the surrounding streets and overpasses to pay homage to the victorious national champion. The gathering was a spontaneous occurrence. No formal plans had been made for the homecoming. It was an amazing outpouring of affection for the modest man golf fans had taken into their hearts as one of the people. The impromptu reception by the wildly cheering audience made it next to impossible for the champion and his friends to get to the awaiting automobiles without a few words. Francis, never expecting such an explosion of emotion, declared, "This is the happiest moment of my life, I did nothing out there to deserve this and all I can say is that I am happy that my fellow townsmen have turned out in such a wonderful way." Newsman Linde Fowler noted that one of the highlights of the celebration occurred when "the $7,000 gold trophy emblematic of the championship, the Havemeyer Cup, was hailed with cheers as it was borne on the stout shoulder of Chay Burgess towards the awaiting motorcade."

After a night's rest, Francis returned to Woodland where the members prepared a very special reception for him. The ceremony took place on the clubhouse veranda, where Chay stood by Francis's elbow as he made his remarks to the assembled crowd. With characteristic modesty, he expressed his appreciation and told of a few intimate incidents that helped him in his march to the championship. He gave his mentor a good share of the credit for pulling him through. "Charlie got me out of one bad hole when I was hurrying my stroke, and he was always there when I needed him." Francis went on to say, "I don't know what I would have done out there without Charlie Burgess. He was a great strong bulwark to lean on at all times. When things were going a little tough you will never know what his encouragement meant." Then to Francis's amazement, the crowd assembled below him on the front lawn of the clubhouse parted to reveal a brand-new Buick Roadster convertible that they had purchased for him, apparently within the permissible guidelines of the USGA, as a token of their esteem. In typical fashion, Francis followed up the festivities with a relaxing round of golf at the club. It was a Scotch foursome, with Francis and Linde Fowler partnered against Chay and Bill Donnolly, another one of Chay's fine young amateur students who was among the field of 151 in Chicago. It resulted in a 79 tie.

• The Nicoll Brothers •

The wonderful adventure Charlie had shared with Francis in 1931 was a pleasant diversion from trying times. Like everyone, he was forced to contend with the constant struggles, shortages, and sufferings of the

1930s. Ironically, as his own fortunes were waning, his nephews and his famous pupils continued to enjoy relative prosperity during the Depression despite the hard times felt by most of the nation.

Each of the Nicoll brothers Chay brought over from Scotland met with considerable success in American golf. The youngest three were Jimmy, Arthur, and Frank. Jimmy first worked in Chay's shop and then spent some time as a teaching professional in Winter Harbor, Maine. He occasionally would visit his brothers Bert and Charlie when they worked at Pinehurst for some noteworthy rounds of golf. On one occasion at Pinehurst, he was paired up against *Golf* magazine founder Bob Harlow, a very powerful opponent. Jimmy shot a disappointing 41 during the first nine holes and was well behind in the match and on the side bets he made. The final nine was a different story. He shot a miraculous 31, which even included a bogey five on the next-to-last hole, for a record finish at the southern resort. Arthur Nicoll came to the States in 1927 at age twenty and, like his older brothers, often wound up working at a Donald Ross or an Alex Findlay-designed course thanks to the long-established friendship their uncle had with each of the great American golf course architects. Among Arthur's professional positions were the Huntington Valley Country Club in Pennsylvania, the Detroit Golf Club, and the Rockledge, Weathersfield, and Wampanoag Country Clubs in Connecticut. Least is known about Frank except that he worked for Chay as a club maker at Woodland upon his arrival in America in 1922, stayed for a season or two, then returned to Montrose to rejoin the golfing trade there.

The most successful Nicoll brothers were the eldest four. Harry, Bert, Willie, and Charlie attracted a lot of attention throughout the country as highly regarded professionals during the twenties, thirties and forties, and in Bert's case right into the seventies. Harry was the first to join Chay at Woodland before taking jobs at Oak Hill in Fitchburg, Massachusetts, and at nearby Haverhill. During the 1930s, he spent some time at the Wiano Club on Cape Cod and finished his career at a driving range he owned in San Antonio, Texas. He also spent a lot of time at Pinehurst and in Miami with his brothers Bert and Charlie.

Herbert, better known as Bert Nicoll, was a very prominent and respected golf professional all up and down the East Coast. Bert was a great performer and was always among the top finishers and money winners in the New England Professional Golfers' outings. His home course was the Donald Ross-designed Belmont Springs (now simply called Belmont) Country Club of Massachusetts.

Beginning in the twenties, Bert spent his winters in North Carolina as Donald Ross's head professional at Pinehurst. After 24 winters there, Bert moved to Palm Beach until his retirement in the early 1970's. At Pinehurst he shot a record 69 on the famous number 2 course and was a perennial best-ball team champion along with his partner Ted Gow at the famous southern resort. Bert is unique among golf professionals because he was the very first professional golfer to get his aviator's license. The famous flying ace Lloyd Yost was his instructor. Bert would often pilot his own plane and fly his fellow pros around the South in pursuit of tournaments or on other golf business.

Bert was very similar in personal temperament and in his teaching style to his uncle Chay. Like his uncle, he also had a sporting connection with Harvard University. In 1931 Bert became the coach of the Harvard golf team and coached the team for a decade. Under Bert's guidance, Harvard tied with Holy Cross College for the New England Intercollegiate Championship in 1936 and won it outright in 1940.

Bert also shared his Uncle Chay's well-known ability to arrange and promote celebrity golf tournaments. In 1937, he arranged an international match play event at Belmont, which was an innovation on the recently established PGA Tournament circuit that year and according to Bert "one which reflected the American interest in developing worldwide competition." Former Belmont caddie Fred Corcoran most likely also had a hand in bringing the match to Belmont. Fred, who first learned the rules and etiquette of golf under the direction of Bert Nicoll, had worked his way up through local and national golf circles as an able administrator and promoter. Corcoran at age twenty-eight had just been appointed as the tour director of the PGA after previously serving as an official with the Massachusetts Golf Association for several years. His close association with Bert Nicoll made Belmont a natural choice for a new PGA event and it is likely that the two men worked together to establish the 1937 tournament.

Byron Nelson, who had just come off of his first major championship at the Masters Tournament, defeated fellow Ryder Cup team member Henry Picard in the inaugural Massachusetts event that offered a $1,200 purse. Both golfers were rising stars on the PGA Tour. Picard went on to win the Masters in 1938 and the following year defeated Nelson in the PGA Championship. Nelson went on to win 54 PGA tour events, including the PGA Championship and the U.S. Open, and is considered one of the most revered figures in American Golf.

As Bert Nicoll aged and took his place as one of America's best and most well known teaching pros, he came to be known as "Mr. Bert" in golfing circles. He also gave up trying to correct the various reporters and journalists who constantly misspelled his last name Nicolls, Nicholl or Nicholls. In fact, all of the Nicoll brothers came to accept the common misspellings of their name throughout their careers.

In his senior years at Palm Beach, Bert gained celebrity as President John F. Kennedy's golf instructor. According to Bert, President Kennedy "duck hooked like the devil, but still could shoot anywhere from a 36 to 39 for nine holes." Bert taught the Kennedy clan for years but would normally not talk about his famous student. In a 1961 newspaper interview he let out a few benign comments saying that the new American President, "has quite a good swing and has the ability to play well and hits the ball like a low handicapper." He went on diplomatically commenting, "I can tell you he has great enthusiasm for the game and I'm sure he would be an excellent player if he played more."

Charlie Nicoll, like Bert, was a snappy dresser on the links and favored a broad-brimmed Panama hat, a trademark of sorts for both brothers. Charlie was so dapper that he was pronounced the best-dressed golfer in New England in 1930. Charlie left Woodland and took a job at the Framingham Country Club in Massachusetts before stints at the Rockledge and Sunset Ridge Clubs in Hartford, Connecticut. He also spent a season at Shenacossett, a Donald Ross-designed course in the Groton-New London area. Like Bert he was also part of Donald Ross's staff of professionals at Pinehurst, beginning at the North Carolina resort in 1926 and working at the Pineneedles and the Mid Pine Golf Courses.

Charlie also worked at Palm Beach with his brother Bert. But Charlie, unlike the genial Mr. Bert, had a volatile temper both on and off the course, a temper that eventually ended his career in golf.

One day in 1959, after young Bobby Kennedy finished up a round of golf, he came into the pro shop asking Charlie to take care of the caddie's fee for him. Apparently young Kennedy had a habit of often asking the pro on duty to cover his caddie fee and had run up a debt of a few hundred dollars, which was a lot of money for Charlie to take out of his own pocket. When Charlie called Bobby on his debt, Kennedy took offense at the pro's impudence for speaking publicly of the matter. According to a witness who worked at the club, "a loud argument ensued." Kennedy was rumored to have a pretty hot temper and so did Charlie Nicoll. The matter escalated to where Bobby threatened to have Charlie fired, but Joe Kennedy, head of the Kennedy clan, stepped in to calm the matter down and paid off his son's debt. The winter season finished up quietly, but when Charlie returned for duty the next season, he found that his services were no longer required by the Palm Beach Country Club. Interestingly, Charlie Nicoll never held another professional golf position there or anywhere else again.

"Little" Willie Nicoll came to the United States in 1919 at age twenty. His first position after leaving his uncle's shop was at the Dedham Country and Polo Club in Massachusetts, an Alex Findlay-designed course. He also worked briefly at another Massachusetts course, the North Andover Country Club, until Donald Ross recommended him for the head position at the Beresford (now Peninsula) Country Club in San Mateo, California. Nicoll was the first pro at the club, and the course was the only one Ross had designed on the West Coast. Willie rode out the Depression very well as a most successful teacher of the game at the far western course. He was the smallest of the Nicoll brothers, only weighing about 120 pounds, but he could hit the ball like a heavyweight thanks to the perfection of this swing, a style he learned from his uncle Chay. Like Chay, he was revered by the members of this club, who referred to him as a "pro's pro . . . without peer as an instructor and a developer of champions." His most well-known pupil was the great amateur Lawson Little, who won the U.S. and British Amateur Championships twice each and was a Walker Cup team member before turning professional in 1936. Dot Kielty, Curtis Cup team member from 1948 to 1950, and Helen Lengfeld, sponsor of many early women's tournaments, were also prominent students of Willie Nicoll. Pioneering woman professional Pattie Berg also made it a point to avail herself of Willie's instructions any time she was on the West Coast.

• A Champion in Defeat •

Charlie's nephews all fared well through the dark days of the great Depression and his star pupils experienced the thirties as successful businessmen and respected senior amateurs. Neither Jesse nor Francis won another major tournament after the 1931 Amateur during the decade, but they continued to be a successful team in four-ball play as they had been during the twenties. Both had been chosen as members of the inaugural Walker Cup team in 1922, then again in 1924 and 1926. Francis went on to play on four more Walker Cup Teams and then was elected as the non-playing captain in 1936. Jesse did not make another appearance in the Walker Cup during the thirties, but remained active in local competitions and made a run at the 1932 National Amateur at the Baltimore Country Club, along with Francis, who was attempting to retain his 1931 crown. Each lost out in the semi-final rounds, Guilford to eventual champion C. Ross Somerville and Ouimet to John Goodman.

For the rest of the decade, Jesse concentrated on his accounting business while Francis followed a number of business opportunities including assuming the position of president of the Boston Bruins Hockey Club in 1931. However, one additional match between them merits mention, as it seems to illustrate the mutual respect and admiration the two former students of Charlie Burgess had for each other as they entered the latter stages of their careers.

In 1933, Francis and Jesse found themselves engaged in a desperate and poignant struggle against each other, as the veteran golfers vied for one last shot at the National Amateur crown they both had once worn. On an unusually dark and rainy August afternoon, 100 or more hopefuls from the New England region were assembled at the Brae Burn Country Club trying to win one of the 10 qualifying spots for the national tournament. The two former champions managed to each finish with 159, enough to tie them for the tenth and last spot in the section's qualifying rounds. Two other golfers, Charlie Clare and Peter Petroske, both from Connecticut, also shot 159s, and so there was a four-way tie for the final qualifying position.

In a "sudden death" play-off, the four contestants faced each other under dismal wet and windy conditions for the right to compete in the National Championship at the Kernwood Country Club in Ohio. The two Connecticut men were quickly out of the running after the first play-off hole getting five's while Jesse and Francis halved the hole with par fours to continue on against each other. Now it was a two-man contest between the aging Woodland heroes. In the words of longtime Boston sportswriter W. A. Whitcomb, a drama unfolded as Ouimet and Guilford "steadfast friends, long-standing rivals . . . stood on the second tee with the necessity of beating each other in order to win themselves."

Francis had been first crowned the nation's Amateur Champion in 1914 as an unknown young man and ex-caddie who had just turned the golf establishment on its head in the 1913 United States Open. He won again in 1931 as a world renowned and mature veteran who had to overcome 17 years of second-place finishes or worse to regain his title. It meant a great deal to Francis to prove himself once again in the National. For Jesse it was just as important. He also knew the thrill of winning the National Championship, and it was just the previous year when both he and Francis came so close to another crown when they each lost in the semi-final rounds. The friendship the two men had for each other for so long now made it difficult for either one to put his heart into beating the other on this particular occasion.

At the second hole of the play-off, Jesse had a chance to finish off the match. Francis hit a short drive and then pitched his second shot into a bunker in front of the green. Jesse had a booming drive and his second shot was a chip of only 20 yards or so onto the green. But to the observers of the contest, he sized up the shot half-heartedly, swung at it listlessly, and dumped the ball into the sand trap next to Francis. Jesse seemed to be in a position of not wanting to win or lose. He had the appearance of wanting to finish the match even, hoping that both he and Francis could qualify. It was a strange match seeing both men playing for a prize that each hoped the other one would win. Instead of a play-off for the last qualification slot for the National Championship, it looked like a friendly match, or a practice round where each contestant was coaching the other along. They remained tied at the end of the second hole.

On the third hole, Francis hit his second shot off line and into a trap to the right of the green. Jesse had another tremendous tee shot and put his second on the green, although again to observers he hardly looked at his lie or line before taking his shot. Jesse was down in two while Francis had trouble with his bunker shot and could not recover well enough to stay even anymore. A longtime friend of Ouimet, reporter Linde Fowler, described the scene as one where "a grim and gruesome shadow stalked in the rain at Brae Burn . . . a shadow of a champion in defeat."

Jesse was the reluctant winner and went on to the National Amateur, while his good friend and friendly rival Francis failed to qualify for the championship for the first time since 1913. Neither Jesse nor any of the other New England qualifiers fared very well at the Nationals after the drama at Brae Burn. The championship went to first-time winner George T. Dunlap Jr., of Garden City, New Jersey, who defeated Max R. Marston, also a first-time finalist, 6 and 5.

• The Deepening Depression •

The New England professionals opened up their annual series of tournaments for the 1933 season with an unusual but time-honored version of team competition. It was a Scotch foursome match where partners would hit alternate shots with the same ball, drives and all. The origins of this type of play is reputedly credited to two ancient Scotsmen who both wanted to play golf one day but they only had a single golf ball to use between them. As a result, the Scotch format was born. One observer in the gallery, unfamiliar with Scotch play and who had been watching the pros go around a bit commented disgustedly, "Heck, I came out here to get away from the Depression for an afternoon and what do I find? Times so bad that *two* professionals are playing with *one* ball!"

The impact of the terrible national economy was starting to be felt more and more acutely by the golf pros across America. Business for Chay and his fellow professionals began to decline in earnest early in the Depression when desperate sporting goods manufacturers began to dump their merchandise at bargain basement rates in order to pay off the banks who were calling in their loans. As a result, the club professionals were seeing the goods in their pro shops being severely undercut by department store golf equipment and they suffered greatly as a result.

By the start of the 1933 golf season, business had slowed down considerably at Woodland, yet Chay had the opportunity to improve his personal situation in another fashion. John Johnstone, the long-time greenskeeper at Woodland retired and vacated the small two-story white clapboard house that he had lived in since before Burgess's arrival at the club. "The Cottage" as it was called sat about one hundred yards to the left of the clubhouse facing east towards Washington Street and the main drive into the club. In the springtime, Chay and Hat moved across the links into their new quarters, just a chip shot away from Chay's pro shop and the first tee, which made life much more convenient for the veteran professional.

Young Charlie and his family lived just down the street from Chay's old Knickerbocker cottage, in a pleasant two-family home in Newton Lower Falls. Little Charlie turned ten years old that summer and was spending a lot of his time at the golf club with his grandparents. The youngster was allowed to begin caddying an occasional round for his grandfather and was learning to play the game himself in earnest. Chay still employed his son at the club whenever he could, but because of the shrinking demand for lessons and the declining membership caused by the Depression, there was little need for another pro. Chay often called upon his friends to see if they might help young Charlie obtain any sort of employment. Thankfully, there was a enough financial stability in the younger Burgess's household during the summer of 1933, to escape the depression for a while and to enjoy a short seaside vacation at Long Beach in Rockport on Massachusetts's rocky North Shore. Charlie, Kitty, little Charlie, and Sister enjoyed a few weeks of fun and relaxation together on the picturesque beach with its wide firm sand flat at low tide and the bone-chilling water from the Gulf of Maine.

On December 5, 1933, Prohibition was repealed, and the Depression had worsened.

Although Chay was keeping his head above water, things were not going well for his son and his family. Bills were piling up. Food and other consumables, once plentiful, were getting scarce. Dunning letters from creditors began to arrive. Chay and Hat were hard-pressed to help Kitty and the children but they did what they could. Charlie got work as a temporary substitute letter carrier and that job provided a few dollars for his family over the Christmas holiday, but it was not enough. They could not pay the rent for the Newton Lower Falls apartment that they considered their home. Kitty found a much cheaper attic apartment in nearby Auburndale, but it was much further away from Chay, and Hat and little Charlie and Mary were forced to transfer to a new school. Kitty returned to her old job as a postal telegraph operator in order to survive. But her job was in Boston and it was easier for her both logistically and economically to eventually move in with one of her sisters who lived in the city of Somerville, northwest of Boston while Charlie looked for work. The children had to move once again in short order, this time to an unfamiliar area far away from the familial warmth and security they had enjoyed with Chay and Hat at the club.

Chay's golf business was barely surviving, as the membership at Woodland was shrinking every month. Fewer members meant fewer lessons, less locker and equipment maintenance income, and less business in the shop. Many other golf clubs across the nation were folding, going bankrupt in the same fashion as the businesses of their once-privileged members. Woodland was still holding on thanks to the prosperity and popularity that Chay, Francis, and Jesse had brought the club over the previous twenty years.

Chay, now nearly sixty, willingly worked from sunup to sundown when necessary to keep things going. He even contracted with Lasell Junior College, a nearby school for women, to give golf lessons to the students as part of their curriculum. Lasell had taken over the old Woodland Park Hotel, and the campus included a small six-hole golf course on Commonwealth Avenue, not far from Woodland's course. Chay managed to stay at Lasell for several seasons, given the slack in his teaching schedule caused by the Depression. Hat, fifty-seven, was forced to go out to work for the city's welfare department doing cooking for the needy in order to make ends meet. She also would take occasional agency positions working as a domestic for wealthy families still able to afford hired help.

In the fall of 1934, young Charlie enlisted in the Civilian Conservation Corps (CCC) to try to better his situation at the combination boot camp, public works, and relief project. The CCC was one of the first agencies newly elected President Franklin Delano Roosevelt created to combat the unemployment crises caused by the Depression. All over the nation, young men were assigned, mostly to rural communities or to national parks and forests, to work with pick and shovel, ax and saw, or stones and mortar to create thousands of public works projects. The men lived in barracks and in a quasi-military environment where they received food, clothing, shelter, and a small stipend. The idea was to get the men off the streets and into a productive work setting that would benefit both the men and the nation.

Charlie was assigned to the CCC Camp in the Spencer State Forest, just a little southwest of Worcester, Massachusetts, while Kitty was back working for Postal Telegraph on State Street in downtown Boston as an operator. She and her children were living in a two-family house in Somerville with her sister and were not far from her family in North Cambridge. Little Charlie and Sis, eleven and nine, would spend the weekends out in Newton with Chay and Harriet—Sis sometimes, Charlie almost always. Everyone prayed and hoped that Charlie would be successful and return to them soon.

Just as in the military, the CCC workers would get leaves and weekend passes which were eagerly looked forward to. Everyone wrote letters to Charlie often and what follows is a sample of the correspondence to Charlie from his family during the long, hard, cold winter of 1934–35, one of the most severe winters on record. The thoughts, sentiments, concerns, fears, and hopes of each writer serve as a poignant reflection of life during the dark days of the Great Depression:

> Dear Charlie—
>
> Received your letter O.K. Saw Chay this afternoon. He says in order to get your check which is coming to you he has to have the name of your company commander so that it can be sent to you then mailed back to me. Needless to say it is badly needed. Am enclosing letters from Chubby [little Charlie] and Sis. Will expect to hear from you soon.
>
> Best of luck and love. Kitty

> Dear Charlie,
>
> Got your letter yesterday when I came home from work but was too tired to write. But I will stick it [domestic work] out for a while anyway. Your father isn't doing much at the

club and if I don't get a raise soon I will quit by Christmas. They called me up from the Mayor's relief so I could always get a day or two from them. See you soon.

Your loving Mother

Dear Charlie,

I am glad you're getting on all right. I am sending $1.00 to pay bus fare if you get home this week. My back is a little better but I have had a nasty pain in my right side for the last few days but hope it will be right again. Gave my first lesson yesterday for the last ten days, two hours to Mr. Brady. He is living at the club and is to have another one Thursday morning. The weather is very cold for this time of the year but I am glad there is no snow yet.

Your loving Father,
Chay

Charlie stayed at the CCC camp from October 1934 until March of 1935. Letters were sent almost daily to him from Hat and Chay. Golf news and activities at the club practically came to a standstill during that long cold winter in the middle of the Depression. No matter how tough things were at home, Chay always slipped a precious dollar or sometimes two in the letter so that Charlie would have bus fare home or some change for the Post Exchange. Kitty would often send a telegraph from work when she could spare a few moments and the children would write just about weekly. Most of the time the news was not good:

Dear Charlie,

It's terrifically cold down here and I have to do something as I'm afraid we'll all get pneumonia . . . The kids are sadly in need of shoes to say nothing of myself . . . I bought a heater at Sears Roebuck, $25.45, $3.00 down and $4.00 a month. I just get sick when I think of Christmas. The poor kids are looking forward to it so and where I'm going to get anything I don't know. Am enclosing two stamps which is all I have . . . Poor Chay had quite a blow today. *The club has cut his salary to just fifty percent.* He is quite broken up about it naturally. I am still waiting for your check for the rent. It is terribly cold tonight . . . To make matters worse we got no pay this week yet. No one seems to know what the trouble is. Chay's back is still painful and I didn't think he looked at all well. It would be wonderful to think that when you get home you may lift the burden from his shoulders, also from yours truly. Sorry not to write but I've been too sick to do anything. I got out of bed to work Friday as I had a tip they were going to lay girls off. . . . There was no school on account of the storm, which has been terrific. The snow is sky high everywhere. Am having a tough time all around just now. Had no pay at all this week of course and the bills are piling up.

Kitty

Throughout the terrible winter of 1934–35 the letters continued—some desperate, some hopeful—as the Burgess family, along with the rest of the nation, suffered through the depths of the Depression. Occasional rays of hope for Chay and his family often came from the friends he had made from golf. Even as his income from lessons and his shop dwindled and the club cut his base salary in half, Chay still was able to put food on his table thanks to the admiration many of the individual club members had for him. Woodland member Joe O'Meara was an example of one such caring individual. Joe was a club member who had established his own very successful grocery business in nearby West Newton. Whenever Chay went to the Joe's market for provisions or called in an order for delivery, Joe would see to it that a few extra items were packed in or would drastically discount the goods without ever saying a word. The kind and subtle act spared Chay his pride and helped his family survive the desperate times.

12 1935–1960

> "The proper finish means complete control of the club and should find the weight on the left leg and the body balanced. The right elbow is straight out. Parallel with the line of flight, and the club shaft almost rests on the shoulders back of the head. Too many good golfers overlook this factor and apparently swing properly but contract near the finish and end up in grotesque postures."
>
> —Charlie Burgess

• Ruth Returns •

One bright spot for Chay in the difficult winter of 1934–35 was the news that his old friend and frequent golfing companion Babe Ruth was returning to Boston to join the struggling Braves of the National

Baseball League. The gregarious Ruth was in the twilight years of his baseball career, the most amazing career of any ball player ever. The Babe Ruth story has been told many times by many writers over the years. Some have emphasized his wilder side, his enormous appetites, and his personal excesses. A few writers have highlighted the rags-to-riches journey of the former "orphan" from Baltimore (he was not really an orphan; he knew his father but was raised in a Baltimore orphanage run by the Christian Brothers). Still others have portrayed Ruth as self-centered, spoiled, and paid so much to hit a baseball that he had no idea of the fact that during the Depression millions were unemployed and thousands of Americans were on the point of actual starvation. Despite any shortcomings he may have had, Charlie Burgess found that Ruth had a big heart, played hard, was extremely generous, and retained an innocence about him that made him always seem like a big kid.

His road back to Boston began eight years after the record-setting season when he hit his incredible 60 home runs, a record that lasted for over three decades. He was still earning the biggest baseball paycheck in history. Even in the middle of the Great Depression, he was making over $80,000 a year. Ruth's career in New York marked the golden age of the New York Yankee Baseball Club, but by 1935, Ruth's usefulness as an everyday player was virtually over. His aging legs seemed no longer able to carry his big body as in the past, his stamina was slipping, and his overall health was suffering from years of more bad habits than good ones. The Babe had ambitions to manage a big league ball club, but he had no chance to take over the Yankees, as Joe McCarthy was secure and competent in that position. Ruth had a binding contract with New York so they could not let just him go, but a proposition from Boston Braves President Judge Emil Fuchs looked like a good deal—for both teams and for the Babe as well.

In 1934, the Braves finished in fourth place. The fan support at the start of that season had been pretty promising until the weather dealt the Braves a box office blow that almost killed their gate receipts for the entire year. The team started the season on the road and did fairly well, but when they returned to Boston, it began to rain heavily and did not let up for 25 days! Important weekend games and doubleheaders that would have brought in desperately needed cash had to be cancelled and

Judge Fuchs looked at the upcoming 1935 season with a sense of financial urgency.

Fuchs was desperate to get the beleaguered Boston franchise out of the red and proposed to entice Ruth to Boston with the implied incentive of having Babe play for a while and then eventually fulfill his desire to manage a big league club—the Braves. But Charles F. Adams, a businessman who also controlled the Boston Bruins Hockey Team, led a group of Braves stockholders that controlled the team and was strongly opposed to the idea. Adams had no intention of letting anyone take over from incumbent Braves manager Bill McKechnie, who had done a great job despite the financial woes of the club and the poor attendance of the fans. So the idea that Ruth could actually become the manager of the Braves was a hollow promise, nothing more than an illusion presented to Ruth by Fuchs who desperately needed some magic, or a miracle, to save his club.

The deal was made. Ruth was released from the Yankees, who were happy to get out of Ruth's expensive contract, and he agreed to come to Boston under what he thought was a promise to eventually take over the team. When the press got a hold of the story, they gave the implied agreement credibility and Ruth's trade to Boston became a publicity windfall for the Braves. Fuchs could see his revenues rising at once.

Chay Burgess was delighted to have his old friend back in Boston. Over the years, Ruth had developed an intense love for golf ever since Chay taught him to play during his first year with the Red Sox. The *Boston American* ran a feature story on the deal that brought Ruth to Boston. It solicited the reactions of many well-known sports personalities, including Yankee star Lou Gehrig, Bob Quinn of the Brooklyn Dodgers, Stuffy McInnis of the Braves, and prominent Boston golf professional Chay Burgess.

When asked what he though about Ruth's return to Boston, Chay responded, "I have known the Babe intimately since he played his first round of golf at Woodland with Harry Hooper, Hal Janvrin, and Joe Wood almost twenty years ago . . . although fame has not changed him, the Babe will change the Braves into a baseball attraction." For a while Chay's optimistic prediction looked like it would come true, but with Ruth there was often always more to the story.

Ruth was a frequent visitor to Woodland, even after he had departed for New York in the infamous deal that Red Sox owner Harry Frazee made in 1920. Ruth had maintained a home in nearby Sudbury, Massachusetts and was still able to get in many rounds with Chay in the off-season as well as on layover days when he was in town with the Yanks.

There are many interesting golf stories attached to the fabled ball player because of his passion for the game, as he played whenever he could at courses all across the country. One tale about his ability to make a golf ball soar came from California when he was playing a round at the municipal course in Los Angeles at Griffith Park. The park is the recreational preserve at the foot of the large hills where the famous Hollywood sign is located. During Babe's visit, the golf course below the hills featured a challenging 453-yard seventh hole. The Babe took a full swing from the tee and sent his drive well down the fairway, at least 275 yards. An impressive shot—but it was his second shot that was remarkable. He took out a brassie (two wood), and sent the ball over a hill that blocked the line of sight to the pin. The ball disappeared momentarily in a cluster of tulips on top of the hill, but came bounding out, caught the slope just right, went down on the green and trickled in to the cup for a two!

Woodland members Tommy McEnamey and John Feeney, both prominent Boston attorneys, were the frequent hosts of Ruth out at the Woodland Links. More often than not, they would call upon their old club pro to join them for a round to make up a foursome. Ruth loved the challenge of playing against another professional and although he never could match Chay's golfing skills, he had the obvious admiration of one professional athlete towards another in regard to his first instructor.

Ruth was a left-handed hitter and drove his golf balls with the same big arcing swing that he hit so many home runs with. One day at Woodland he stepped up to the second tee and smacked the ball what seemed like a mile high, slicing it clear over the clubhouse which was more than 300 yards away. The ball was never found. The next drive he hit was fairly well on line landing in the rough, pin high to the green, another wallop of at least 300 yards from the tee! The caddies and his partners were wide-eyed with amazement.

It was true that the larger-than-life Ruth had the bad habit of using profanities in his everyday speech almost unconsciously. Chay, on the other hand, rarely if ever used that sort of language and would gently remind his friend George to be careful about his language, especially around the young caddies. One day Ruth was in town with the Yankees and had the chance for a round of golf at Woodland. He particularly liked going around with Chay because when they reached the back holes near the old Knickerbocker, Ruth would look forward to a quick sandwich or a bowl or two of Hattie's ever-present stew for a snack.

On this particular occasion, Ruth barreled into the pro shop full of energy and enthusiasm ready for his round of golf. Little Charlie was about ten or eleven at the time and was hanging around his grandfather as he often did. Needless to say he was mesmerized, as were several club members also in the shop, by Ruth's sudden and boisterous entry. As he approached the counter, Ruth declared in a loud comedic tone, "Where's that old son of a bitch Charlie Burgess? I'm feeling damn good and I think I'm going to kick his God damn ass out there today!" Chay, who had been working in the back room on some clubs, slowly walked out into the shop and without a word surveyed the scene. There was Ruth larger than life in his knickers, tam o'shanter, and loud argyle pullover vest smiling broadly at Chay, while little Charlie and the several members present in the shop were slack-jawed and silent. Chay quietly said to Ruth in his most fatherly fashion, and of course with his authoritative Scottish burr, "George, I dinna know how many time I've told ye, ye canna swear like that in front of the wee laddie!" Ruth looking sheepish, apologetically replied, "Jesus Charlie, you're right! God damn it, you'll never hear me swear like that again—I promise!"

Ruth joined the Braves for their spring training camp in St. Petersburg, Florida, and Judge Fuchs was eagerly selling thousands of tickets in advance for the home opener in Boston. But Chairman of the Board Charles Adams was having no part of the so-called plan for Ruth to become the club's manager even though the newspapers and the radio commentators gave the story credence. The team's train from the South arrived in Boston with Ruth on board, and an exhibition series with the neighboring Red Sox was scheduled for Babe's Boston debut. April weather in Boston is notoriously unpredictable, and on the opening day of the exhibition series, rain poured down in torrents and the air was cold and raw. The rain went on relentlessly for three days and all of the games were a wash-out. The cash that Fuchs had counted on from the cross-town series went down the drain as well. Finally on the official opening day of the regular National League schedule, the Braves were able to play their first home game with Ruth in the lineup and they beat the New York Giants. Ruth hit a home run that proved to be the game winner, and Fuchs could not have been happier! Alas, the next home game fell victim to more rain and then the team went on the road where things really began to unravel. The team started to lose and Ruth was neither hitting nor helping the team at all.

Soon Ruth's lack of usefulness as an everyday player for the Braves was apparent to everyone and even he could see that the promise of his becoming the team's manager was just a fiction. He grew disenchanted with the team and his situation. One day in early June, when the Braves were back in Boston, Babe stomped off the field in a huff, packed his car, and drove back to his apartment in New York with his wife. When asked what his plans were by inquisitive reporters, Ruth shot back, "I'm going to play golf!" It was the end of the Babe's brief fling with the Boston Braves.

• Bing Crosby •

With Ruth's departure, the Braves continued to flounder both financially and on the field, and the team had a perennial "for sale" sign out for the rest of the decade. In 1940 it was almost bought by a visiting Hollywood star who had a strong liking for golf, Woodland, and Boston. The star was Bing Crosby who, in his early days as a crooner with the Rhythm Boys and Paul Whiteman's Big Band, satisfied his early infatuation with golf by taking many lessons from Chay at Woodland. It was believed that Crosby actually took a room at the Woodland clubhouse while performing in the ballroom at the nearby Norumbega Amusement Park. He returned to Woodland on several occasions throughout the thirties when he was traveling with his bandleader brother Bob and was often the frequent guest of Woodland member Ed Wiener, the owner of the exclusive Boston Ritz-Carlton Hotel.

The 1940 visit of Bing Crosby to Boston was in regard to the purchase of the Braves. Former Belmont Country Club caddie Fred Corcoran was by this time very active in the affairs of professional golf as the tournament director of the PGA of America and was well connected in sporting circles in Boston and throughout the country. His official duties for the organization often saw him travel to the West Coast. He met Crosby out there and in casual conversation suggested that Crosby might consider purchasing the struggling Boston team. Bing was very interested and was all set to take over the team until the ironhanded commissioner of baseball, Judge Kenesaw Mountain Landis, stepped in to block the sale. Judge Landis was the man that baseball turned to in 1919 after the infamous Chicago "Black Sox" scandal when members of the team were judged guilty of fixing games. Landis did not tolerate any hint of gambling around baseball and Crosby had an interest in, and was president of, the Delmar Race Track just outside of Hollywood.

The Crosby deal fell through, but another well-connected golfer became involved with the purchase of the beleaguered Boston baseball franchise. After the 1941 season the team, which had recently changed its name to the Boston Bees in a desperate attempt to generate a new image, was taken over by a syndicate of investors headed by Boston businessman Bob Quinn. Quinn served as president of the organization and Francis Ouimet, now an equally successful Boston broker, was appointed as the vice president of the club. In 1942, the Bees changed their name back to the Braves and remained so until the financially plagued team moved to Milwaukee in 1953.

• Big League Sluggers •

Baseball and golf have always had a certain degree of connection to each other, perhaps because of the central principle of swinging at and trying to hit a ball as far as one could. It was not surprising that American homebred heroes of the links were also attracted to the "national pastime" and vice versa. Bobby Jones was a stockholder in the Atlanta Baseball Club, which at the time was a minor league team in the Southern League. Walter Hagen once owned the Rochester Baseball Club in the International League for a year and was himself a major league prospect before turning to golf in 1913.

In 1914, Jesse Guilford and Francis Ouimet were invited to the Detroit Tigers ballpark to put on a golf ball hitting demonstration. The Tiger ballplayers were astonished to see Francis casually tee up a ball at home plate and blast it out over the centerfield wall. They could not believe their eyes when Guilford, the Siege Gun, followed with a shot that lost itself in the sky somewhere over downtown Detroit. It was really no big trick to perform, but to a public that had not been exposed much to golf at the time, it was a feat that was practically a front-page news story.

Throughout the thirties, many big league baseball players often played golf at Chay's club with influential members and the veteran professional. Joe Cronin, the star infielder/manager of the Boston Red Sox from 1935 to 1945, was a member at Woodland and brought out scores of enthusiastic golf-loving ball players, most of whom benefited from a lesson or two with Chay.

After Ruth, perhaps the best-known slugger in baseball was James "Jimmie" Foxx who was with Boston from 1936 to 1942. Foxx led the American League in home runs in 1932 (58) and again in 1933, 1935, and 1939 with 48, 36, and 35 home runs respectively. The prodigious slugger, a powerful golfer, and a favorite of the Woodland caddies because of his friendly nature, was also a very *serious* golfer.

One afternoon in the late 1930s, little Charlie Burgess the Third, now a young teen, had the chance to caddie the round that Foxx was having with Joe Cronin and his grandfather. At the time, the seventh hole of Woodland ran southward along the extreme western edge of the club's property. A deep ravine choked with trees and bushes ran all the way down one side of the long par five hole. Foxx teed off at the seventh with a screaming line drive that quickly went out of sight deep into the woods and gully to the right. He took his next shot from the tee again (the out of bounds ball only penalized him one stroke). He cursed at shot number two, a rocket of a shot, which followed his first into the deep gully, lost and out of play again. On his third try he stubbornly teed up again rather than drop a ball somewhere near the out of bounds spot. He hit the ball so hard on his third drive that little Charlie thought the ball would be shattered to pieces. It was a straight shot so far down the fairway Foxx only needed an easy chip shot to get on the green, where he took one putt to hole the ball. Three hits off the tee and the powerful Foxx still got the par! Jimmie's love for golf continued after his retirement from baseball and he owned and operated several resort golf courses in Florida.

Another Boston baseball legend that tried his hand at golf at Woodland with Chay was Ted Williams. Fred Corcoran invited him out to the club. Corcoran, the tournament director of the PGA, was also one of the country's first sports agents. At the time, he represented Williams, Sam Snead, and many other stars of the day in business deals that developed because of their fame as sports figures. Fred was one of five brothers who were all active in golf to varying degrees. Fred had been the executive secretary of the Massachusetts Golf Association (MGA) from 1926 until 1936 when he left to assume his job as PGA Tournament Director. His brother John, a prominent Woodland member, succeeded him at the MGA. Another brother, George, became a professional golfer and worked in Greensboro, North Carolina. Thus, the large Corcoran clan was closely linked to Burgess in many ways and Fred had worked closely with Chay and his organization of New England pros especially when arranging the many celebrity affairs that were held at Woodland.

Williams joined the Sox as a rookie in 1939 and, like many of his teammates, had the opportunity to try golf for the first time under Chay's instruction at the Newton course. Although Williams had perhaps the best swing in baseball, he could not make the adjustment to a proper golf swing. Time and again Williams would wind up and spray the ball all over the course. Worse, he would coil back in a beautiful back-swing only to fluff or dub the ball on his way down at it. After several frustrating holes, the "Splendid Splinter" took his new bag of clubs from his caddie, and according to the story that was often repeated in the caddie shack, tossed them into one of the Woodland ponds. He allegedly said, "The hell with this! I'll stick to fishing" and walked away back to the clubhouse. For years, until he retired from baseball, the only water hazards Williams ever saw were the ones where he could pull out a largemouth bass or a rainbow trout. Williams became world famous as a dedicated outdoorsman and fisherman in addition to his Hall of Fame baseball career. After his retirement from baseball, he eventually tried golf again and actually did very well, often teaming up with his agent Corcoran at clubs in Florida and near his summertime youth baseball camp in Lakeville, Massachusetts.

• A Special Order •

Through the years, Francis Ouimet always remained a headliner among the steady stream of famous personalities that played with Chay on the Woodland links and his continuing friendship with his mentor helped ease the tedious concerns about the stagnant economy in the thirties. Francis's ascension into the ranks of the Boston establishment was pleasing to his old golf coach. His onetime pupil now had the distinction of being one of the world's most admired and respected figures in golf as he neared forty. Even though the poor son of a gardener was now practically a Boston Brahmin, he never forgot where he started and who his friends were. Francis was particularly sensitive to Chay's well being and always kept in touch with him, if only to see how he was getting along.

Ouimet remained relatively untouched by the widespread effects of the Depression. Throughout the period, he retained his position at White, Weld and Company and had the opportunity to invest in several interesting ventures, the Bruins hockey club, and the Boston baseball Bees (Braves) included. Typical of Francis, he went out of his way to insure that his old mentor would not be forgotten when he purchased a new set of clubs in 1936. After talking with Chay beforehand, Francis went into Wright and Ditson and picked out his new clubs. Rather than buy them direct from the sporting goods outlet, he charged them to Chay's account so that Chay would realize the commission from the sale. Francis sent Chay the money for the clubs along with this note:

> January 17, 1936
>
> Dear Charlie,
>
> I am enclosing, herewith, a check for $132.50, which covers the purchase of a set of Jones Clubs. These, as I advised you, were charged to your account at Wright and Ditson. I received ten irons at $8.50; one dynamiter, which they told me retailed for $7.50; and four wooden clubs retailing at $10.00 each . . . I am leaving for the sunny South Sunday and expect to be gone three weeks. I do not want you to feel funny about

> this at all. I have not bought a set of clubs for a long time and I do want you to get full benefit out of this purchase. Had I made this purchase from Wright and Ditson direct it would have cost me the same amount and you know I would much rather have you the gainer. Keep up your courage, and with warm regards, I am
>
> Sincerely, Francis

The gesture was typical of Ouimet, a kind and thoughtful act, giving a little encouragement back to the man who had done so much for him, in so many ways, for so many years.

• Snead Shunned •

Chay had a reputation as a friendly, unassuming gentleman who rarely had an unkind word for anyone. His good nature was severely tested one day in the very late 1930's when a famous new golf star visited Woodland—Sam Snead, soon to be known as Slammin' Sammy. Snead was the 1937 runner-up in the U.S. Open, a member of the 1937 and 1939 Ryder Cup Teams (the 1939 team never officially played due to the outbreak of War in Europe), the runner-up to Byron Nelson in the 1938 PGA Tournament, and the holder of many regional titles at the time. Snead would eventually win every major golf championship except the U.S. Open and would be inducted into the Golf Hall of Fame. When he visited Woodland, Snead was in his late twenties and was already used to being the center of attention whenever he arrived at a new golf club, or anywhere at all for that matter.

Born near Hot Springs, Virginia, he became known in the golfing world as the Virginian Hillbilly. Snead was a colorful figure and his natural ability at the game won him many admirers. It was said that he never had a lesson, that he just picked up the game from watching the members play at the Cascades Club in Hot Springs where he worked as a caddie when he was a boy. Snead was a golfing sensation who was quickly capturing the imagination of golf fans as the successor to the legendary players like Ouimet, Jones, Sarazen, and Hagen. Becoming a celebrity on the national scene as the 1940's approached, Snead was part of a new generation of touring professionals that included Scotland's Tommy Armour, and America's Byron Nelson and Ben Hogan as its stars.

Snead was another new client of sports agent Fred Corcoran and was his guest at Woodland that day. Chay was in his mid-sixties at the time of Snead's visit and was considered a golfing icon by all of the members of the club after nearly 30 years of honorable service at Woodland.

Snead had carelessly dropped his very expensive and impressive-looking bag of clubs haphazardly on the walkway in front the clubhouse before he went inside for some pre-match refreshments. Later Snead and his party would head out for a round with Corcoran, the club president, and—by tradition—with the club pro, old Charlie Burgess.

During the time that Snead was in the clubhouse, Chay emerged from his pro shop to discover Snead's bag lying on the path. Fearful that the bag might get stepped on, he directed one of the young caddies to pick up the bag and bring it over to him for safe keeping. Just as the boy handed the set of clubs over to Burgess, Snead and his party exited the clubhouse. Snead looked over at Chay, who now had hold of his bag, and yelled out to Corcoran (and was heard by many of the other members and caddies who had gathered to see the famous Snead), "Hey what the hell is that old man doing with my clubs. Tell him to put them down!" Clearly embarrassed, Corcoran whispered to Snead, "It's all right Sam, that's the club pro, Charlie Burgess." Snead replied offhandedly and unapologetically, "Oh, well, how the hell was I suppose to know that?" and muttered words to the effect that the old man didn't look like much of a pro to him, as he continued toward Chay and his clubs. Chay gently placed the bag back down on the ground and walked away without saying a word.

A short while later, the club president went over to the Burgess cottage and asked Chay to join in the round with Snead. Chay politely declined. Snead may have been a rising golf star but was not much of a gentleman in Chay's humble opinion. Snead, in later years, was often described as the greatest golfer that never won the U.S. Open. He was also the first and only celebrity golfer at Woodland that the affable Chay Burgess refused to play with!

• The Other Babe •

Fred Corcoran's growing stable of sports celebrities during the late 1930s included another young golfing sensation that Chay was very pleased to play golf with many times. "Babe" Didrickson Zaharias was acclaimed to be the world's greatest woman golfer just four years after she first picked up a club for the first time when she was in her mid-twenties.

Her relatively late start in golf followed an incredible and successful career in a host of other sports and athletic endeavors, starting as a schoolgirl in Beaumont, Texas. She was born Mildred Didrickson in 1914 and soon earned the nickname "Babe," some say after Babe Ruth, in a tribute to her tremendous athletic prowess. She was a great high school basketball player who later excelled in tennis, track and field, baseball, swimming, diving, cycling, skating, bowling, as well as golf. As a youngster, she took the singles and doubles titles in the first tennis tournament she ever participated in. Several days before the tournament, she had watched a few games, borrowed a racquet, and mastered the sport easily.

Babe was chosen as America's leading woman athlete three times, and in 1947 was the first American ever to win the British Woman's Amateur Golf Championship after capturing the U.S. Amateur the year before. She led the 1932 American Women's Olympic Track Team setting World and Olympic Records for the javelin throw and the hurdles. She also tied for first place in the high jump.

Babe had just married professional wrestler George Zaharias in December of 1938 when she embarked on a spring exhibition golf tour, including Woodland, arranged by her manager Fred Corcoran. While on the tour, she offered a cash prize of several hundred dollars to any man who could out-drive her off the tee. No one at the club, including Chay and legendary long ball hitter Jesse Guilford, collected from Zaharias that day or at any other time she was at Woodland.

Corcoran remained associated with Didrickson-Zaharias as her manager for years and in 1948 she was among the top women pros that Corcoran organized into the Ladies Professional Golf Association (LPGA).

Fred Corcoran was the very embodiment of the changing world of golf during the 1930s, 40s, and 50s because of his many related endeavors. Besides his involvement with the LPGA and his sports agent business he managed the Ryder Cup teams of 1937, 1939, and 1953, and was the founder of the Golf Writers Association of America. For his lifelong contribution to golf, Corcoran was elected into the World Golf Hall of Fame in 1978.

• Ted Bishop •

Before Chay finished out the 1939 season and prepared for his eventual retirement from the game, he was presented with another young amateur golfer who appeared to be a possible successor to his legendary students Ouimet and Guilford. Stanley E. "Ted" Bishop had been an "under thirty" junior member at Woodland since 1935, after a short spell as an assistant professional at a club in nearby Framingham, Massachusetts. Bishop sought and received his amateur reinstatement from the USGA and concentrated on preparing for the National Amateur under the guidance of Burgess. In 1937, he had attracted a lot of local attention when he won a match play tournament at Commonwealth Country Club and later won a NEPGA Pro-Am tournament held at Woodland that same year when he teamed up with Wellesley Country Club professional, Tom Howe. In 1939 Chay's newest pupil set a Woodland record of 64, one stroke better than Jesse Guilford's mark of 65 set in 1925. Having the opportunity to work with still another fine young amateur before his retirement was a rewarding and exciting finale to Chay's memorable career.

• Charles the Third •

Perhaps the most important young amateur golfer to Chay that year was his own grandson, Charles the Third. Little Charlie was sixteen and had spent almost every weekend and all of his school vacations at the club with Chay and Hattie since he was eight or nine years old. Young

Charlie had become a regular caddie at Woodland and often carried his grandfather's bag and the bags of many fine golfers. He also had developed into a pretty fair golfer himself, shooting close to the mid-eighties on a good day.

There were two classifications of caddies then: schoolboys and day caddies. Schoolboys were available to carry clubs after school, during vacations, and on the weekends. These younger boys would be graded as "A", "B", or "C" caddies depending on their age or experience. The most inexperienced, the C-caddie would get a lighter ladies bag or perhaps an older member's bag to carry around on a "loop" or round of golf. The A-caddie was older, more experienced and would carry the bags of the club's better players, sometime two bags at once—"doubles".

Charlie was by virtue of his age and experience a higher-level caddie than most of the other schoolboy caddies, somewhere in between the schoolboys and the day caddies, who were in fact young men. Most of them were in their early to mid-twenties, some even older, and were available for the better golfers all day and throughout the entire season. The day caddies had a certain worldliness about them as they easily carried doubles around the course—twice a day when they had the chance.

Most of the day caddies had little education or skills for other employment, and many of them seemed to enjoy spending what little money they earned on cigarettes, gambling, and drinking. However some were quite skilled at playing golf and had aspirations to move up in the club's hierarchy to clubhouse work, perhaps into the pro shop as an assistant. Woodland had a well-respected day caddie known simply as Sam the Caddie to everyone. Sam was an excellent golfer and was the captain of the Woodland caddie golf team that played against the other area clubs and was permitted to practice on the course every Monday when the demand by the members was lowest.

On one occasion during the summer of 1939, the Woodland caddie team was scheduled to play against its archrivals, the caddies at the neighboring Brae Burn Country Club. So intense were the competitions that even the club members would take an interest and some pride in the achievements of their caddies if they beat another club's team. The younger Woodland caddies were fiercely loyal to their team even though their neighborhood friends, cousins, or brothers might caddie at the opposing club. Sam was by far the most skilled member of the Woodland caddie team, but he took ill just before the long-anticipated Brae Burn match. Without a full team, the match would have been a forfeit. The team needed a substitute and Sam suggested young Charlie.

Charlie was both flattered and frightened at the offer. He had never played in a serious tournament before and had never played on the Brae Burn links where the match was going to be held. But he played often and fairly well, so he apprehensively stepped in as the substitute for the ailing Sam. As he went round the Brae Burn course, he kept waiting for something to fall apart in his game, and he was fearful that he would let the team down during the important match.

When he had left home that morning, the pride in his grandfather's eyes strengthened his resolve. The feeling stayed with young Charlie hole after hole as the match got underway, and instead of falling apart as he feared he might, he began to play better and better. He could hardly believe how well he was doing, and soon he knew that this was going to be the best round of his young life. When the match was over, he had done more than just fill in for the older caddy Sam. The team won and Charlie's victory was the deciding match. On a course he had never played on before, he shot an incredible 73!

Chay Burgess had played, coached, and observed thousands of golf matches in his lifetime. It is doubtful that any one of them could have meant more to him than did the match that his grandson won that day.

• Retirement •

By the end of 1939, Chay had quietly retired from Woodland after 30 years as the club's professional. Close friends and family observed the occasion, but because of the Depression and the specter of another World War looming on the horizon, the formal celebration was minimal. The club presented Chay with a $100 monthly pension and the use of the little cottage next to the clubhouse for as long as he wished to remain living there. At age sixty-six, Chay was happy to remain available to assist his young successor Johnny Thoren, who had been a local club professional for six years and had a brief fling on the PGA tour.

Thoren had taken on Johnny Fitzgerald, a well-known professional hockey player for the Boston Olympics, as an assistant. Many hockey players, like baseball players, seemed to have a natural affinity and aptitude for golf. Young Fitzgerald certainly did and he spent many hours being coached by the retired Burgess on the Woodland practice tee as he developed his game and teaching skills. In the early 1940s, the National Hockey League was stocked almost exclusively with Canadian-born athletes. Fitzgerald was one of the top American players of the era who starred in the highly competitive American League, the minor league of pro hockey at a time when there were only six National Hockey League teams. The colorful hockey star remained at Woodland with Burgess and Thoren for several seasons during the forties.

Francis was now a successful businessman in his late forties and he and his wife Stella were busy raising their two teenage daughters. He was a senior member of the nation's golfing establishment and was elected to serve a three-year term on the USGA's Executive Committee. The Professional Golfers' Association of America also honored him as an original inductee in the PGA's Hall of Fame. The Hall of Fame was established in 1940 and Francis joined three other great amateurs honored by the professional organization that year: Jerry Travers, Chick Evans, and Bobby Jones.

Throughout the golf season of 1940, Johnny Thoren followed in Chay's footsteps by linking up with Woodland's premier amateur in many competitions. Like Chay, who often paired up with Ouimet and Guilford, Thoren and Ted Bishop became a formidable duo in many New England PGA Pro-Ams. In September of 1940, the pair combined to capture the "Downeast" New England crown that Burgess and Guilford once wore. The Thoren–Bishop team also took top honors at the season's final Greater Boston Pro-Am held at their home club, with a low gross score of 132 for the 36-hole tournament.

Chay was enjoying his retirement playing an occasional round of golf while living frugally on the modest pension provided by the club. Hat, although slowed down a bit by her chronic stomach ailment and the added aches and pains caused by her domestic work during the Depression, could still cook and bake a grand Scottish banquet for her family and friends. Charlie the younger was forty-three and after nearly 10 years of seeking regular employment during the Depression finally landed a position with the Dole Cam Corporation (later Honeywell) as a machinist. He and his family returned to nearby Newton Corner, after young Charles the Third graduated with honors from Cambridge High and Latin School at age sixteen in June of 1940.

The younger Burgess was a very gifted student and was double promoted during his elementary school years, which accounted for his matriculation from the Latin School at such a young age. Young Charlie spent the summer of 1940 at Woodland assisting the caddie master and in the fall joined the Austin-Hastings Machinery Company in Cambridge as a clerk. His mother had long hoped that Charlie would take advantage of the academic scholarship he was offered and attend Harvard, but Charlie steadfastly insisted on doing his part to help out the family and went to work instead.

One mild Saturday afternoon in early December, "Chuck," who had turned seventeen in August, and several of his pals from the Auburndale area, met at a diner near Woodland for a soda and to plan their evening adventures. He was the only one of the group to have a driver's license, and better yet he had his grandfather's car.

One of the gang had heard that some girls on the other side of town were going to have a house party that evening and that their parents would be away! They all piled into Chay's big Dodge sedan and Charlie found his way to the address of the supposed party, only to find the house quiet and still. While the boys lingered in the running automobile in front of the house, a beautiful brunette just about their age stepped out of the front door to see if they were lost or needed help. Young Charlie was instantly smitten with the lovely Rita Sullivan who innocently answered their inquiries about the party rumored to be at her house. In a scene reminiscent of an old Andy Hardy movie starring Mickey Rooney and Judy Garland, young Charlie was cast into the part of a lovestruck teenager. Charlie quickly hatched a plan. He convinced his friends to forget about the party and to go to a movie theater instead. Once he drove them there, he made up an excuse that he forgot he had to get the car home early and left. In minutes, he was back in Newton Center, and he and Rita made their first date that very next week, courting until still another World War changed their lives and the lives of millions of other young couples and families everywhere.

• Back to Duty, WWII •

Chay's successor John Thoren was developing a solid following among club members and was exceedingly busy in the pro shop and on the practice tee as the membership began to fill up slowly once again. He was also very active in many New England PGA events during the summer of 1941. Thoren had just left Woodland for a fling at the winter professional touring circuit when the devastating news of December 7, 1941 flashed across America. The fate of the nation was once again placed in harm's way as America prepared for another World War. Thoren soon joined hundreds of other PGA professionals as they enlisted in the Armed Forces. After Thoren's enlistment in the Army, Arthur Wedgeworth took over as Woodland's professional. He also teamed up with Ted Bishop to become a very successful professional-amateur team during the early years of the war.

At the beginning of World War II, the draft age was set at twenty, but thousands of teenagers flocked to the recruiting stations anxious to do their part in the fight against the totalitarian aggressors in Europe and the Far East. Charlie the Third was only nineteen when he enlisted in the Army Signal Corps in 1942, and although he was deeply in love with his sweetheart Rita, the patriotic call to arms drew him and many young men away from their homes and loved ones. Like so many other young couples, Charlie and Rita married in 1943 just three weeks before Charlie shipped out to the West Coast for eventual duty in the Pacific Theater.

America quickly moved into a wartime economy and many of the things taken for granted, even during the Depression, were now in short supply because of the war effort. Rubber, for example, became a top military need and the domestic production of new rubber products almost came to a halt. The United States Rubber Company shifted production lines in early 1942 to an "All-out-for-winning-the-War" basis and ceased the production of U.S. golf balls. The company froze all stocks of golf balls and instituted a voluntary rationing system of distribution to the PGA professionals across the nation.

The USGA voted to hold a "Hail America" Open golf tournament in June of 1942 to replace the National Open. The Hail America match was planned for the dual purpose of raising funds for war relief and for promoting the physical fitness program sponsored by the U.S. Office of Civilian Defense. Because so many young men became engaged in the war and armed service, almost all of the major golf competitions were put on indefinite hiatus. The U.S. Open and National Amateur were not held from 1942 through 1945, and the British Open and Amateur championships were canceled in 1940 and did not resume until 1946.

In 1944, Chay received a call from Woodland's president requesting him to come out of retirement and take over his Woodland duties once again as Arthur Wedgewood was also called to active duty. Chay had just turned seventy years old the previous November, was still a formidable player for his age, and had not lost his ability to teach and run the club. The biggest challenge to any club professional during the war was to make sure that the members' equipment lasted for the duration and that golf balls were available. The PGA of America warned, "The golf ball problem is becoming more acute as time goes on. [Every] PGA member must start immediately to obtain all the old golf balls available for the purpose of reprocessing, and . . . new balls still remaining must be apportioned wisely if the game is to continue during the duration of the War. Golf Clubs may be forced to close down due to the lack of a sufficient supply of balls." Fortunately Chay had always been thrifty with his supplies and was still very skilled at making old clubs serviceable when they needed repair or an overhaul.

His grandson was stationed in the Hawaiian Islands prior to his participation in what was considered the Pacific D-Day, the invasion of the Japanese-held island of Saipan in June of 1944. Hawaii had an abundance of plush and famous golf courses that were available to any GI if he had his own clubs and golf balls. Young Sergeant Burgess was pleasantly surprised one day to receive a package of a dozen brand-new balls from his grandfather, a gift that even a general would envy! One day when he was off duty and out for a round of golf on a beautiful seaside course, he partnered up with a distinguished older gentleman who he found out during the round was a very high-ranking naval officer on the staff of the Pacific Command. When the admiral admired the stock of golf balls the twenty-one-year-old GI had to play with, Charlie wisely and unselfishly offered several to the admiral. For the rest of the round, the two played along like they were lifelong friends.

Chay's second tour of duty back at Woodland passed unremarkably, at least as far as any major or noteworthy golf events were concerned. Like the rest of the nation, the Woodland folks were listening to the radio and reading the daily papers hoping for an end to the hostilities. Finally in August 1945, the surrender of Japan meant that young Charlie would be coming home from his Pacific duty. Once on American soil, he was reunited with his wife, Private First Class Rita Burgess of the newly formed Marine Corps Women's Reserve, who was stationed at Camp Pendleton, California, after enlisting in 1944.

During the war, Chay's granddaughter Mary met and married a young Marine. The couple had a baby boy who became one of the first members of the famous post war Baby Boom. Ironically in a family that already featured three generations of Burgess men named Charles, Mary's husband was named Charles as well, and their little boy became Charlie Tower, Jr.!

Soon all of the Burgess clan who served in the war, including young Charlie and the Nicoll brothers—Willie, Charlie, and Bert—returned home safely. Old Charlie Burgess was ready to retire for good at age seventy-two, but Woodland still insisted that their long-term professional remain connected to the club in some way. Even though Yancy Doyle, a young Holy Cross College golf star, was appointed as the first postwar professional at the club, Chay remained at home, only yards away from the pro shop for his counsel and assistance when needed. Chay continued to work with Woodland's new amateur star Ted Bishop and saw him win the 1946 State Amateur Crown at the Charles River Country Club and the New England Amateur Crown over at nearby Brae Burn.

• A Third National Champion •

Ted Bishop had just recently returned to Massachusetts from service in England during the war. He entered the Army in 1943 and was discharged during the early summer of 1946. His return to competitive golf began when he joined many of his fellow returning veterans for an All-Servicemen's Golf Tournament at Woodland sponsored by the club, the Massachusetts Golf Association, and the Greater Boston Wartime

United Services Organization or USO. The amateur record holder at Woodland showed the field he was ready to play again as he shot a 70 for the low gross top prize in the match. His victories in the Massachusetts and New England Amateurs soon followed. Bishop settled in nearby Dedham, Massachusetts, after the war and Ted joined the nearby Norfolk Golf Club as he began his quest for national recognition.

Bishop continued his winning ways in September of 1946 in the National Amateur held at the Baltusrol Golf Club in Springfield, New Jersey, where Chay's old friend and popular former National Open Champion Johnny Farrell was head professional. The 1946 National Amateur meeting was the first held after the war and interest in the event was high, reflected by the largest galleries recorded since the 1930 Championship. Ted faced 150 contestants in the tournament, each of whom had survived grueling sectional qualification rounds.

Of the 150 entrants, only 64 qualified further for the championship rounds. Bishop did so with a medal round total of 148 for the 36 holes, a very respectable average of 74 per round. Ted faced a series of tough opponents in the match play rounds and most of the early contests were extremely close. In the first three rounds he defeated John Dawson 2 and 1, Charles Kocsis 2 and 1, and then Dick Chapman, a former national champion, again by the margin of two holes up with one to play. In the fourth round, he beat Charles Lind 4 and 3. Surprisingly his easiest win came in the semi-finals when he dispatched Robert Willits of Kansas City 10 and 9.

The final round was a closely matched duel that ended in a tie requiring an exciting sudden death play-off between Bishop and Stanley Quick of Los Angeles, the reigning Public Links Champion.

Both Bishop and Quick were World War II veterans. Bishop served in the European Theater, while Quick had landed on the Japanese-held island of Tarawa in the Pacific. Quick was a Navy Seabee and still suffered a nervous tic that was visible when he addressed the ball. The disability was said to have resulted from the incessant bombings by the enemy on Quick's position after he landed with the first wave of invading troops. Bishop also still carried a reminder of the recent war as his lanky frame was carrying much less weight than normal, down to about 160 lbs.

When the two veterans teed off, Bishop at 6'3" and Quick at 5'6", it looked like a "Mutt and Jeff" match up. But the finale was far from a comic book affair as it was quite dramatic right to the very end, requiring an exciting extra play-off hole. Bishop prevailed and beat Quick, 1-up for the National Championship. With the victory, Ted became the first player ever to win the Massachusetts, New England, and United States Amateur Championship in the same year. A golfing Triple Crown! When Ted returned from his victory at Baltusrol, Woodland conferred an honorary membership on him, thus perpetuating his long time affiliation with the Newton club.

Bishop's victory at Baltusrol made Chay Burgess unique among American teaching pros. Never before had one golf club professional nurtured a trio of National Amateur Champions. His longevity as a great teacher was demonstrated as his pupils captured their national championships over a span of four decades. Their considerable accomplishments made him America's foremost teacher and coach of champions. In his native Montrose, Chay once competed against the famed Great Triumvirate of Harry Vardon, James Braid, and John H. Taylor. In his adopted land he had taught and developed his own triumvirate of great American champions: Francis Ouimet, Jesse Guilford, and now Ted Bishop.

• Final Rounds •

Celebrations reigned at Woodland during the fall and winter months. First, a grand event was staged for Bishop, honoring him for his great accomplishment. Chay, of course, joined the rest of his Woodland family for the special homecoming event as an honored guest. Shortly after the testimonial to Bishop was over, the Woodland members began planning still another tribute to their beloved retired professional and his wife. Chay and Hat celebrated their fiftieth wedding anniversary in January of 1947 and the club wanted to make it a special event for them. The anniversary was made a bit more special for Chay because his entire family would be present, including the newest addition, another baby Burgess. Chay and Hat were delighted when grandson Charlie and his wife Rita started their family with an eight-pound blue-eyed baby boy they named—what else—Charles!

Charles Burgess the Fourth was now "Baby Charlie" to the family, but things got a bit confusing when Mary and Charlie Tower were visiting with their "Baby Charlie." Grandfather Burgess [Charles the Second] stepped in to relieve the confusion by calling wee Charlie Burgess "Bougie"—a playful nickname he had for his father back in the twenties. Baby Charlie Tower was called Dougal, or "Dougie" for short.

Once again the members of Woodland took the opportunity to show their genuine affection and respect for the man described as "Woodland itself." The president of the club sent out a request to the membership to contribute to a generous purse of "at least a thousand dollars" to remind Chay and Hat "that their many friends and acquaintances had not forgotten them in their declining years." The master of ceremonies at the special event was naturally Chay's great friend and special pupil Francis Ouimet.

Shortly after their anniversary, Hattie began to experience increasing medical difficulties, many harking back to her long-endured intestinal problems. In addition, the years of hard physical labor that she put in during the Depression and a weakened heart began to take its toll. After a prolonged illness, Harriet died at age seventy-four in October of 1949 at the Newton-Wellesley Hospital, which was located just across the street from her Woodland home.

After Harriet passed away, young Charlie, Rita, and baby Charlie moved into the little cottage at Woodland to care for and provide companionship for Chay. Charlie had enrolled at Boston University under the post war "GI Bill" of educational rights for veterans, while Rita cared for Chay and the baby. Even at his advanced age, Old Chay was reputed to still be able to shoot in the 80s and was often requested to play a round with some of the older members at the club. He was also always a welcome visitor to the clubhouse and pro shop, but spent most of his time doting on his great-grandson.

In 1951, Francis was afforded the greatest honor that any golfer from the United States had ever been given. He was elected Captain of the Royal and Ancient Golf Club of St. Andrews, the first American ever so honored. Chay was thrilled that his former student was now enshrined alongside so many of the great golf heroes he once knew so well in his native land.

Chay's last official act as Woodland professional came in 1952 when the club celebrated the 50th anniversary of its incorporation. His two "young" amateur stars were on hand to play an exhibition round. Francis, fifty-eight, and Jessie, fifty-seven years old, shot rounds of 78 and 79 respectively. The two Woodland stars shared the spotlight with their old coach and mentor at the evening's gala banquet, where they received special commemorative plaques and Chay once again was rewarded by his club with a generous purse.

Chay remained happy and content in his small course-side cottage for the next several years as his grandson pursued his college education and worked at various part-time jobs. The old golfer's days were filled with the pleasure of attending to the newest Little Charlie. As baby Charlie grew, learned to walk, and became a little boy, Chay made the entire golf club his great-grandson's playground and even had him enrolled as a member of the club when he was less than a year old!

One day in the springtime of 1954, when Chay was eighty years old, a representative of Woodland came to the little cottage to inform him that the club desired to expand their operation in light of the modern demands of their members. The club was going to install a new family swimming pool and make other improvements and as a result, they needed the land on which Chay's home stood. What they did not tell him was that they were also going to reduce his pension by half, which they did just a year later.

It was understandable and almost inevitable that this day would come. The governing boards and directors of any organization come and go. Committees evolve and change. By 1954, there were few members left at the club who remembered the verbal promises and the gentleman's agreement from long ago that assured Chay he would always have a pension and a place to live provided by the club. Chay stoically listened to the rationalizing of the official and, with his characteristic nod of the head and with few words, made arrangements to leave.

Charlie, Rita, and the children moved to an apartment just west of Wellesley, Massachusetts, where the recent Boston University graduate had landed a job as a high school history teacher. By this time, the youngest Burgess family had expanded by two. Baby girl Kathleen had been born in 1951 and David, the newest Burgess was only months old.

Charlie and Kitty lived nearby in Newtonville. Charlie was now a mid-level executive in the Dole Cam Corporation (later Honeywell) working on guidance systems for the intercontinental ballistic missiles that the country was developing during the initial years of the Cold War. Kitty had continued to work as an operator for Postal Telegraph, now called Western Union. She had transferred some time before from Boston to a branch of the company located in the Newton Corner railroad station, the very same station that Chay and Francis triumphantly returned home to after the National Amateur in 1931.

For the first time in over 80 years Chay Burgess would not be living on or near a golf course as he moved in with Charlie and Kitty. Golf links had defined and shaped his life. From his first encounters with Bob Dow, Tom Morris, and the other grand old men of the game to his own experiences as a mentor of champions, Chay had always been a part of golf and golf had been a part of him in so many interesting ways.

Chay lived a quiet life at the home of his son and observed the changing world through the newspapers and the wondrous new invention that transformed American homes during the 1950's—television. Imagine the thoughts of a man who learned the game of golf on the sandy links of Scotland in the 1800's watching the images of the new stars of golf like Gene Littler, Ben Hogan, Julius Boros, Gary Player, and Arnold Palmer right in his own living room. In the summer of 1954 he sat with his son, grandson, and eight-year-old great-grandson Charles the Fourth, watching the exciting one-stroke victory of Ed Furgol over Gene Littler in the first televised U.S. Open. It had been 44 years, before television, before even radio had been invented, that Chay had played in his first U.S. Open. And it had been 41 years since his star pupil had changed the course of American golf in that same tournament. It was a remarkable day of reminiscences for the old pro to share with his family.

As the years passed, Chay suffered a mild stroke that sometimes left him confused in regard to common, everyday matters. During these times he would, however, recall with amazing clarity the events and people in his life from years before. Occasionally, he would pick up one of the several golf clubs he kept in his old leather bag. His large and callused hands would still gracefully and naturally hold the club with the expert grip he learned as a boy in Scotland and he would take a practice swing—an act he had performed countless times in his life. Chay picked up his clubs for the final time in May of 1960, and at the age of eighty-six his remarkable journey ended.

As a young boy in Scotland, Charlie Burgess thought that he was destined to spend his life as a stonemason building structures and foundations designed to last for years—block by block, building by building. Instead, he helped to build something even more lasting. He and his fellow pioneering professionals built the foundation of the modern game of golf—lesson by lesson, student by student, and match by match. They guided the evolution of the game from the days of Old Tom Morris into the twentieth century, paving the way for today's new heroes to emerge. Chay and his contemporaries were also the craftsmen who forged the seminal links connecting the past, the present, and the future of the golf—"Golf Links."

Acknowledgements

I would like to thank the many helpful individuals who supported my efforts, and who shared their time, energy, talents, and knowledge with me. No one has been more instrumental in the development of this book than my wife. Above all, her encouragement, support, and faith in me made it possible. I would also like to recognize the importance of my extended family to me, particularly my mother, my children, and my grandson Charles Dylan Burgess for being my own very special "links."

My sincere appreciation and gratitude is extended to all of the other people and organizations that have in various and countless ways, made this book possible. I hope that I have remembered you all, my sincere apology to anyone that I may have missed, without you this work would not have been accomplished:

Bob Benson, Head Professional of the Palm Beach Country Club
Carolyn Boday, Historian of the Women's Golf Association of Massachusetts
Jim Bodreau, Head Librarian, Lasell College, Newton, MA
Rod Burgess, London, Burgess family genealogy
Carolyn Cooney Burns, Hatherly Country Club
John Crawford, Director of the Montrose Football Club

William Coull, Montrose golf historian and member Montrose Mercantile Golf Club

Michael T. Costello, Sr., my late father-in-law who honored the heritage of golf and the people in this book long before I thought to chronicle their stories

Brian DeLacey, golf historian and friend

Bob Denny, Director of Media Relations, and the West Palm Beach administrative staff of the PGA of America

Bob Donovan, Director, and the entire staff of the Francis Ouimet Scholarship Fund

Peter Georgiady and the many members of the Golf Collectors Society that I had the pleasure of meeting in Dayton and elsewhere

Bob Gormley, former editor of the Northeastern University Press—the promise has been kept

Robert A. Graham, Bristol, Connecticut—formerly of Montrose, Scotland—for his 1970 correspondence

David Forbes, Associate Director of the Dundee Football Club

Ted Hansberry, former Woodland Golf Club President, President of the Francis Ouimet Scholarship Fund, and friend

The late "Bun" Howie

Chrissey Howie and family, Stan Rygula, and Muriel Addison, for everything— especially their wonderful Scottish hospitality

Alan Jackson, British Golf Collector's Society

Michael Jamieson, Peninsula Country Club, San Mateo, CA

Kris Januzik and the staff of the Tufts Archives, Pinehurst, NC

Randon Jerris, Pattie Moran, and the entire staff of the United States Golf Association Archives at the Golf House, Far Hills, NJ

Richard Johnson, Director of the New England Sports Museum

Willie Johnson, Montrose Football Club

Anne King, Scottish genealogist—for her help on the Burgess family tree

Claudette La Bonte, LPGA, friend, and advisor

Don Lyons, President Emeritus of the New England PGA

Tee Martin, Editor of the *Little Black Book of Golf*

Tom Martin, Publisher of the *Little Black Book of Golf*

Valerie Mitchell, Director General of the English-Speaking Union, London, and special thanks to the Boston Branch of the English Speaking Union for the opportunity to travel and study in the UK

The New England Professional Golfers' Association, with special thanks to Ed Carbone, Executive Director, and to the 2003 Hall of Fame selection committee for honoring Chay in such a wonderful way

J. Louis Newell, Historian of The Country Club, Brookline, Massachusetts

The wonderful Ouimet family—"Bro" and Barbara (Ouimet) McLean, John and Jane (Ouimet) Salvi

Richard Owen, Historian of the Portsmouth Football Club

J.M. Piggins, "Freeman of Montrose," for his 1970 correspondence

Denis Rice, former editor, *Montrose Review*, Montrose, Scotland

Paul Richards, Historian of the Beverly Country Club of Chicago

John Rigg, Historian of the Muirfield Golf Club, Scotland

Susan Roberts, for her valued word processing skills and tutorials

Aaron Schmidt, and the staff of the Boston Public Library print department

Michael Sherret, Sydney, Australia—Clark family historian

Eidith "Babs" Smith, of the Montrose Burgess family

Peter F. Stevens, author, historian, and valued advisor

David Sullivan, Historian of the Millwall Football Club

Ian Sykes, Secretary of the Royal Montrose Golf Club

Mary Burgess Tower, the late Charles S. Tower, Sr., and the entire Tower family—especially Charlie for his early Burgess family research and Jimmy for his support

Lisa Tuite, Head Librarian, *Boston Globe* newspaper

Robert S. West, former Secretary of the Montrose Mercantile Golf Club

Judy Van Woert, and the family of Jesse Guilford

Bob Wood of Keene, New Hampshire, son of baseball legend "Smokey" Joe Wood

Finally—special thanks to Bill Nowlin for his belief in this project, and to the entire staff of Rounder Books, especially Steven Jurgensmeyer, Steve Netsky, and Brad San Martin, for their fine work in the development of this book

Works Cited

Allen, G. F. *Luxury Trains of the World*. Everest House 1979

American Golfer, The. December 1905, September 1911, October 1913

Bertagna, Joe. *Crimson in Triumph*. Stephen Greene Press, Lexington, MA 1986

Boston American. 1935

Boston Evening American. 1953

Boston Evening Transcript. 1909, 1913, 1916, 1921, 1927

Boston Globe. 1909, 1910, 1913, 1914, 1928, 1929, 1941, 1947, 1999

Boston Herald. 1919, 1924, 1931

Boston Post. 1931

Boston Sunday Globe. 1914, 1921, 1946

Boston Sunday Herald. 1988

Boston Traveler. 1915, 1916, 1919, 1921, 1922, 1928, 1931

Boston Transcript. 1916, 1920, 1921, 1922, 1923, 1926, 1927, 1934

Burgess, Charles, I. personal papers, correspondence, and remembrances

Burgess, Charles, II. personal papers, correspondence, and remembrances

Burgess, Charles, III. personal papers, correspondence, and remembrances

Braynard & Miller, Eds. *Fifty Famous Liners.* Norton Co., NY and London 1982

Chicago Tribune. 1931

Christian Science Monitor. 1934

Corcoran, Fred with Harvey, Bud. *Unplayable Lies.* Duell, Sloan and Pearce, NY 1965

Cotton, Henry. *A History of Golf.* Lippencott Co. NY 1975

Cousins, Geoffrey. *Golf in Britain.* Routledge & Kegan Paul, London 1975

Coull, William. *Golf in Montrose.* Wm. Coull, Montrose, Scotland 1993, revised 2004

Darwin, Bernard. *Golf Journal,* "Mr. Ouimet Makes History (1913)." 1940, reprinted 1988

DeLacey, Brian. *A Willie Campbell Remembrance—The Scottish Influence on Golf in Greater Boston.* Relux Press, Malden, MA 1999

DeLacey, Brian. *Battlefield of the Best: The Historic Golfing Glories of Mussleburgh.* Relux Press, Malden, MA 1999

Gibson, Nevin. *A Pictorial History of Golf.* Barnes and Co., NY 1968

Glasgow Herald. June 8, 1905

Golf. "Our Boston Letter." May 1914

Golf Illustrated. September 9, 1904; October 21, 1904; June 30, 1905

Golf Magazine. April 1913

Golfers Magazine. June 1916, October 1926

Graffis, Herb. *History of the PGA.* Thomas Y. Crowley Co., NY 1975

Graham, Robert A. correspondence. Bristol, RI 1988

Grimsley, Will. *Golf, Its History, People and Events.* Prentice Hall, NJ 1966

Henderson, I.A.N. *Angus and the Mearns.* John Donald Publishers Ltd., Edinburgh, Scotland 1990

Hickok, Ralph. *New Encyclopedia of Sports.* McGraw-Hill Book Co., NY 1977

Hirshberg, Al. *The Braves—The Pick and the Shovel.* Waverley House, Boston 1948

Hollander, Zander. *The American Encyclopedia of Soccer.* Everest House, NY 1980

Lardner, Rex. *The Great Golfers.* Putnam's Sons, NY

Manchester, City of. *Manchester (NH) City Directory.* 1915

Martin, H. B. *50 Years of American Golf.* Dodd, Mead & Co., NY 1936

Maclean, Fitzroy. *A Concise History of Scotland.* Thames and Hudson, London 1970

Meany, Tom. *Babe Ruth—The Big Moments of the Big Fellow.* Grosset and Dunlap, NY 1947

Morrison, Ian. *100 Greatest Golfers.* Brompton Books Corp. 1988

Minutes of the Mercantile Golf Club Committee. Montrose, Scotland 1898–1908.

Minutes of the Executive Committee of the PGA of America, 1916–27

Minutes of the Royal Albert Golf Club. Montrose, Scotland 1903–1908

Montrose Review. 1860–1922

Montrose Standard and Angus And Mearns Register. 1922

Movius, Geoffrey H. *The Second Book of Harvard Athletics.* Harvard Varsity Club, Cambridge, MA 1964

Mulvoy, Thomas F., ed. *Wollaston Golf Club Diamond Jubilee.* 1970

Murphy, Thomas J. *Woodland: Seventy-five Years of Golf.* Woodland Golf Club, Newton, MA 1977

Murray, James. *Millwall: Lions of the South.* Millwall F. C. publication 1988

Neasom, Mike, Cooper, Mick, & Robinson, Doug. *POMPEY- The History of the Portsmouth Football Club.* Milestone Publications, Portsmouth, England 1984

New England Professional Golfers' Organization, Incorporation Charter #380–83, Commonwealth of Massachusetts. February 2, 1921

Newcastle Football Club. *The Black and White Alphabet.* team publication

Newton, City of. *Newton Census Directory.* 1913, 1917

Newton Graphic. 1918, 1920, 1931

Newton Times. 1919, 1920

Newton Journal. 1921

Nicoll, Harry. personal correspondence.

Norumbega Park Centennial program book. City of Newton publication 1997

Oraton, George W. ed. *College Soccer.* Spalding's Athletic Library Yearbook. 1913

Ouimet, Francis D. *A Game of Golf.* Houghton Mifflin Co., Boston & NY 1932

Ouimet, Francis D. *Golf Facts for Young People.* The Century Co., NY 1921

Ouimet, Francis D., personal correspondence. 1929, 1936

PGA Publications. *Media Guide* 1994, 1998

Pinehurst Outlook. Vol. XVII, January 24, 1914, 1922, 1930

Piper, George. *Golf in America: The First One Hundred Years.* Abrams Publishers, NY

Portsmouth Evening News. 1900–1902

Professional Golfer of America. May 1920, June 1921, April 1924, 1929, 1932, 1937, 1940, 1946

Professional Golfer's Association, Apollo House, West Midlands, England, Promotions and Information office, correspondence. 1998

Rice, Grantland, ed. *Spalding's Athletic Library Golf Guide.* American Sports Publishing Co., NY 1914, 1915, 1916, 1917

Rice, Grantland. *The American Golfer* "The Siege Gun Gets the Range." October 1921

Richards, Paul. research material for the 90th anniversary of the Beverly Country Club of Chicago, Illinois

Richardson, William D. & Werden, Lincoln A., eds. *The Golfer's Yearbook 1933.* The Golfer's Yearbook Co., NY 1933

St. Nicholas. August 1921

Scottish Tourist Board. *Scotland Home of Golf.* 1978

Simmath Sporting Series. *History of the Montrose Football Club.* Simmath Press Ltd. Dundee, Scotland 1948

Sloan, S. W. Director of the Portsmouth Football Club, correspondence. 1988

Smelser, Marshall. *The Life that Ruth Built.* Quadrangle Publishers 1975

Steel, David. *Golf Records, Facts and Championships.* Guinness Superlatives Ltd., Enfield, Middlesex, England 1987

Stevens, Peter F. *Links Lore.* Brassey's Press, Washington, London 1998

Sullivan, David. Millwall Football Club historian, interview notes. 1999

Tufts, Richard S. *The Scottish Invasion.* Pinehurst Publishers, Pinehurst, NC 1962

Waltham Newton News Tribune. 1947, 1977

Woodland Golf Club. *50 Years in Golfing.* Published by Woodland Golf Club, Newton, MA 1952

Wilding, E.W. Millwall Football Club historian, correspondence. 1988

United States Golf Association. *Constitution, By-Laws, and Rules.* 1898 Edition, Revised Edition, 1909

United States Golf Association. *Official USGA Record Book.* Far Hills, NJ

United States Golf Association. *Yearbook.* 1920

Index

Aberdeen, Scotland 47
Charles F. Adams 234, 236
All-Professional Tournament (Montrose) 55, 56
All-Serviceman's Golf Tournament 252
Amateur Championship at Sandwich (see British Amateur)
The American Golfer 79, 131
Carl Anderson 87
James Anderson 10
John G. Anderson 108, 113, 169
Apawamis Country Club 128
Apple Tree Gang 30
Tommy Armour 16, 243
William Auchterlonie 41
Colin Aylmer 190
Laurence "Laurie" Ayton 163–165, 171
Judge Bacon 155
Baltimore Country Club 224
Baltusrol Golf Club 253
Jim Barnes 105–107, 109, 110, 115, 117, 118, 139, 164, 166, 167, 171, 189, 198, 199
Belmont Springs Country Club 143, 150, 174, 221, 237
Thomas Bendelow 35
Beresford Country Club (now Peninsula) 207, 223
Pattie Berg 223
Beverly Golf Club 163, 211–218
Bing Crosby Pro-Am 184
Stanley E. "Ted" Bishop 2, 245, 248, 250, 252–254
Jock Blair 160, 161, 172
Bill Blaney 206
Florence Boit 32, 33
Aubrey Boomer 199
Boothby-Campbell Shield 40, 54, 56, 60, 63, 84, 143, 164
Julius Boros 257
Boston Braves 141, 232–234, 237, 238, 241
Boston Griscom Cup 175
Boston Newspapermen's Golf Association 177
Boston Red Sox 141, 142, 153, 159, 234–236, 238–240
C. Harry Bowler 172, 173, 175, 178, 194
John Brady 161
Mike Brady 88, 92, 99, 100, 107, 110–12, 115, 116, 150, 161, 167, 171, 189, 196, 199
Brae Burn Country Club 70, 74, 141, 146, 155, 161, 175, 178, 179, 201, 206, 224, 226, 247, 252
James Braid 2, 41, 49, 50, 52, 55, 56, 59, 60, 185, 254
The Breakers Golf Course 66
British Amateur 133, 189, 190, 201, 251
British Open (The Open Championship) 9, 17, 18, 23, 39, 41, 48–52, 55, 56, 58, 67, 74. 99, 111, 133, 136, 162, 171, 178, 186, 189, 198, 201, 251
British Professional Golfers' Association (see also The Professional Golfers' Association) 79, 150
British Professional Golfers' Association Championship (see PGA Match Play Championship)
British Women's Amateur Golf Championship 244
Brookline High School 85, 87, 88, 92, 93, 203
David "Deacon" Brown (Davie Brown) 20, 21, 74
Oscar Bunn 113
Buresford Country Club 207
Anne Campbell Burgess 6
Catherine "Kitty" Burgess 177, 181–183, 188, 194, 212, 218, 227–231, 249, 257
Charlie "Chay" Burgess 1, 2, 3, 5, 8–30, 36–66, 68–86, 88–103, 106, 107, 109, 110, 114–116, 120, 121, 123, 124–129, 133–139, 141–145,

147, 150–154, 148–166, 168, 170–172, 174, 175, 177, 179–181, 183–190, 192–194, 196, 200, 201, 203–209, 211–213, 215–221, 223, 224, 226–237, 239–241, 243–245, 247, 248, 250–252, 254–258
Charles Beattie "Young Charlie" Burgess 23, 39, 49, 59, 60, 71, 72, 94, 97, 98, 153, 154, 160, 162, 174, 177, 178, 181–186, 188, 190, 192, 194, 200, 202, 212, 215, 218, 227–230, 238, 254, 257
Charles Burgess III 191, 194, 215, 227–229, 236, 239, 245–251, 255, 256
Charles Burgess IV 255–257
David Burgess 6, 23, 38, 53
David Burgess 256
Harriet "Hattie" Low Burgess 22, 23, 39, 49, 61, 62, 71, 72, 160, 180–184, 187, 194, 218, 227–230, 236, 245, 248, 254, 255
Kathleen Burgess 256
Rita Sullivan Burgess 249, 250, 252, 254–256
Billy Burke 209–211
Jack Burke 172
Jack Burns 17
Robert Burns 11
George H. W. Bush 189
George W. Bush 189
Chris Calloway 104, 109
Alex Campbell 74, 99, 100, 109, 110
Georgina Stuart Campbell 74
John Campbell 7
Matt Campbell 192
Willie Campbell 17, 32, 35, 74
Canterbury Golf Club 181
Carnoustie, Scotland 5, 17, 42, 45, 47, 50, 51, 55
Cascades Club 242
Dick Chapman 253
Charles River Country Club 159, 193, 252
Bonnie Prince Charlie 11
Chicago Golf Club 30
Edmund Childs 194
Civilian Conservation Corps 228–230
Charlie Clare 224
C. Peter Clark 156
John Clark 70
Thomas Clark 70
Walter Clark 70
Glenna Collette 175
Tony Colombo 126
Edward Colthard 55
Commonwealth Golf Club 88, 160, 188, 245
Archie Compston 199
Frank Connolly 215
Fred Corcoran 106, 221, 237, 240, 243–245
George Corcoran 240
John Corcoran 240
Coronation Tankard Championship 53, 54, 60, 63, 64, 164
William Coull 5, 61
The Country Club (Brookline, Massachusetts) 17, 30, 32, 35, 70, 74, 85–87, 89, 94, 99, 103–106, 109, 114, 119, 120, 125, 140, 179
John Cowan 176, 191
Wiffie Cox 210
John Craven 190
Geordie Croll 38
Joe Cronin 239
Bing Crosby 2, 154, 184, 237, 238
Bob Crosby 237
Pearly Crosby 206
Robert A. Cruickshank 196
Bill Cunningham 213–215
Julian W. Curtis 67
Bernard Darwin 125, 190
Charles Darwin 125
Jock Davidson 12, 13
Willie Davis 112
Dedham Country and Polo Club 107, 223
George Dernbach 172
Detroit Golf Club 220
Leo Diegel 167, 172, 188, 199, 210
Donald Ross Trophy 176, 177, 188
Bill Donnolly 219
Dornoch, Scotland 32
John "Jock" Douglas 54, 55
Bob Dow 2, 8, 9, 10, 18, 23, 37, 48, 57, 61, 63, 85, 257
Patrick Doyle 140
Fred Driscoll 176
George Duncan 171, 176, 185, 199, 211
Dundee 47
Dundee Football Club 21–23, 25, 28
Dundee Telegraph Cup 55
George T. Dunlap, Jr. 226
Willie Dunn 74, 112, 113
Morrie Dutra 210
Eastern Amateur Championship 175
J. D. Edgar 164
Edinburgh, Scotland 23, 58
King Edward I 11
King Edward VII 42, 53
Edzell, Scotland 42, 116
Ekwanok Golf Club 141, 144
Howard Emerson 155
Englewood Golf Club 164
Earl, Lord Esk 60, 61, 62
Al Espinosa 199, 210
Chick Evans 103, 108, 141, 147, 169, 170, 172, 189, 190, 248
Evanston Golf Club 165
Johnny Farrell 164, 189, 199–202, 210, 253
John Feeney 235
Willie Fernie 17, 45
Alexander H. Findlay 30, 31, 32, 33, 63, 64, 65, 66, 67, 68, 69, 70, 71, 87, 137, 149, 220
Fred Findlay 51, 57, 60, 63, 64, 69
Findlay Medal 63
Hamilton Fish 97
Johnny Fitzgerald 248
Henry Flagler 66
William Flynn 88
Rubin Forknall 156
Forfarshire Cup 8
Linde Fowler 34, 121, 146, 173, 203, 213, 215, 216, 219, 226
William C. Fownes, Jr. 108, 145, 190

Jimmie Foxx 239
Framingham Country Club 222
Franklin Park 34, 35, 70, 87, 132
Harry Frazee 159, 235
C. B. Frye 26
Emil Fuchs 233, 234, 236, 237
Ed Furgol 257
George Gadd 199
Robert A. Gardner 147, 169, 170, 189, 190
Judy Garland 249
Lou Gehrig 234
Glamorgan 45
Johnny Golden 188, 199
Golf Hall of Fame 242
Golf Illustrated magazine 52
Golf magazine 17, 220
Golf Writers Association of America 245
John Goodman 224
Elizabeth Gordon 175
R. R. Gorton 145
Ted Gow 221
Herb Graffis 167
John Graham 5
William Gray 5
Greater Boston Inter-Scholastic Golf League 93
Greater Boston Pro-Am 248
Jesse P. Guilford 2, 145–147, 149, 161, 165, 168–170, 176, 186, 189, 190, 193, 206, 208, 211, 212, 224–226, 228, 239, 244, 245, 248, 254, 256
Louise Guilford 169
Walter Hagen 3, 110, 113–115, 118, 139–141, 159, 162, 164, 166, 167, 171, 186, 189, 198–202, 210, 238, 242
Hail America Open 250
Frank G. Hale 155
Harry Hampton 163–165, 167, 215
Happy Hollow Golf Club 31
Frank Hardiman 155
Andy Hardy 249
Bob Harlow 220
Harvard University 71, 84, 96–100, 129, 133, 134–136, 141, 153, 221
Hatherly Country Club 194
Havemeyer Cup 219
Theodore Havemeyer 113
Haverhill Country Club 151
Arthur Havers 199
Alexander Herd 41, 51, 55, 185
Fred Herreshoff 108
Ben Hogan 243, 257
Charles Hope 136
C. V. L. Hooman 190
Harry Hooper 142, 234
Houston Invitational 189
Tom Howe 245
Billy Howell 216
W. I. Howland 145
Huddersfield 41
Arthur Hunnewell 33
Bob Hunter 24, 25
Willie Hunter 55
Huntington Valley Country Club 220
Jock Hutchinson 41, 45, 52, 55, 56, 57, 164, 167, 171, 172, 189
Intervale Country Club 146
Inverness Club 165, 171, 209
Inwood Country Club 115, 196
Paul Jackson 216
Jackson Park Golf Course 213
Hal Janvrin 142, 234
Harrison "H. R." Johnson 169, 207
John Johnson 94
John Johnstone 227
Herbert Jolly 199
Al Jolson 154
Robert T. "Bobby" Jones 159, 169, 186, 189, 190, 193, 196, 200–202, 210, 214, 218, 238, 242, 248
John J. Keenan 172, 194
Alex "Sandy" Keillor 16, 20, 22, 38, 39, 48, 53, 54, 60, 63
John F. Kennedy 222
Joseph P. Kennedy 223
Robert F. Kennedy 222
Kernwood Country Club 225
Tommy Kerrigan 107, 115, 167, 189
Dot Kielty 223
Edward Kimball 155
Jack Kirkaldy 45
Andrew Kirkcaldy 17, 52, 55, 57
Hugh Kirkcauldy 17
Joe Kirkwood 198
Charles Kocsis 253
LaBoulie, France 39, 104, 136
Ladies Professional Golf Association 244
Herbert Lagerblade 191, 192
Kenesaw Mountain Landis 238
Johnny Lehman 214
Helen Lengfeld 223
Charles Lind 253
Abraham Lincoln 9
Lawson Little 206, 213, 223
Gene Littler 257
Fred Low 192
Mary Low 22
Eddie Lowery 109, 118, 122–124, 168, 174, 177, 184
MacBeth 11
Bob MacAndrew 74
Flora MacDonald 11
R. G. MacDonald 112
James MacGregor 163
Rob Roy MacGregor 11
W. W. MacKenzie 190
Willie Maguire 107
Francis Mahan 93
Lawrence Manley 89
H. H. Marden 174
Mary Queen of Scots 11
Max Marston 190, 226
W. R. Marston 145
Massachusetts Golf Association 147, 155, 156, 176, 206, 221, 240, 252
Massachusetts Open 175, 176
Massachusetts State Amateur Tournament 103, 136, 141, 146, 184, 189, 252, 254

Arnaud Massey 41, 52, 57, 171, 178
Masters Tournament 221
Match Play Tournament 96
Eugene McCall 99
Joe McCarthy 233
John J. McDermott 99, 100, 110, 111, 115, 117, 123, 139, 171, 196–198
Tommy McEnamey 235
Stuffy McInnis 234
Bill McKechnie 234
Tom McNamara 99, 100, 107, 109, 110, 115, 170, 171, 181, 182
Ed McPhail 174
Bill Mehlhorn 167, 188, 199, 210
James Melville 5
Mercantile Club Championship (see Coronation Tankard Championship)
Merion Cricket Club 193
Miami Golf Links 66
Lee Mida 213, 215
Midlothian Country Club 139
Mid Pines Golf Course 222
Edward Millar 31
Millwall Athletic Football Club 24, 25, 27, 28
Misquamicut Golf Club 163
Abe Mitchell 171, 176, 185, 211
Monfieth 47
William H. Monroe 81
Montrose, Scotland 2, 5–25, 28, 30, 31, 37, 48, 58, 60, 63, 71, 72, 183, 186, 213, 220
Montrose Golf Club 14
Montrose Football Club 8, 12, 14, 19, 20, 24, 39, 40
Montrose Links Championship (see Boothby-Campbell Shield)
Montrose Mercantile Golf Club 8, 23, 37–39, 42, 43, 46, 47, 49–54, 56, 57, 62, 71, 74, 163, 164
Montrose Tournament of 1888 15
Gus Moreland 214
J. P. Morgan 72
George Morris 163
Jamie Morris 18
"Old" Tom Morris 2, 8, 9, 10, 15, 17, 18, 23, 32, 60, 63, 85, 257, 258
Tom Morris, Jr. 9
Muirfield, Scotland 23, 58
Musselburgh, Scotland 17, 20, 70, 74
Myopia Hunt Club 140, 176
Nashua Country Club 160, 161
Nassau Golf Links 66
National Amateur Championship of the United States 87, 89, 93, 94, 96, 103, 104, 108, 130, 144–146, 169, 176, 184, 186, 189, 206, 207, 209–218, 224, 251, 253, 254, 257
National Open (see U.S. Open)
Daniel Needham 99
Byron Nelson 184, 221, 222, 242, 243
Newcastle United 25, 26
New England Amateur-Pro Championship 193, 194, 206, 245, 248
New England Professional Championship 176
New England Professional Golfers' Association 188, 190, 191, 194, 200, 202, 205, 220, 245, 250
New England Professional Golfers' Organization 172–179, 184, 187, 188, 195, 200
New Hampshire State Amateur 145
Newport Country Club 30
News of the World tournament 52, 55, 56, 150
Bernard Nicholls 68
Brayton Nicholls 135
Gilbert Nicholls 68, 69, 71, 110, 113, 171, 176, 177, 179, 188, 189
Arthur Nicoll 84, 220
Charlie Nicoll 84, 151, 220, 222, 223
Francis "Frank" Nicoll 84, 187, 220
Harry Nicoll 83, 94, 95, 134, 137, 142, 143, 150, 153, 162, 181, 220
Herbert "Bert" Nicoll 84, 134, 137, 142, 150, 162, 172, 174, 175, 220–222
Jeannie Burgess Nicoll 60, 83, 151
Jimmy Nicoll 84, 220
Willie Nicoll 84, 151, 181, 182, 201, 206, 213, 220, 223
Norfolk Golf Club 253
North Andover Country Club 164, 223
North Berwick, Scotland 17, 52
North-South Championship 175, 189
Oak Hill Golf Club 181, 220
Oakland Hills 164, 195
Oakley Country Club 32, 70, 74, 175, 191
Oak Park Country Club 196
Willie Ogg 173
Frederick Law Olmstead 34, 132
Olympia Fields 201
Olympic Games 125, 130
Joe O'Meara 231
Ormond Country Club 66
Arthur Ouimet 86
Barbara Ouimet 217
Francis Ouimet 1, 2, 68, 85–96, 98, 100, 102–137, 139, 141, 144–152, 159, 161, 165, 166, 168–170, 172, 184, 189, 190, 193, 194, 197, 201, 204–208, 211–219, 224–226, 228, 238, 239, 241, 242, 245, 248, 254–257
Francis Ouimet Caddie Scholarship 2
Janice (Jane) Ouimet 217
Mary Ouimet 86
Raymond Ouimet 86
Stella Sullivan Ouimet 151, 168, 217, 248
Wilfred Ouimet 86, 87, 174
Palm Beach Country Club 162, 221–223
Arnold Palmer 2, 257
Willie Park, Jr. 9, 17, 39, 60, 181
Willie Park, Sr. 10, 17
Alan Paton 49
Larry Paton 187
William Jameson Paton 42, 43
John Nelson Patrick 31
Pebble Beach 206, 207
Peninsula Country Club (see Beresford Country Club)
Herb Pennock 142
Peter Petroske 224
Henry Picard 221, 222
Pinehurst 132, 133, 146, 162, 220–222
Pinehurst Outlook 33, 34

Pineneedles Golf Course 222
Gary Player 257
Ponce de Leon Golf Club 66
Portsmouth Football Club 26–28
Prestwick, Scotland 5, 17, 133, 136
The Professional Golfers' Association (PGA) 38, 41, 42, 44, 47, 50, 62, 79, 106, 150
Professional Golfers' Association of America 150–152, 160, 161, 163–168, 172–174, 187, 188, 191, 195, 196, 198–203, 209, 221, 222, 238, 240, 247, 248, 250, 251
Professional Golfers' Association Hall of Fame 1
Professional Golfers' Association Match Play Championship 47, 52
Stanley Quick 253, 254
Bob Quinn 234, 238
Rainier Golf and Country Club 214
Edward Ray 110, 171, 172
Ted Ray 1, 104, 106, 110–112, 114–120, 122–125, 128, 139, 146, 171, 179, 197, 199, 216
John Reid 30, 31, 53, 110, 114–119
Wilfred Reid 104, 112, 179
T. G. Renoof 41
Grantland Rice 67, 137, 146
Robert the Bruce 11
Fred Robson 199
Mickey Rooney 249
Franklin D. Roosevelt 228
Alex Ross 70, 71, 74, 92, 109, 110, 115, 146
Donald Ross 32, 66, 70, 71, 133, 142, 150, 162, 164, 174, 176, 177, 181, 188, 190, 207, 220–223
Rockledge Country Club 220, 222
Royal Albert 37, 38, 40, 43, 47–49, 51, 52, 57, 60–64, 78
Royal Albert Golf Club (see Royal Montrose Golf Club) 14
Royal and Ancient Golf Club / St. Andrews 1, 2, 5, 8–10, 15, 17, 18, 23, 30, 32, 39, 41, 45, 47, 49, 51–52, 55, 63, 70, 71, 74, 80, 84, 160, 164, 190, 255
Royal Montrose Golf Club 14
Babe Ruth 2, 141, 142, 159, 232–237, 239, 244
Ryder Cup Challenge 162, 170, 198–203, 209, 221, 242, 245
St. Andrews Royal and Ancient Golf Club (see Royal and Ancient Golf Club)
St. Augustine Country Club 66
St. Louis Country Club 169, 170
Sam the Caddie 246, 247
Sandy Burr Golf Club 206
Gene Sarazen (Geno Saraceni) 3, 128, 164, 166, 167, 186, 189, 198–202, 210, 242
George Sargent 115
Ben Sayers 41, 42, 83
Walter Scott 11
Frank H. Scroggie 55
Shackamaxon Country Club 196
Shenacossett 222
John Shields 214
Shinnecock Hills Golf Club 30, 112, 113, 117
John Shippen 110, 112, 113, 115, 117
John Sim 49
Andrew Simpson 39, 40
Archie Simpson 17
Bob Simpson 42
George Simpson 111
Rob Simpson 55
Alex Smith 110, 112, 171, 196
Heinrich Smith 113
MacDonald Smith 110, 115, 118, 139, 196, 198, 199, 210
Bob E. Smith 184
Willie Smith 110
Sam Snead 240, 242, 243
C. Ross Somerville 224
South Shore Country Club 206
A. G. Spalding 67, 137
Spalding Sporting Equipment Company 67, 68, 82, 137,
Tris Speaker 142
Springfield Country Club 70
Joe Stien 161, 162, 198
Andrew Strath 10
Herbert Strong 115, 117
Amos Strunk 153
James Stuart 53
John "Jack" Sullivan 147, 152
Sunset Ridge 222
Jesse Sweetser 169, 189, 190
William Howard Taft 108, 109
David G. Tait 172
James Henry Taylor 41, 49, 50, 51, 52, 54, 55, 56, 60, 185, 254
Tekoa Golf Club 70
Louie Tellier 104, 107, 109, 110, 114, 115, 117, 136, 139, 161, 167, 171, 173, 175–179
Paul Tewksbury 132
Charlie Thom 115, 117
Ralph Thomas 206
Johnny Thoren 247, 248, 250
Jim Thorpe 130
Cyril Tolley 190
Walter Toogood 51
W. B. Torrance 190
Charlie Tower, Jr. 252, 255
Mary Alice Burgess Tower 195, 215, 227–229, 252,
Jerome Travers 103, 108, 110, 113, 115, 136, 145, 147, 218, 248
Walter J. Travis 145
James Walker Tufts 132
Joe Turnesa 199
Unicorn Club 192
United States Amateur (see National Amateur)
United States Golf Association 69, 79, 80, 89, 93, 104, 106, 109, 111, 130, 131, 146–149, 152, 174, 189, 191, 195, 199, 212, 219, 248, 250
U. S. Open 50, 80, 103–107, 136, 164, 167, 168, 184, 186, 189, 196, 197, 198, 199–202, 209, 210, 222, 242, 243, 251, 257
    1894 74
    1896 113
    1900 67
    1907 70
    1911 100

1913 1, 76, 107–127, 137, 140, 141, 190, 225
1914 139, 141
1920 165, 167, 168, 171
1924 196
1963 106
U.S. Women's Amateur Championship 175, 244
Van Cortlandt Golf Course 35
Harry Vardon 1, 2, 36, 41, 42, 49, 50, 51, 55–57, 60, 67, 68, 104, 106, 109–111, 114–120, 122–125, 128, 136, 139, 140, 171, 172, 179, 185, 197, 216, 254
Tom Vardon 109
Ken Venturi 184
Donald Vinton 172
George Von Elm 169, 189, 208–212
Jack Wade 163
Ronald Waitt 89
Walker Cup 170, 189, 190, 201, 223, 224
Cyril Walker 163, 164
George A. Walker 189
William Wallace 11
Walton Heath 50, 56, 59
Al Waltrous 198, 199
Wampanoag Country Club 220
Rodman Wanamaker 149, 150
E. Harvie Ward 184
Robert Watson 103, 104, 109, 112
Jack Way 181
Weathersfield Country Club 220
Dewey Webber 169
Arthur Wedgewood 251
Wellesley Country Club 107, 245
Western Golf Association Amateur 148, 149
Western Open 189
Jack Westland 214, 217
Roger Wethered 190
Alex Wheatley 54
W. A. Whitcomb 225
Charles A. Whitcombe 199
Jack White 41, 51, 52, 55, 116
Paul Whiteman 237
Whitemarsh Valley Country Club 197
Howard Whitney 148
Wiano Club 220
Ed Wiener 237
Ted Williams 240
Robert Willits 253
Winchester Country Club 173
Winton Brothers 82, 137, 185, 186
Lothrop Withington 97
"Smokey" Joe Wood 142, 234
Tiger Woods 2
Wollaston Golf Club 74, 87, 103, 107, 178
Woman's Western Open 213
Women's Golf Association of Boston 174, 175
Woodland Golf Club 68, 69, 73, 74, 75, 85, 88, 89, 92, 93, 96, 100, 103, 110, 129, 131, 134, 136, 141, 142, 147, 148, 153–155, 162, 165, 168, 169, 174–176, 179, 181, 184, 188, 190, 192, 194, 201, 203–206, 209–212, 219, 220, 222, 227, 228, 231, 234–256
Woodland Park Hotel 71, 81, 152, 228
Worcester Country Club 165, 196, 199
Wright and Ditson 32, 33, 66, 68, 82, 87, 93, 132, 137, 153, 241, 242
Fred Wright 189
George Wright 33, 34, 35, 70
Lloyd Yost 221
George Zaharias 244
Mildred "Babe" Didrickson Zaharias 244

This book was typeset in Minion, a typeface designed by Robert Slimbach, inspired by classical, old-style typefaces of the late Renaissance. The line-drawing at each chapter start was provided by the author: it was originally used on Chay Burgess's golf-pro stationery.

Designed & typeset by
Windhaven Press
Auburn, New Hampshire
www.windhaven.com